Charles F. Whitley
Koheleth

Charles F. Whitley

Koheleth

His Language and Thought

Walter de Gruyter · Berlin · New York
1979

Beiheft zur Zeitschrift für die alttestamentliche Wissenschaft

Herausgegeben von Georg Fohrer

148

Gedruckt mit Unterstützung der Deutschen Forschungsgemeinschaft

CIP-Kurztitelaufnahme der Deutschen Bibliothek

Whitley, Charles F.:
Koheleth : his language and thought / Charles F. Whitley. – Berlin,
New York : de Gruyter, 1979.
  (Zeitschrift für die alttestamentliche Wissenschaft : Beih. ; 148)
  ISBN 3-11-007602-0

Preface

It is over seventy years since G. A. Barton wrote his *International Critical Commentary* on Koheleth. During the decades that immediately followed there were relatively few publications on the subject. But since the discovery of the Ras Shamra tablets and the Qumran documents much interest has been shown in the book by German, French, Italian and American scholars. In consequence there are various and conflicting views on the origin, language and thought of the author. It is against this complex and challenging background that the present work was undertaken.

In the preparation of the book I received much help from more than one scholar. Professor W. D. McHardy of Oxford offered valuable criticism of the first draft of the linguistic section. Professor P. A. H. de Boer of Leiden read the entire typescript and made many discerning comments. Professor Bernhard Lang of Tübingen read the proofs and supplied much bibliographical information.

During the revisionary stage of the work I was privileged to be invited to the Oxford Centre for Postgraduate Hebrew Studies as a Visiting Scholar. Not only were the research facilities at my disposal considerable, but I was able to discuss certain problems with members and scholars of the Centre. As editor of the BZAW series, Professor Georg Fohrer took a kindly and helpful interest in the work and brought his experience and wide knowledge to bear on the ultimate division and classification of parts of the material.

Finally I would like to acknowledge my debt to the *Deutsche Forschungsgemeinschaft*, Bonn-Bad Godesberg, for a generous grant towards the cost of publication, and also to express my appreciation of the care and patience which Walter de Gruyter & Co. exercised on the printing and production of the book.

Bangor, March, 1979   C. F. Whitley

Contents

Contents

A. Introduction

Koheleth, according to Renan, is "the only pleasant book that was composed by a Jew"[1]. Certainly it is the most unorthodox and varied of the writings of the Hebrew bible. It contains elements ranging from the pessimism of the ancient Egyptians and Babylonians to the fatalism and hedonism of the Stoics and Epicureans. It ostensibly stems from Solomon (1 1. 12), but as Franz Delitzsch remarked, "if the book of Qoheleth were of Solomonic origin, then, there is no history of the Hebrew language"[2]. Many constructions in the book are obscure, and its syntax as a whole is cumbersome. It thus lacks the lucidity and elegance of the classical age, and clearly belongs to the decadent period of the language.

Koheleth has indeed some affinities with the language of the later books of the Old Testament such as Chronicles, Ezra-Nehemiah and Esther, but it has other linguistic features which are especially characteristic of the book itself[3]. Thus the Waw Consecutive, so common in classical Hebrew, occurs but three times (1 17 4 1. 7). The article is often omitted, while, on the other hand, we find a preponderance of particles such as גם, כי and כאשר. The participle is again frequently used, and the ל"א verbs often assume the inflections of the ל"ה verbs. The form ש for the relative pronoun, though found elsewhere in the Old Testament, occurs here almost as often as the classical אשר. Aramaic forms and constructions appear throughout the book[4], while a number of words and expressions resemble the Hebrew of Ben Sira and the Mishna.

---

[1] Renan, L'Antichrist, 1873, 101.

[2] The Song of Songs and Ecclesiastes (Eng. trans. 1885) 190.

[3] Renan thought that in the whole of Hebrew literature the language of Koheleth forms "a sort of islet apart" (L'Ecclésiaste, 1882, 16).

[4] Cf. Kautzsch, who has pointed out that there are 29 Aramaisms in Koheleth out of a total of 122 in the entire Old Testament. He thus calculated that Koheleth contains 24 per cent of the Aramaisms of the Old Testament, although the book itself only constitutes 1.2 per cent of the Old Testament (Die Aramaismen im Alten Testament 1, 1902, 102). See also the tabulation presented by Wagner, Die lexikalischen und grammatikalischen Aramaismen im alttestamentlichen Hebräisch, 1966, 142 and especially 145, where he calculates that 3.1 per cent of Koheleth is Aramaic in origin.

Unusual phrases and vocabulary further emphasise the peculiar nature of the language of Ecclesiastes.

This peculiarity has been the subject of much speculation, and has been explained in various ways. The generally accepted view, found, for example, in the Commentaries of Barton, Podechard, Hertzberg, Gordis, Zimmerli, Kroeber and Strobel, is that Koheleth is representative of the Hebrew language during the period of the fourth to the third centuries B.C.[5]. Other scholars have, however, seen a more extraneous element in the text. Margoliouth thought that the idioms of Koheleth are to be explained on the assumption that it is based on a work of Indo-Germanic origin[6]. So Burkitt suggested that the book is a translation from a lost Aramaic original[7]. This, he thought, might account for the disconcerting style and "the crabbed and unnatural lingo" (26) in which the work is composed. Zimmermann welcomed this translation hypothesis and argued that the obscurities and awkwardness of the language disappear on retrogression into the original Aramaic[8]. Zimmermann's arguments attracted the interest and gained the approval of Torrey[9], and, with some modifications, were later supported by Ginsberg[10].

Again, Dahood has proposed the theory that Ecclesiastes was originally written by an author who employed Phoenician orthography and whose composition shows heavy Canaanite-Phoenician literary influence[11]. A basic feature of this orthography is that it did not use vowel letters, and therefore, argues Dahood, a later scribe, copying from a Phoenician *Vorlage*, would encounter many ambiguities in the text. This would particularly apply to verbs where one and the same consonantal form would be used for both singular and plural. Dahood further maintains that we have examples of Phoenician morphology, syntax and vocabulary in the book.

---

[5] Barton, The Book of Ecclesiastes, ICC, 1908; Podechard, L'Ecclésiaste, 1912; Hertzberg, Der Prediger 1963²; Gordis, Koheleth — The Man and his World, 1951; Zimmerli, Das Buch des Predigers Salomo, 1962; Kroeber, Der Prediger, 1963; Strobel, Das Buch Prediger (Kohelet), 1967.

[6] JE V (1903), 33b.

[7] JTS 23 (1932), 22–26. Cf. also Fernández, Bibl. 3 (1922), 45–50.

[8] JQR 36 (1945–46), 17–45; JQR 40 (1949), 79–102.

[9] JQR 39 (1948), 151–160.

[10] Studies in Koheleth (1950); VTS 3 (1955), 138–149; The Quintessence of Qoheleth, in: Biblical and other Essays, 1963, 47–59.

[11] E. g. Bibl 33 (1952), 30–52. 191–221; also 39 (1958), 302–318; and 47 (1966), 264–282.

This diversity of opinion and approach indicates the perplexity of the linguistic problems encountered in Ecclesiastes. In the following pages, then, we will attempt a fresh examination of the language of the book. In so doing we will give special attention to those words and phrases which are difficult or unusual, and which are the basis for the various opinions on the nature of the language of the work; but we will also note some expressions which, though not problematical, are representative of the author's familiarity with the language of the Old Testament. We will then attempt an assessment of the theories of Zimmermann and Dahood, and subsequently offer our own view of the language of the book. In a final section we will discuss the sources and content of Koheleth's thought.

B. An Examination of the Language of Koheleth

I. CHAPTER 1

1₁ קֹהֶלֶת. The superscription represents the work as deriving from Koheleth, son of David, king in Jerusalem. The intention, as 1₂ indicates, was thus to associate it with Solomon. The word קהלת occurs in seven places in the book (1₁. ₂. ₁₂ 7₂₇ 12₈. ₉. ₁₀), but uncertainty attaches to its precise meaning. Structurally it is that of the Qal feminine participle of קהל "to assemble", but we have no other biblical instance of this form of the verb. Nor indeed does קהל occur in the Qal elsewhere in the Old Testament, although it is frequently used in both the Niphal (e.g. Ex 32₁) and Hiphil (e.g. IReg 12₂₁). According to Rabbinical tradition the title *Koheleth* was suggested for the book by the contents of IReg 8₁ff., in which Solomon is represented as assembling (יקהל v. 1) and addressing an assembly (קָהָל v. 22)[1]. This interpretation of *Koheleth* seems to be supported by the Greek translation Ἐκκλησιαστής. The word occurs in Plato (e.g. Gorg 452 E; Apol. 25 A) and elsewhere in Greek literature, and means a member of the ἐκκλησία, which was itself an assembly of the citizens summoned to the legislature (e.g. Thuc. 2₂₂; Plato, Gorg 456 B). The verb ἐκκλησιάζω means to hold an assembly or to debate therein (e.g. Xen Anab 5₆. ₁₃₇). The Vulgate *Ecclesiastes* is but a transliteration of the Greek, while the Peshitta ܩܘܗܠܬ and the Targum קהלת are but transliterations of the Hebrew.

קהלת finds structural parallels in the terms סֹפֶרֶת and פֹּכֶרֶת which are amongst the lists of names in Ezr 2₅₅. ₅₇. These terms originally pertained to the office of "scribe" and "gazelle-tender" respectively, but were subsequently used as personal names[2]. So, used with the article in 7₂₇ (amended) and 12₈, *Koheleth* seems to retain a functional meaning[3]. It is to be noted too that the term משטמה, though feminine in form, signifies the office of "accuser" or "plaintiff" in the Community Rule

---

[1] "Why was Koheleth's name so called? Because his words were uttered in public (בהקהל) as it is stated, Then Solomon assembled (יקהל) the elders of Israel, IKgs. viii: 1", Midrash Rabbah, Ecclesiastes (Trans. by Cohen, 1939).

[2] Cf. Bauer, ZAW 48 NF 7 (1930), 73–80.

[3] See, however, under 7₂₇ below.

of Qumran[4]. In the Mishna again we meet with such feminine forms as מְשׁוּחוֹת "surveyors" (Eru 4₁₁) and דְּרוּכוֹת "grape-treaders" (Ter 3₄). The use of the feminine for the holder of an office is likewise discernible in the Arabic خليفة, originally meaning "successor", but later assuming the significance of a personal title[5].

The meaning of קהלת as one who speaks in an assembly has been accepted by most exegetes[6]. Zapletal, however, thought that it meant an assembler of proverbs as suggested by Koh 12₁₀[7], and indeed in Prov 30₁ we find words attributed to one by the name of "Augur" which means "gatherer". Renan regarded the term as a cryptogram[8], and Zimmermann likewise sees it as a cryptogram for Solomon. In accordance with his view of an Aramaic original for the work, he points out that the lexical and grammatical equivalents of קהלת are to be found in the Aramaic feminine participle כָּנְשָׁה. He then ingeniously demonstrates that the combined numerical value of the letters כנשה amounts to the same total as the letters of the word שלמה[9]. However, Ginsberg considers this argument fallacious on two counts. Firstly, he holds that the identification of "the Convoker" with Solomon is not original with the author, and that therefore קהלת must be regarded as deriving from an Aramaic קהלה(א) rather than from an assumed כנשה. Secondly, he observes that the equation of one set of numerical letters with another would be impossible in a pre-Christian book, since the use of the Alphabet for numerical reckoning appears first on the coins of the Jewish Revolt in 66–70 A.D.[10].

However, while there are difficulties in the theory of an Aramaic origin of the book, the common view of קהלת as meaning one who

---

[4] E.g. The Manual of Discipline, III 23 (ed. by Burrows, Trevor and Brownlee in The Dead Sea Scrolls of St. Marks Monastery, II 1951). See also Habermann, Megilloth Midbar Yehuda, 1959, 159.

[5] Cf. Milik, RB 59 (1952), 591, who mentions Nabatean masculine names which are feminine in form.

[6] E.g. Barton, The Book of Ecclesiastes, 68; Podechard, L'Ecclésiaste, 187f.; Gordis op. cit. 164; Hertzberg, Der Prediger, 53; Zimmerli, Das Buch des Predigers Salomo, 143; Kroeber, Der Prediger, 1; Strobel, Das Buch Prediger (Kohelet), 1967, 23–24; Barucq, Ecclésiaste, 8–9; Galling, Der Prediger, 1969², 75. Cf., however, Braun (Kohelet und die frühhellenistische Popularphilosophie, 1973, 178) who thinks that the term denotes a public teacher and is applied as a synonym to our author by the first epilogist.

[7] Das Buch Koheleth, 1911², 5f.

[8] L'Ecclésiaste 13.

[9] JQR 36 (1945/46), 43f.

[10] Studies in Koheleth 31f.

addresses an assembly is scarcely adequate. For Koheleth's views are
so unorthodox and his arguments so disconnected that he would hardly
be likely to publish them in the traditional manner[11]. It is probable,
moreover, that we can discern a meaning other than "assemble" in the
term קהלת. In Neh 5₇ we read "and I pleaded (ואריבה) with the nobles
and potentates . . . and I delivered against them a great קְהִלָּה". This
Hebrew word is rendered by the Versions as "assembly". But "assembly"
makes little sense here, since, as the context indicates, we require a term
with a meaning similar to ריב such as "indictment" or the like[12]. Nehe-
miah accuses the nobles and officials of ruthlessly exacting usury from
the returned exiles. We are then told that, confronted with such a קְהִלָּה
גדולה—"grave indictment"—, the officials "were silent and could not
find a word to say" (v. 8). Again, despite some textual difficulty, in
Job 11₁₀, the term יַקְהִיל seems to have a juridical force: "If he seizes[13],
imprisons and *adjudicates* (יקהיל), who can prevent him?" So in addition
to meaning "to assemble" the Syriac ܟܰܫ has also the force of "to
consider", and in the Pa. "to consider attentively"[14]. In discussing the
issues of life and existence, the author of our book displays all these
attitudes and moods. Thus sometimes he questions (e. g. 2₁₉. ₂₂ 3₂₁
8₁₆. ₁₇), other times he considers (e. g. 1₁₃. ₁₇ 2₁₂ 7₂₅) and again he passes
judgment (e. g. 5₁₃. ₁₈ 7₂₇₋₂₈). It would accordingly be difficult to describe
such a complex character by one term. It may be that the Hebrew קהלת
has such a comprehensive connotation, but, if it is to be represented
by one term in English, perhaps "The Sceptic" would have some measure
of adequacy.

   1₂ הֶבֶל. This word is used more than thirty times in Ecclesiastes[15].
Here, as in 12₈, we have the construct state of the absolute form הֶבֶל,
but the pointing הֲבֵל instead of הֶבֶל (cf. Heb. abs. עֶבֶד, cons. עֶבֶד)
suggests Aramaic influence; so the Targum הֲבֵל הבליא, and compare
Aramaic עֲבַד (or עֲבֵד), cons. עֲבֵד (Dan 6₂₁) and Aramaic צְלֵם, cons.
צְלֵם[16]. הבל primarily means "vapour" or "breath". Thus in Isa 57₆ it

---

[11] Accordingly Joüon's view, Bibl 3 (1921), 53f., of the term as denoting the
   preacher "par excellence" is hardly relevant.
[12] Cf. Ullendorff, VT 12 (1962), 215, who suggests "the arguer".
[13] Reading יחטף instead of יחלף ("passes by") with e. g. BH³.
[14] Syriac Dictionary, ed. Smith, 1903, 491b.
[15] BDB mentions 31 times, and 3 instances of הבל־הבלים, 210b.
[16] See also Du Plessis, in: De Fructu Oris Sui, Van Selms Festschrift, Pretoria
   Oriental Series 9, 1971, 169, who draws attention to other Aramaic construct
   forms in non-Aramaic books of the Old Testament; e. g. שְׁגַר, abs שֶׁגֶר (Deut
   28₄. ₁₈. ₅₁), חֲדַר abs חֶדֶר (I Reg 20₃₀).

appears as a parallel to רוח "wind", and in Prov 21₆ we find the expression הבל נדף "a fleeting vapour". So הבל is used with תֹהוּ "nothingness" in Isa 49₄, while in Isa 30₇ it is similarly used with ריק "emptiness". Again in Deut 32₂₁ the plural הבליהם parallels לא אל "that which is not a god", and in Jer 8₁₉ הבלי is likewise used with פסליהם "idols". Such references indicate that הבל denotes not merely what is vaporous and evanescent, but also that which is without substance and false. Burkitt was of the opinion that הבל represents an original Aramaic הבלא which denoted "exhalation", and therefore suggestive of a mere waste product which rapidly vanishes. But while he considered this "a scientific" rendering, he thought that "bubble", which is indicative of the unsubstantial and evanescent, might, as a "poetical" equivalent, be nearer to the thought of Ecclesiastes [17].

1₃ יִתְרוֹן. In the Old Testament this word is peculiar to our book (e.g. 2₁₁.₁₃ 3₉); but it is found again in Rabbinical literature [18]. It derives from the root יתר, which, as in the cognate languages, means "to remain over". Here its meaning is that of "advantage" or possibly "profit" [19].

בְּכָל־ עֲמָלוֹ. It is possible to translate here "from all his labour" as בעמלו in 5₁₄c where ב clearly has the force of "from" [20].

שֶׁיַּעֲמֹל. It is estimated that ש is used as the relative particle sixty-eight times in Koheleth, while אֲשֶׁר is used eighty-nine times [21]. The element ש is probably Proto-Semitic [22], and is therefore likely to be as old as אשר. It is obviously cognate with the Phoenician ש, although the commonly held view that it is also to be etymologically identified with the Phoenician אש [23] has been recently questioned [24]. We meet ש in some early Hebrew literature, thought to be of northern provenance

---

[17] JTS 23 (1922), 27–28. Staples, JNES 2 (1943), 95–104, claims that the word denotes what is incomprehensible to man. But this is not based on linguistic grounds.

[18] E.g. Midrash Rabbah on Leviticus (sec. 22), and Midrash Rabbah on Koheleth 6₈.

[19] Cf. Dahood, Bibl 33 (1952), 221, who lists it as one of the commercial terms in the book.

[20] See below under 5₁₄c. Dahood regards such passages as showing signs of Ugaritic and Phoenician influence, Bibl 47 (1966), 265.

[21] So Wright, The Book of Koheleth, 1883, 499.

[22] See Harris, Development of the Canaanite Dialects, 1939, 69.

[23] E.g. Harris, A Grammar of the Phoenician Language, 1936, 55; Friedrich-Röllig, Phönizisch-Punische Grammatik, 1970, § 121. 54.

[24] Gevirtz, JNES 16 (1957), 124–127, who argues that the Phoenician אש is not to be regarded as ש with a prothetic א but is rather to be identified with the Hebrew יש/אש, Ugaritic it and Aramaic (אית(י.

(e.g. Judg 5₇ 6₁₇ 7₂₂ IIReg 6₁₁). It appears, however, with increasing frequency in the later biblical books: for example, Pss 122₃₋₄ 124₁. ₂. ₆ Lam 4₉ 5₁₈ IChr 5₂₀ 27₂₇ and, apart from the superscription, exclusively in Canticles. This form of the relative appears throughout the Mishna, אשר, with one exception (Pes 10₆), being used only in biblical quotations[25]. The fact that ש in proportion to אשר is used in the ratio of 7 to 9 in Ecclesiastes is one of the grounds on which Dahood bases his theory of a Phoenician origin of the book[26].

תַּחַת הַשֶּׁמֶשׁ. This phrase is peculiar to Koheleth, occurring no less than twenty-nine times in his book[27]. Some scholars regard it as a Graecism, ὑφ᾽ ἡλίῳ[28], although we find it in the Phoenician inscriptions of Tabnit (6th cent. B.C.) and Eshmunazar (5th cent. B.C.)[29], and again in an Elamite document of the twelfth century B.C.[30]. The phrase תחת השמים is also found in our book in the same sense (1₁₃ 2₃ 3₁), but this occurs elsewhere in the Old Testament (e.g. Ex 17₁₄ Deut 7₂₄ 25₁₉ 29₁₉).

1₅ וְאֶל מְקוֹמוֹ שׁוֹאֵף זוֹרֵחַ הוּא שָׁם. Literally, "and unto its place it (the sun) pants, it rises there". Thus the phrase as a whole is cumbersome, while the application of שואף to the sun is unusual and forced. Its primary meaning is that of "gasp" or "long for"; compare Isa 42₁₄ where it is used of a woman gasping in travail, and Job 7₂ where it expresses the longing of a slave for the shadow.

Zimmermann attributes the awkwardness of the phrase to a faulty translation of an Aramaic original, which he reconstructs thus: וּדְנַח שִׁמְשָׁא וְעַל שִׁמְשָׁא וּלְאַתְרֵיהּ תָּאֵב דְּנַח הוּא תַּמָּן. He accordingly thinks that the Hebrew translator took the Aramaic תאב as תָּאֵב "desire" (= Heb שׁוֹאֵף) instead of תָּאֵב, the Aramaic participle of תוּב "return". Similarly, the translator read the second דנח as "shine" (= Heb זוֹרֵחַ) instead of דְּנַח, a combination of the adverb ד and נָח, the perfect of נוּחַ "to rest". Zimmermann then proposes that the Hebrew should read: וְזָרַח הַשֶּׁמֶשׁ וּבָא הַשֶּׁמֶשׁ וְאֶל מְקוֹמוֹ שָׁב אֲשֶׁר נָח הוּא שָׁם "The sun shines and the sun sets;

[25] Mittwoch notes that אשר is used only four times in the Mishna, and that three of these are quotations from the Pentateuch, in: Essays Presented to J. H. Hertz, 1942, 327.

[26] Bibl 33 (1952), 44–45.

[27] So Barton op. cit. 32.

[28] E.g. Plumptre, Ecclesiastes, 1885, 104; regarded it as "essentially Greek in character" and cited Euripides, Hippol., 1220; and Theognis 158. Cf. too Ranston, Ecclesiastes and the Early Greek Wisdom Literature, 1925, 55f.

[29] KAI I, 13₇ and 14₁₂ (p. 3); cf. also DSIO, 310.

[30] See J. Friedrich, Orientalia 18 (1949), 1ff. especially 28–29.

and he returns to his place where he rests"[31]. But remarkable as this reconstruction is, it is scarcely germane to the sense of the passage; for the idea of the sun resting is not suitable to the context, which is rather concerned with its continuous motion. As the next line states, "it goes unto the south and veers to the north"[32].

On the other hand, the Versions vary and seem uncertain in their rendering of שׁוֹאֵף. The Septuagint reads ἕλκει (drags), the Targum שָׁתִיף (crawls), while the Peshitta does not represent it at all. The reading שָׁב אַף, proposed by Graetz, has been accepted by Joüon[33], but again this scarcely improves the logic of the verse. Hence, although generally accepted by commentators[34], it is doubtful if the phrase וְאֶל־מְקוֹמוֹ ... שָׁם is authentic. Rather, the original passage relating to the sun would seem to have been: "The sun rises and the sun sets[35], it goes unto the south and veers to the north". We would then have a natural reference to the four points of the compass, without the cumbersome intrusion of וְאֶל־מְקוֹמוֹ ... שָׁם. The phrase was probably inserted under the influence of verse 7b where there is a similar, and probably an original, elaboration of the preceding line.

1₆ וְעַל־סְבִיבֹתָיו שָׁב הָרוּחַ. It is probable that עַל is here to be rendered "from"; "And from its circlings the wind returns"[36]. This meaning of ʿal is fairly widespread in the Semitic languages. We meet it in Akkadian, Phoenician, Moabite, Aramaic and Hebrew. Thus Esarhaddon is represented as saying, riddu kînu eli aḫḫēya ittabik (loyal conduct was taken away from my brothers)[37]. In the Ahiram Phoenician inscription we read, ונחת תברח עלי גבל (And may tranquility flee from Gebal)[38]. Again in the Moabite Stone we read ויאמר לי כמש לך אחז את נבה על ישראל ואהלך בללה (And Chemosh said to me, Go, take Nebo from Israel, and I went by night . . .)[39]. Likewise in Aramaic we find ושנתה נדת עֲלוֹהִי (Dan

---

[31] JQR 36 (1945–46), 23–24.

[32] The Targum and Vulgate rightly take the words וסובב אל־צפון with "the sun", and not with "wind" in the next clause.

[33] Graetz, Kohélet oder der Salomonische Prediger, 1871, 55f.; Joüon, Bibl 11 (1930), 419.

[34] E.g. Gordis op. cit. 195; Hertzberg op. cit. 68 n. 5; Zimmerli op. cit. 147.

[35] Cf. Gen 28₁₁ and Ps 104₁₉ where בא applies to the setting of the sun. So in the Phoenician Inscription, Karatepe, we find the expression במבא שמש "in the setting of the sun" (KAI I, IA, 18–19, 5).

[36] See Dahood, Bibl 47 (1966), 265.

[37] See Driver, JSS 9 (1964), 349.

[38] KAI I, 1₂ (1).

[39] KAI I, No, 181₁₄. (32).

6₁₉, and his sleep fell *from* him). So in Hebrew we find, for example: אָמַרְתְּ לַיהוה אֲדֹנָי אָתָּה טוֹבָתִי בַּל־עָלֶיךָ (Ps 16₂, I said O Yahweh (לֹ) thou art my God, my good is indeed (בל) *from* thee)[40]; וּשְׁנָתוֹ נִהְיְתָה עָלָיו (Dan 2₁, and his sleep went *from* him). Similarly in the Mishna we read: אִם יֵשׁ לָהֶם עָלָיו מְזוֹנוֹת (But if they receive food *from* him, Maas 3₁).

1₈ כָּל־הַדְּבָרִים יְגֵעִים. Zimmermann thinks that יגעים is a mistranslation of an Aramaic מְשַׁלְהִין (from Shaphel of לְהֵי "to weary") which could be either passive or active[41]. He implies that the sense requires the active and transitive, and should therefore be rendered by the Piel מִיגְעִים. We have an example of יגע used in the Pi. in an active sense in 10₁₅, but there is no reason for thinking that the sense required here in 1₈ should be other than adjectival: "all things are wearisome". We may compare Deut 25₁₈ and II Sam 17₂ where יָגֵעַ is used in the singular as an adjective.

1₉ מַה־שֶּׁהָיָה הוּא שֶׁיִּהְיֶה. The phrase מה־שהיה is common throughout Koheleth (1₉ 3₁₅.₂₂ 6₁₀ 7₂₄ 8₇ 10₁₄). מה is generally used in classical Hebrew in an interrogative sense, and it is interesting that both the Septuagint and Vulgate so take it, though wrongly, here. There are a few instances in biblical Hebrew where מה has the force of an indefinite substantive as, for example, I Sam 19₃ וְרָאִיתִי מָה וְהִגַּדְתִּי לָךְ (and if I see anything I will tell you) and II Sam 18₂₂ וִיהִי מָה אָרוּצָה־נָּא (and whatever happens I will run). Apart from a few cases in late books (I Chr 15₁₃ לְמַבָּרִאשׁוֹנָה for that which was at first; II Chr 30₃ לְמַדַּי to what was sufficient; Est 9₂₆ מָה רָאוּ, what they saw)[42] its use as the relative "what" is not attested in Hebrew, אשר being used instead. Some scholars have identified מה־שׁ with the Phoenician מאשׁ[43], and, accepting this identification, Dahood regards it as another instance of Phoenician influence on the author of Koheleth[44]. This etymological equation has, however, again been questioned by Gevirtz who argues that the Phoenician מאשׁ is rather to be equated with the Hebrew מה יש (I Sam 21₄ II Sam 19₂₉ II Reg 4₂)[45]. But even if the Phoenician מאשׁ were to be explained in terms of the Hebrew מה־שׁ it should be noted that both structurally and philogically מה־שׁ is also to be identified with the biblical Aramaic

---

[40] On the positive use of בל in Hebrew, see Whitley, ZAW 84 (1972), 215–219.
[41] Loc. cit. 41.
[42] BDB 553a.
[43] *Kilamuwa* (KaI I, 24₄, p. 5). See, e.g. Lidzbarski, Ephemeris III, 227; Harris, A Grammar of the Phoenician Language, 82.
[44] Bibl 33 (1952), 45.
[45] Loc. cit. 126b.

מה־די (e.g. Dan 2 28-29 where מה די להוא = Heb. מה־שיהיה) and again
with מה ז of the extra-biblical Aramaic documents[46]. מה is also used in
the Mishna in the same sense as in Koheleth; for example, Aboth 5 7
על מה שלא שמע (regarding what he has not heard) and Baba Bath 6 7
מה שנתן נתן (whatever he gave, he gave).

1 10b כְּבָר. This word occurs in biblical Hebrew only in Koheleth.
The root basically means "much" or "great" (cf. Assy. *kabáru*[47], Arabic
كبر[48], Aramaic כבר[49], "to be rich, great"). In Gen 35 16 48 7 and II Reg
5 19 we meet the nominal form כברת (con) with the meaning "stretch"
or "dimension" of land. כבר would thus seem to connote length or
duration of time, and it is accordingly used here and elsewhere in Koheleth (e. g. 2 12. 16 3 15 4 2) in the adverbial sense of "already". It also occurs
in the Mishna with this meaning; for example, Erub 4 2 שכבר הייתי מסתכל
(I have already observed).

1 10b הָיָה לְעֹלָמִים אֲשֶׁר הָיָה מִלְּפָנֵנוּ. Because of the plural form of the
antecedent לעלמים some MSS and critics read the second היה as הָיוּ[50].
Dahood too favours the plural and regards the error as arising from the
purely consonantal הי of the Phoenician *Vorlage*, which a scribe could
have taken as singular or plural[51]. However, עלמים appears to have the
force of a singular in certain biblical passages. Thus it qualifies a singular noun in Isa 26 4 (צור עולמים), Isa 45 17 (תשועת עולמים) and Dan 9 24
(צדק עלמים). עולמים has also an adverbial force in such passages as
I Reg 8 13 לשבתך עולמים (for thy dwelling always) and Ps 61 5 אגורה באהלך
עולמים (I will dwell in thy tent always). Again we find the singular עולם
in Ps 85 6 הלעולם תאנף־בנו (wilt thou be angry with us for ever?), but
the plural עולמים in Ps 77 8 הלעולמים יזנח אדני (will the Lord spurn for
ever?)[52]. It is thus likely that while עלמים here in Koheleth is an emphatic term for a long period of time, it may be construed in the singular:
"already it was in *the age* which was before us".

---

[46] E.g. Letter 12 8. 9, in Driver's Aramaic Documents of the Fifth Century
B.C., 1957, 36.
[47] Bezold, Babylonisch-Assyrisches Glossar, 1926, 137a.
[48] Freytag iv, 3b.
[49] *Zenjirli*, KAI I, 215 9 (39).
[50] A few MSS mentioned by de Rossi (Varie Lectiones Veteris Testamenti, III
1786, 247a) read the plural; so BH³.
[51] Bibl 33 (1952, 36. So Jenni, ZAW 64 (1952), 245, seems to prefer the plural.
[52] We find similar usages elsewhere in the Old Testament. E.g. מארץ מרחק in
Jer 6 20, but מארץ מרחקים in Jer 8 19; ערי מצורה in II Chr 14 5, but ערי מצורות
in II Chr 11 10. See Sperber, A Historical Grammar of Biblical Hebrew, 1966,
86.

1₁₁ ... זִכְרוֹן לְ. The classical absolute form is זִכָּרוֹן (e.g. Ex 13₉
Jos 4₇). Delitzsch accordingly thought that, like יִתְרוֹן and כִּשְׁרוֹן, this
is a late form of the absolute state[53]. However, the form זִכָּרוֹן appears
in the next line, and זִכְרוֹן is thus probably to be regarded as the construct before the preposition *Lamedh*. Such examples occur in Ps 58₅
חֲמַת־לָמוֹ (their anger) and Prov 24₉ וְתוֹעֲבַת לְאָדָם לֵץ (and the scoffer
is an abomination to men)[54]. The construct before the preposition לְ
also occurs in the Mishna; for example, Aboth 5₁₄ הוֹלְכֵי־לְבֵית־הַמִּדְרָשׁ.

1₁₃ לָתוּר "to spy out, explore", from the root תּוּר. So in Num 13₂.
16. 17 it is used of "spying out" the land of Canaan. Hence, here and 7₂₅
Koheleth uses לָתוּר of mental exploration. This is a natural semantic
development from earlier biblical usage[55], and there is therefore no need
to assume with some scholars that the term depends on the philosophic
Greek term σκέπτεσθαι[56].

1₁₃ᵦ ... לַעֲנוֹת בּוֹ. עִנְיַן רָע. עִנְיָן in biblical Hebrew is confined to the
book of Koheleth (2₂₆ 3₁₀ 5₂ 8₁₆), but it is used frequently in the Talmud
in the sense of business or affair: for example, Kid 6a עֲסוּקִין בְּאוֹתוֹ עִנְיָן
(employed with this matter); Baba Bath 114b מֵעִנְיָנָא לְעִנְיָנָא (from one
matter to another). There are four meanings of the root ענה in the Old
Testament[57]. 1. "to answer"; 2. "to be occupied with" (Syriac ܥܢܐ),
which seems to be confined to Koh 1₁₃ and 3₁₀; 3. "to be oppressed or
afflicted"; 4. "to sing or chant". It is likely that the meaning of the root
underlying לענות בו here in our text is that of 2, "to be occupied with".
Gordis contests this on the ground that apart from here and 3₁₀ the
verb occurs nowhere else in the Old Testament or in the Mishna, and
he accordingly translates "to be afflicted with"[58]. However, ענה does
appear in the Hebrew version of Ben Sira in the sense of "being occupied with"[59]. As in Koheleth the verb is followed by ב, ענה בזנות (occupied with harlotry), and this is also the construction of the Syriac
version ܥܢܐ ܒ.

---

[53] Franz Delitzsch, The Song of Songs and Ecclesiastes, 1885, 225; so Hertzberg
op. cit. 68 n. 11.

[54] Cf. GK § 130a (p. 142).

[55] Cf. Hertzberg op. cit. 82, and Ellermeier, Qoheleth, Pt. I, Abschnitt I, 1967,
175f.

[56] E.g. Wildeboer, Der Prediger, 1898, 125; Pedersen, RHPR 10 (1930), 331;
Levy, Das Buch Qoheleth, 1912, 14.

[57] BDB 772ff.

[58] Op. cit. 200.

[59] 42₈ B. Marginal. Cf. Yadin, The Ben Sira Scroll from Masada, 1965, 23.

1₁₄ וּרְעוּת רוּחַ. There are three meanings of the root רָעָה in Hebrew. The first is "to feed or tend", the second "to associate with", and the third "to strive or desire". It is possible that רעות here and elsewhere in Koheleth (2₁₁. ₁₇. ₂₆ 4₄. ₆ 6₉) derives from the last meaning of the root[60]. That רעה has this meaning may be seen from Hos 12₂, אפרים רֹעֶה רוח וְרֹדֵף קדים (Ephraim strives after the wind and pursues the east wind)[61] where it is used as a parallel to רדף (pursue)[62]. This meaning of the root רעה is to be associated with the Aramaic רְעָה "to desire" which corresponds phonemically to the Hebrew רצה "to be pleased with"[63]. In the Aramaic of Ezr 5₁₇ and 7₁₈ we find רְעוּת as the construct state of the (absolute) noun רְעוּ (will, pleasure)[64]. The meaning "desire" for the Hebrew verb רעה may also be discerned in Prov 15₁₄ where there is mention of a fool "desiring folly", יִרְעֶה אִוֶּלֶת, and again in Ps 37₃ וּרְעֵה אֱמוּנָה (and take pleasure in security). The semantic development from "desire" to "thought" is exemplified in such passages as Prov 15₂₈ which describes a fool "bubbling out thoughts", יַבִּיעַ רָעוֹת, and Dan 2₃₀ where we read of רַעְיוֹנֵי לִבְבָך "the desires (thoughts) of thy heart". In Syriac too ܪܥܝܢܐ means "mind, intellect".

1₁₅ לְתַקֵּן. The term derives from the root תקן (to be straight) which is found in biblical Hebrew only in Koheleth. This is the sole instance of the verb in the Qal. Elsewhere in the book (7₁₃ 12₉) it is used in the Pi., and often in both the Pi. and Hi. in the Mishna (e. g. Git 4₅ תְּקָנְתֶּם and 4₂ התקין). The form in Ben Sira 47₉ is again that of the Piel תִּקֵּן. We also meet the Pa. form in an Aramaic inscription from Palmyrene[65], while the Ho. of the verb occurs in Dan 4₃₃ עַל־מַלְכוּתִי הָתְקָנַת (I was established upon my kingdom). The ancient Versions seem to presuppose a passive here in Koheleth; for example, the Septuagint ἐπικοσμη- θῆναι, and the Vulgate corriguntur. Some commentators accordingly read

---

[60] Cf. the LXX προαίρεσις πνεύματος "a purposeful desiring of wind".

[61] With this expression in Hosea we may compare Prov 27₁₆ צֹפֵן־רוח "hoards the wind", and Akkadian sâk(i)el (šā)riim "who hoards the wind". See Held, JCS 15 (1961), 1–26, especially 6, 1. 7 (text) and 12a.

[62] Isa 44₂₀ רֹעֶה אֵפֶר is doubtful; "he desires? feeds on? ashes".

[63] Cf. Wagner, Die lexikalischen und grammatikalischen Aramaismen im alt- testamentlichen Hebräisch, 1966, No. 287 (107).

[64] רעות also occurs in Punic inscriptions with the meanings "decision" and "pleasure", as Dahood points out (Bibl 33, 1952, 203f.); but this is probably due to Aramaic influence. It would seem that וּת is the Aramaic abstract feminine ending like Hebrew מלכות which in Aramaic was shortened to מלכו (abs. st.). Cf. Rosenthal, A Grammar of Biblical Aramaic, 1961, 28.

[65] See Cook, A Glossary of Aramaic Inscriptions, 1898, 122; DISO, 333, 1. 40.

the Niphal לְהִתָּקֵן[66], while Driver suggests that we have an example of the rare form of the Pual infinitive construct לְתֻקָּן[67]. Gordis defends the text on the analogy of עֵת לָלֶדֶת, "a time to be born" in 3₂, where he remarks that, though the sense is passive, the infinitive Qal is used[68]. But this expression is idiomatic, and grammatically could be translated "a time to give birth". A passive meaning is, however, required of the verb here in 1₁₅. Driver's proposal preserves the consonantal text, but the Niphal may be expected in view of its usage in the following and parallel verb (לְהִמָּנוֹת).

1₁₅. וְחֶסְרוֹן. From חָסֵר "to lack". This nominal form appears here only in the Old Testament, but the notion of "need" or "poverty" is expressed elsewhere by מַחְסוֹר (e.g., Judg 18₁₀ Prov 11₂₄). In its context in Koheleth חסרון means "loss" or "deficit"; and the word is also used with this meaning in Talmudic literature: for example, Kid 32b, שאין בה חסרון (in which there is no monetary loss).

1₁₆. דִּבַּרְתִּי אֲנִי. The first person singular of the verb with the personal pronoun is characteristic of the book. In common with other late works, such as Haggai, Ezra and Esther, Koheleth uses אני to the exclusion of אנכי. This is likewise the practice of the Mishna where אנכי is used only in biblical quotations and in allusions to biblical material[69].

1₁₆. עִם לִבִּי. A common biblical usage; for example, עם לבבך Deut 15₉ עם לבבי Jos 14₇ and Ps 77₇. On the other hand, we find בלבי in 2₁ (אמרתי אני בלבי) and 2₁₅, with which we may compare Aḥiqar (l. 25) אף אמר בלבה (and said in his heart).

1₁₆. הִגְדַּלְתִּי וְהוֹסַפְתִּי "I magnified and increased". It is claimed that the second verb is here modified adverbially by the first, and that the phrase should be translated "I increased greatly"[70]. The Septuagint, however, renders "behold I have increased and have acquired...", thus recognising the independent verbal status of והוספתי. The form וְגָדַלְתִּי והוספתי occurs in 2₉, and some scholars emend accordingly here[71]. But the change of conjugation scarcely meets the sense required by our text. It would appear that the Qal of גדל is used intransitively

---

[66] E.g. Siegfried, Prediger Salomonis und Hoheslied, 1898, 30; BH³; Zimmerli op. cit. 87.

[67] VT 4 (1954), 225.

[68] Gordis op. cit. 201. So Hertzberg op. cit. 78 prefers the MT on the grounds of *lectio difficilior*.

[69] Segal, A Grammar of Mishnaic Hebrew, 1927, 39. So Kuhn, Konkordanz zu den Qumrantexten, 1960, 19–20, noted that אנכי occurs only 3 times in the Scrolls while אני is found no less than 20 times.

[70] So Gordis op. cit. 201 f.; see too Wright op. cit. 319; Barton op. cit. 86.

in biblical Hebrew. For example: Gen 26₁₃ וַיִּגְדַּל הָאִישׁ ... עַד כִּי־גָדַל מְאֹד (and the man increased ... until he was very great); I Sam 26₂₄ כַּאֲשֶׁר גָּדְלָה נַפְשְׁךָ ... כֵּן תִּגְדַּל נַפְשִׁי (as your life was precious, so may my life be precious); Jer 5₂₇ עָל־כֵּן גָּדְלוּ וַיַּעֲשִׁירוּ (therefore they have become great and gain riches). The Hi., on the other hand, is used in a transitive and reflexive sense. Thus, Ps 138₂ ... אִמְרָתֶךָ כִּי הִגְדַּלְתָּ (for thou hast magnified thy word); Koh 2₄ הִגְדַּלְתִּי מַעֲשַׂי (I magnified my works); Isa 9₂ הִגְדַּלְתָּ הַשִּׂמְחָה (thou hast increased the joy); Dan 8₂₅ וּבִלְבָבוֹ יַגְדִּיל (and in his heart he will magnify himself). Inasmuch, then, as the verbal construction of 1₁₆ is that of a transitive verb governing חכמה the use of the Hi. is normal. In 2₉, on the other hand, the Qal is natural in a sentence where the verb is intransitive: "I improved and increased more than any who were before me in Jerusalem". There is, therefore, no need to assume with Zimmermann that the different forms of the verb in 1₁₆ and 2₉ arose from a misreading of the Aramaic רְבֵית (I grew = Heb גָּדַלְתִּי) and רַבֵּית (I increased = Heb הִגְדַּלְתִּי)[72].

Dahood proposes that אֲנִי at the beginning of this line (1₁₆b) should be read as אוֹנִי (my wealth), thus providing a parallel for חכמה at the end of the line. He thinks that the Massoretic reading is due to a scribe mistaking the Phoenician spelling of an original אני[73]. The reading אוֹנִי for אֲנִי is indeed suggestive, but אני need not necessarily be the Phoenician form of אוני. It could be the orthographical variant of a scribe who happened to write defectively here: compare אוֹפָן (wheel) Isa 28₂₇, but אֹפָן in Ex 14₂₅; אֳנִיּוֹת (ships) Deut 28₆₈, but אוֹנִיּוֹת in II Chr 8₁₈[74].

1₁₆c עַל כָּל־אֲשֶׁר־הָיָה לְפָנַי עַל־יְרוּשָׁלָם. One MS recorded by de Rossi[75], the text of the Septuagint, Vulgate and Peshitta, read the plural for היה. Dahood too regards the MT as a "grammatical blunder", and thinks that it is another example of a scribe mistaking the identity of a consonantal הי[76]. There is, however, no compulsion to regard כל־ here as plural, or even as a collective noun: it could equally well be taken as "any". We may compare I Chr 29₂₅, אֲשֶׁר לֹא־הָיָה עַל־כָל־ מֶלֶךְ לְפָנָיו

---

[71] E.g. Graetz op. cit. 58; Galling op. cit. 54. The LXX, of course, reads ἐμεγαλύνθην in both passages, and it has been noted that the ה of הגדלתי in 1₁₆ could be due to dittography from the preceding הגה (cf. e.g. Zimmerli op. cit. 154 n. 1).

[72] JQR 36 (1945–46), 41.

[73] Bibl 47 (1966), 266.

[74] See further below p. 112f.

[75] Op. cit. III, 248a.

[76] Bibl 33 (1952), 37.

עַל־יִשְׂרָאֵל, where כל clearly means "any". So in Koh 2₉ we have a similar reference to a predecessor, and the scribe consistently wrote היה.

1₁₇ הוֹלֵלוֹת. From the root הָלַל, with the meaning "to boast". In Ps 5₆ we find a reference to "the boastful", הוללים, who should not stand before God; and in Ps 75₅ we read, אמרתי להוללים אל־תהלו (I said to the boastful, do not boast). The singular form is apparently הוֹלֵלָה (cf. Rabbinical הוֹלֵלָה)[77], but we do not find it in the Old Testament nor is הוללות found there outside Ecclesiastes. The plural form appears also in 2₁₂ 7₂₅ and 9₃, but a singular form הוֹלֵלוּת occurs in 10₁₃. The morphology appears to be that of the abstract ending וּת attached to the Qal participle[78].

1₁₇ וְשִׂכְלוּת. The context requires the meaning "folly". Thus in many MSS[79] and elsewhere in Koheleth (2₃. ₁₂. ₁₃ 7₂₅ 10₁. ₁₃) the form is סכלות, a term which derives from a root סָכַל meaning "to be foolish" (e.g. Gen 31₂₈ II Sam 24₁₀ Isa 44₂₅)[80]. The root שׂכל, on the other hand, means "to be wise", "act prudently" (e.g. Gen 3₆ I Sam 18₁₄ Prov 19₁₄). The occurrence of שׂ for ס, and ס for שׂ, is, of course, attested in late biblical Hebrew. Thus in Job 5₂ 6₂ 10₁₇ and 17₇ we find כעש for כעס (anger), while in Ezr 4₅ we have סכרים for שׂכרים (hiring).

This phonemic interchange between שׂ and ס is also discernible in Biblical Aramaic. For example, in Dan 5₃₀ we have כשׂדיא (Q כשׂדאה), but כסדיא (Q כסדאה) in Ezr 5₁₂. So in Dan 3₁₀. ₁₅ we find שׂבכא, but סבכא in Dan 3₅[81]. The tendency of שׂ to become ס seems to be more pronounced in extra-biblical Aramaic. Thus we find שׂכלתנו in Dan 5₁₁. ₁₂, but סכל in Aḥiqar l. 47. So we find שׂרשׁו (Q שׂרשׁי) "punishment" in Ezr 7₂₆, but in an Aramaic document from Egypt, a word with the same meaning, and basically the same form, begins with ס, סרושׁיתא[82]. In Syriac the development from שׂ to ס is complete[83], and ܣܟܠ means both "to be wise" and "to be foolish".

---

[77] Jastrow I, 339a.

[78] Cf. Barth, Die Nominalbildung in den semitischen Sprachen, 1913, 414f.

[79] See de Rossi op. cit. III, 248bf.

[80] Cf. Roth, VT 18 (1968), 69–78, who notes that "the basic notion of the verb in the Old Testament is that of intellectual inability or failure", 77. He further observes that since the root is well attested in Akkadian, but not in Aramaic and Ugaritic, it is likely to be a loan word from Akkadian (ibid.).

[81] Although the variant שׁבכא is found; see BH3.

[82] Letter 31. ₆ in Driver, Aramaic Documents of the Fifth Century B.C., 23. Driver, however, suggests that the word here may be Persian in origin, 47 n. 6.

[83] On S as the latest development of the sibilants, see Murtonen, JSS 11 (1966), 147f.

1 18 יוֹסִיף ... וְיוֹסִיף. There is some uncertainty whether these terms are to be taken as participles or imperfects. The Septuagint renders ὁ προστιθεὶς ... προσθήσει, thus taking the first as a participle and the second as an imperfect. The Peshitta employs the Aphel participle in both instances, while the Vulgate equivocally translates by the present indicative, *qui addit ... addit*[84]. Some commentators have regarded the terms as Qal participles on the analogy of such passages as Isa 29 14 הנני יוֹסף להפליא (behold I will again act wonderously) and 38 5 הנני יוֹסף (behold I addeth) where יוסף must be accepted as a Qal participle, pointed with *plene* vowels[85]. Franz Delitzsch, however, considered both instances of יוסיף as Hiphil imperfects, citing Prov 12 17 יָפִיחַ אמוּנה יַגִּיד צדק (he who speaks the truth declares righteousness) as a parallel[86]; and in this he is followed by other scholars[87]. Acceptance of יוֹסיף as a participle depends on the assumption that it is an anomalous form. On the other hand, the Hi. imperfect is frequently attested in biblical Hebrew (e. g. Deut 25 3 Jos 23 13 I Sam 3 17). It is therefore probable that it is this form, used in a gnomic capacity, which is to be recognised in the יוֹסיף of our text. The fact that the Hiphil infinitive is used in 3 14, in a phrase which is no more causative in meaning than here, tends to support this conclusion.

---

[84] The rendering of the Targum is too free and expansive to deduce its interpretation of these Hebrew forms.

[85] See e. g. Wright op. cit. 322, and Galling op. cit. 87. It may be noted that the Qal participle plural is found in Deut 5 22, and the Hi participle plural in Neh 13 18.

[86] Op. cit. 232.

[87] E. g. Barton op. cit. 88; Gordis op. cit. 204; Hertzberg op. cit. 79.

2₁ אֲנַסְּכָה. In rendering *affluam* the Vulgate took the root as נסך "to pour out". But the Septuagint (πειράσω σε) and the Peshitta (ܐܢܣܟ) rightly identify the root as נסה "to test, try". The final element כה . . . is accordingly the *plene* spelling of the 2nd person singular masculine suffix: compare Gen 10₁₉ בֹּאֲכָה . . . עַד עַזָּה בֹּאֲכָה סְדֹמָה (as thou goest to Gazah, as thou goest to Sodom); Jer 40₁₅ יַכֶּכָּה (smite you). The *plene* spelling occurs often in the Dead Sea Scrolls, and seems to be regularly employed in the *Hodayot*, where we find רצונכה (thy will), לכבודכה (for thy glory), בחוכמתכה (by thy wisdom), and many other instances[1]. Torczyner (Tur Sinai) proposed that the phrase ביין את־בשרי ולבי נהג in verse 3 should immediately follow אנסכה (I will try my flesh with wine, and my heart leading me in cheer)[2]; and accepting this order of the text, H. L. Ginsberg reads אֵיטִיב "gladden" for אנסכה[3]. But this transposition of the clause ביין . . . נהג disrupts the construction of verse 3, while אנסכה (I will test or try) is more natural to the experimental signification of verse 1.

2₂ מַה־זֹּה עֹשָׂה "What does this achieve?". זה here is the feminine form of the demonstrative pronoun זֶה. It is also the form used in 2₂₄ 5₁₅. ₁₈ 7₂₃, and זאת does not appear in the book at all. Dahood notes that seven MSS read זאת, and another seven read זו. Such variants, he argues, could not have arisen if Koheleth had been written in the "scriptio plena" of the fourth-third century Hebrew orthography. The Phoenician ז which represents both the feminine and masculine of the demonstrative pronoun "this" is, he assumes, the basis of the ambiguity[4]. But it is doubtful if these MSS witness to anything more than mere scribal

---

[1] See Baumgarten-Mansoor, JBL 74 (1955), 115, especially plate 35, 1.8–14, 117. So we may compare בחנתיכה of the Isaiah Scroll (a) 48₁₀ with the Massoretic בחרתיך.

[2] Dunkle Bibelstellen, in: Vom Alten Testament Karl Marti zum Siebzigsten Geburtstage gewidmet, ZAW 41 (1925), 279.

[3] Studies in Koheleth, 1950, 6.

[4] Bibl 33 (1952), 37. The variants in question are recorded in Kennicott, Vetus Testamentum Hebraicum: cum Variis Lectionibus II, 550 and in de Rossi, Variae Lectiones Veteris Testamenti III, 249.

variants; for in the one case we have the more usúal זאת, and in the other
the Mishnaic זו. The fact that הז appears as the feminine form in earlier
biblical texts (e.g. II Reg 6 19 Ez 40 45; cf. also Judg 18 4) suggests that
it is original here.

2 3 לִמְשׁוֹךְ בַּיַּיִן אֶת־בְּשָׂרִי. מָשַׁךְ has the primary meaning of "draw,
pull". Compare Gen 37 28 ימשכו "drawing" out of a pit; I Reg 22 34 משך
"drawing" a bow. The Septuagint (ἑλκύσει), Vulgate (*abstrahere*), and
Targum (לנגדא) likewise read "draw" or "pull". However, the idea of
"drawing" the flesh with wine is somewhat forced. It has thus been
suggested that we read לִשְׂמוֹךְ "to support", transposing the first two
letters of the root and regarding שׂ as an orthographical variant of ס
in סמך as in Cant 2 5, סמכוני באשישות (refresh me with raisins) [5]. Joüon
again proposed לְשַׂמֵּחַ "to make glad" on the basis of Ps 104 15 ויין
יְשַׂמַּח לבב־אנוש [6]. It may be noted too that Corré sees in משך the meaning
"to render uncircumcised" and reads בייו as כיין (as the Greeks) [7].

Zimmermann contends that the difficulty lies in a literal translation
from the Aramaic original. For while the Aramaic גְּרַר means "to draw"
or "pull" it also means "to stimulate the appetite", and is used in this
sense in the Talmud (e.g. Bera 35 b דגרריה לבביה). But, concludes
Zimmermann, this is a nuance which the Hebrew משך fails to reproduce [8].
However, as well as "draw", משך has also the meaning "sustain". For
example Jer 31 2 משכתיך (I have sustained you); Ps 36 11 משך חסדך
(prolong thy steadfast-love). Compare also the Arabic مسك "to hold,
grasp" [9], and the Aramaic משך "a covering, protection" (*Aḥiqar* 118).
"Sustain" is thus a suitable rendering here in Koh 2 3 [10].

2 3 נהג. In classical Hebrew this verb means "to drive or lead".
For example, Deut 4 27, to drive (ינהג) into exile; II Reg 4 24, to drive
(נהג) a beast; Ps 78 52, to lead (ינהגם) a flock. In our text here, however,
the meaning is rather that of "behaving or conducting oneself". The
word has this meaning likewise in Ben Sira 40 23, לעת ינהגו (behave

[5] E.g. BH³; Kroeber, Der Prediger, 78; cf. too Zimmerli, Das Buch Prediger,
40, who renders "zu laben" (refresh).
[6] Joüon, Bibl 11 (1930), 419–423; see here 419.
[7] VT 4 (1954), 416f.
[8] JQR 36 (1945–46), 37.
[9] See Freytag, iv. 179a.
[10] Delitzsch maintained that משך in the Talmud occurs in the sense of "refresh",
and translated a passage in Hag 14a as "The Haggadists refresh the heart of
man as with water" (op. cit. 234). See, however, Corré (loc. cit. 416 n. 2)
who contends that the point of comparison in this Talmudic passage is "in
the ease of drawing, not in the refreshing qualities of the water".

seemingly). So also in the Mishna it is used in the sense of "behaving" or of "being accustomed to". For example, Ab Zar 3₄ אֶת־שֶׁנּוֹהֵג בּוֹ מִשּׁוּם אֱלוֹהַ (one against whom one behaves as a God). Similarly in the Targum on Koh 10₄ we read דִי הֲוֵיתָא נָהֵג לְמִקַם בֵּיה (where thou wert accustomed to stand). We may accordingly translate here in 2₃, "my heart comporting itself in wisdom".

2₃ᵇ אֵי־זֶה טוֹב. What is the good? אֵי־זֶה has the force of the interrogative "what"; cf. I Reg 13₁₂ אֵי־זֶה הַדֶּרֶךְ הָלַךְ (which is the way he went?).

2₅ פַּרְדֵּסִים. The singular form פרדס occurs in Neh 2₈ and Cant 4₁₃. The plural appears here only in biblical Hebrew, but we find it in the Targum (e. g. Judg 4₅ Job 2₁₁) and again in Rabbinical literature (e. g. Arac 3₂ Metz 103a). The term is borrowed from the Persian *pairi-daēza*, a park or forest enclosure[11]. The Greek παράδεισος is likewise a transliteration, and was first used in Greek literature by Xenophon (e. g. Anab 1₃. ₇ Cyrop 1₃. ₄). It is used often in the Septuagint to translate גַן (e. g. Gen 2₈ 13₁₀).

2₆ מֵהֶם. "From them (masc.)", referring to the antecedent "pools" which is, however, feminine. This preference for the masculine third plural suffix is also found elsewhere in our book (2₁₀ 10₉ 11₈ 12₁). The fact that no suffixal form for the third person feminine plural is known in Phoenician leads Dahood to postulate a Phoenician influence again here[12]. But this tendency to use the form of the third person masculine plural instead of the feminine is evident in other parts of the Old Testament. In Judg 21₂₂ we have לֹא אַתֶּם נְתַתֶּם (ye did not give *them*, masc.) where the antecedent is אִישׁ אִשְׁתּוֹ (men's wives). So in Job 1₁₄ we find עַל־יְדֵיהֶם (beside *them*, masc.), the antecedent of which is הַבָּקָר הָיוּ חֹרְשׁוֹת (oxen were ploughing). Again, as Kropat has shown, the third person plural feminine form occurs neither in the verb nor the noun in Chronicles[13]. Likewise in the Manual of Discipline (IQS) there are three instances of masculine plural suffixes whose antecedents are feminine nouns[14]. So, of course, the Mishna has discarded the imperfect form תקטלנה, the second and third feminine plurals; both genders use תקטלו and יקטלו[15].

---

[11] See, e. g. Handbuch des Altpersischen, Brandenstein-Mayrhofer, 1964, 137.

[12] Bibl 33 (1952), 43–44.

[13] ZAW 16 (1909), 61.

[14] See Leahy, Bibl 41 (1960), 156.

[15] Segal, A Grammar of Mishnaic Hebrew, 1927, 71. We may note too that out of 13 instances of plurals which are feminine in Canticles only three retain

2₈ וּסְגֻלַּת מְלָכִים וְהַמְּדִינוֹת. סְגֻלַּת is the construct of סְגֻלָּה, a term which in Exodus (19₅) and Deuteronomy (7₆ 14₂ 26₁₈) signifies Yahweh's "possession" of Israel. In I Chr 29₃ it denotes "treasure" as here in Koheleth[16]. Syntactically והמדינות is a combined genitive with מלכים, but as מלכים is indefinite the use of the article with מדינות has led some scholars to question its authenticity. Thus the reading וַחֲמָדוֹת (and delightful things) has been proposed[17], and so has המון מְדִינוֹת (the riches of provinces)[18]. However, as Podechard observed, we should expect some such term as "governors"[19]. Dahood accordingly thinks that we can identify the Hebrew with the Ugaritic *mdnt*. In Anat II 15–16 we find *mṭm tgrš šbm bksl qšth mdnt* (with two clubs she drives out the ancients, with the heavy part of her bow the prefects)[20]. If, then, *mdnt* has the force of "prefects" it may be possible to see in מדינות a similar connotation.

2₈ᵦ וְתַעֲנוּגוֹת. From the singular תַּעֲנוּג, though elsewhere it takes a masculine plural (e.g. Cant 7₇ Mic 1₁₆). The root ענג connotes "softness or delicacy". In Mic 2₉ and Prov 19₁₀ it is used in the general sense of luxury, as also in Ben Sira 41₁ (לקבל תענוג, to enjoy luxury). In Cant 7₇ (בתענוגים) it is, however, used in an amorous sense (cf. Arabic غَنِج "to behave amorously"), and that is also probably the meaning here in Koheleth: "the amorous pleasures of man".

שִׁדָּה וְשִׁדּוֹת. This expression occurs here only in the Old Testament, and has been variously rendered by both ancient and modern interpreters. The Septuagint takes it as "a cupbearer and female cupbearers", οἰνοχόον καὶ οἰνοχόας apparently presupposing a Hebrew text שֹׁדֶה וְשֹׁדוֹת. The Syriac similarly reads ܫܩܝܐ ܘܫܩܘܬܐ (cupbearers and female cupbearers), and Aquila κυλίκιον καὶ κυλίκια (a cup and cups). The Vulgate reads *scyphos et urceros* (siphons and water-pots), while the Targum paraphrases as "baths and bath-houses with tubes which poured forth

---

the classical forms, while ten have the forms of the Mishna, which make no distinction between masculine and feminine. See Chomsky, JQR 42 (1951–52), 211.

[16] We may compare the Akkadian *sikiltum* (*sakâlu* "to aquire") which means "treasures" of rich men and kings, and also "possessions" of a god or goddess. See Held, JCS 15 (1961), 1–26, especially 11c. *Sglt* appears too in Ugaritic (UT 2060: 7, 12) and Dahood connects Koheleth's use of the term with this (Bibl 47, 1966, 267; 50, 1969, 341).

[17] E.g. BH³.

[18] Zimmerli op. cit. 1962, 156 n. 4.

[19] L'Ecclésiaste, 1912, 264.

[20] Bibl 47 (1966), 268 (Text, UT, 253a).

tepid water and tubes which poured forth warm water". But none of
these renderings suits the context. Indeed it is probable that שדה ושדות
is an amplification of the immediately preceding phrase "the amorous
pleasures of man". Hence of the ancient interpreters Ibn Ezra seems to
have come nearest to the correct meaning of the term when, relating
שדה to שָׁדַד "to seize", he thought it signified a woman captured in
war[21]. Most subsequent commentators have seen in שדה some reference
to woman. Thus Friedrich Delitzsch associated it with the Assyrian
šadâdu which he rendered "love"[22], while Gordis would connect it with
שַׁד "breast" (cf. Cant 7₄ 8₁, and Arabic ثدي "breast")[23]. Galling regards
שדה ושדות as "many women", but regards it as secondary and uncertain[24].

New light on the meaning of שדה now derives from Amarna and
Ugarit. In one of the Amarna tablets we find the ideogram salumún,
one meaning of which is "concubine". Significantly, the Canaanite gloss
is šaditum, which is probably to be identified with שדה of our text. This
root is also found in Ugaritic št (from šd-t, woman), and in turn is to be
equated with the Arabic ست "lady"[25]. We may accordingly render "a
mistress and many"[26]; compare Judg 5₃₀ רחם רחמתים "a woman or two".

2₉ אַף חָכְמָתִי עָמְדָה לִי. Here, as in 8₃, עמד has the force of "remain":
"yea, my wisdom remained to me". עמד has likewise this meaning in
Ps 102₂₇ המה יאבדו ואתה תַעֲמֹד (they perish but thou remainest), and in
Jer 48₁₁ טעמו על־כן עָמַד (therefore his taste remains)[27].

2₁₀ שָׂמֵחַ מִכָּל־עֲמָלִי. The idiom "rejoiceth from" is unusual, and some
MSS read בכל[28]. Prov 5₁₈ presents an example of such a usage: וּשְׂמַח
מֵאֵשֶׁת נְעוּרֶיךָ (and rejoice in the wife of thy youth), but this too has been
emended to באשת[29]. However, we now find smḫ followed by the pre-

---

[21] Ginsburg, Coheleth, 1881, 286.
[22] Prolegomena eines neuen Hebräisch-Aramäischen Wörterbuchs zum Alten
Testament, 1886, 97. This, however, is only a derived meaning of the term,
its primary meaning being "to draw, pull"; see Bezold, Babylonisch-Assyrisches Glossar, 1926, 266a.
[23] Op. cit. 209.
[24] Der Prediger 87. 89. So Driver thinks that the phrase may be a gloss indicating "costly furniture", VT 4 (1954), 240. The NEB does not translate the
words, regarding them as "unintelligible".
[25] See Milik, RB 59 (1952), 590.
[26] Cf. Kroeber "sehr viele Frauen" (op. cit. 81); so Zimmerli (op. cit. 156) and
Strobel (op. cit. 40) "Frauen in Menge".
[27] Cf. also Driver, ZAW 78 (1966), 5, who points out that in II Chr 20₁₇ Neh 7₃
and Job 32₁₆ עמד has the meaning of "standing still".
[28] Kennicott op. cit. II, 550b records three.
[29] E. g. BH³.

position *mn* in Ugaritic: *wum tšmḫ mab* (and may my mother draw her happiness from my father)[30].

2₁₁ וּבֶעָמָל. עמל has here the force of "wealth, gain" rather than "labour". It has this meaning too, as in other places in the book, in 2₁₈. There the participle עָמֵל has the signification of "amass, acquire" rather than "labour"[31]. The verb has also this meaning in the Aramaic inscription of Barrakib: ובית אבי עמל מן כל "and the house of my father *amassed* more than any"[32]. We may compare also the Qumran Manual of Discipline (I QS) IX 22 לעזוב למו הון ועמל כפים (to leave to him wealth and gain of hands) where עמל כפים is synonymous with הון "wealth". So in the later Talmudic literature עמל may denote "acquisition, income, rent"[33]. We may then render Koh 2₁₁a, "And I turned my attention to all my works which my hands performed and to all my wealth which I strove to acquire, and behold . . .".

2₁₂b כִּי מֶה הָאָדָם שֶׁיָּבוֹא אַחֲרֵי הַמֶּלֶךְ אֵת אֲשֶׁר־כְּבָר עָשׂוּהוּ: An obscure and uncertain line which Ehrlich regarded as "hopelessly corrupt"[34]. The translators of the ancient Versions were equally perplexed by the passage as their largely unintelligible renderings indicate. The Septuagint rendered "For who is the man who will follow after counsel (βουλῆς) in whatever things he uses" (τὰ ὅσα ἐποίησεν αὐτήν). It thus takes מה האדם as מי אדם[35], and המלך as the Aramaic מְלַךְ (counsel, cf. Dan 4₂₄). Symmachus likewise reads βουλῆς but Aquila reads τοῦ βασιλέως. The

---

[30] See Virolleaud, Palais Royal d'Ugarit, II 1957, 31: Dahood, Ugaritic-Hebrew Philology, 1965, 30. Some scholars, of course, think that *mab* may be a scribal error for *mad* "much" on the grounds that "much" would make better sense, and that this is the first text in which Ugaritic *mn* "from" is found (see Greenfield, HUCA 30, 1959, 143 and 144 n. 14, and M. H. Pope, JBL 85, 1966, 465; cf. also Barr, Comparative Philology and the Text of the Old Testament, 1968, 176, who denies the existence of Ugaritic *mn* "from"). Gordon (UT 148) accepts the reading *mab* but thinks it is due to dialectical interpenetration. But Dahood claims to detect the preposition *mn* in Ugaritic *mrhqtm* (= *mn* + *rhqt* + enclitic *m*) "from afar" (Sacra Pagina 1, 270). More recently de Moor declared (UF 2, 1970, 312, 314) himself as accepting the existence of the Ugaritic *mn* "from" and would render the Ugaritic *yrh mkty* as "Yarihu *from* Katti".

[31] Cf. Ginsberg, Studies in Koheleth, 3 n. 2a, and Dahood, Bibl 47 (1966), 269.

[32] Text as Donner and Röllig, KAI I, No 216 7-8 (40). These scholars, however, translate "eifriger als alle" (more zealous than all), II 233.

[33] See the references in Jastrow II 1089a. It may be noted too that עמל has a similar meaning in Samaritan Aramaic; see Greenfield (Bibl 50, 1969, 101).

[34] Ehrlich, Randglossen zur hebräischen Bibel, VII 1914, 62.

[35] McNeile, An Introduction to Ecclesiastes, 1904, 140, however, regards this as the pre-Akiban reading.

Vulgate, Peshitta and Targum all attest to "king", but otherwise they seem to have little bearing on the Massoretic Text. Many commentators insert יעשה between מה and האדם (What does man do?)[36], and its omission may indeed be explained through *homoioteleuton*[37]. The plural form (עשוהו) of the verb is difficult, although it is defended by such scholars as Wright and Hertzberg[38]. It is preferable to read the singular עָשָׂהוּ, with many MSS[39], and this is also presupposed by the Septuagint, Peshitta and Vulgate. Perhaps the superfluous *waw* may have been originally prefixed to את with the force of "but". We may accordingly render the line, "And what does the man do who comes after the king but that which he has already done"[40].

2₁₅ᵦ גַּם־אֲנִי יִקְרֵנִי "It befalls even me". גם־אני serves as an emphatic accusative and is in apposition to the verbal suffix נִ. Compare Gen 27₃₄ בַּרְכֵנִי גַם־אָנִי (bless me, even me) and Zech 7₅ הֲצוֹם צַמְתֻּנִי (have you fasted even for me?) where נִ is similarly used in an emphatic sense. So we find אני ידי (my hands indeed) in Isa 45₁₂, and אתה ידך (thy hand indeed) in Ps 44₃. This use of the personal pronoun is also found in Ugaritic: *tḥt p'ny ank* (under my very feet)[41]; *šmk 'at ygrš* (thy name indeed is Yagrash)[42]. Likewise in a Phoenician text from Karatepe we read ובימתי אנך (but in my days)[43].

2₁₅ᵧ וְלָמָּה חָכַמְתִּי אֲנִי אָז יוֹתֵר. Although accepted by most commentators[44], the particle אז is difficult, and is omitted by some Greek MSS,

---

[36] E.g. BH3, Kroeber op. cit. 80; Strobel op. cit. 42; so Galling op. cit. 90–91, but he would also delete "king" and read אחרי "after me" for אחרי"after".

[37] Hertzberg explains the omission of the verb as an example of *Aposiopes* (op. cit. 76 and 80). But it is doubtful if a verb would be thus suppressed in what is a comparatively short sentence.

[38] Wright op. cit. 333; Hertzberg op. cit. 80.

[39] Driver mentions 68 in BH².

[40] The line, of course, is commonly regarded as misplaced. Thus, citing such authorities as Siegfried, Budde and Vischer, Kroeber (op. cit. 115) thinks that it should precede 12a, while the NEB, translating, "What sort of a man will he be who succeeds me, who inherits what others have acquired?", transposes it to the end of v. 18. But there are no convincing grounds for transposing the line. In v. 12a the author says that he is turning to consider wisdom, madness and folly, and then comments as 12b; that is, he is merely recalling 1₁₇ where he had stated that it was characteristic of him who ruled over Jerusalem to take account of such matters.

[41] Aqht II 6₄₄₋₄₅ (UT 249a).

[42] UT 68₁₁₋₁₂ (180); also UT § 6₁₄ (37).

[43] KAI I, No. 26, II, 5 (5).

[44] E.g. Gordis op. cit. 212; Zimmerli op. cit. 160; Kroeber op. cit. 81. Cf. too Hertzberg's translation: op. cit. 76 and his Commentary 80.

the Syriac, Vulgate and Coptic Versions. The Septuagint too takes יותר
with the following clause (περισσὸν ἐλάλησα). Dahood at one time
thought that such textual variants arose from the "scriptio defectiva"
of the original, and regarded the correct reading as אֵי זה יותר (where
is the advantage?)[45]. More recently, however, he expressed the view that
אז is to be taken as the Phoenician demonstrative ז preceded by the
prosthetic Aleph, and translates, "Is this an advantage?"[46] We would
indeed expect that the letters אז should contain some note of interrogation
as a balance to למה in the first part of the line[47]. It is probable, however,
that אז is a corruption of an original אֵי (where?), the י of which was
mistaken by a copyist for ז. An instance of such a mistake is to be found
in Ben Sira 41 18c. In the B Text we have על זר (regarding a stranger),
but in the B Marginal and the Masada Scroll we have על יד (regarding
sleight-of-hand). An example of the confusion of ר and ד is also seen
here in the B Text, and the Greek περὶ κλοπῆς (concerning theft) supports
the reading[48]. We would, therefore, read אי for אז and accordingly
translate our line "And why am I wise, where is the advantage?".

2 16 עם. אֵין זִכְרוֹן לֶחָכָם עִם הַכְּסִיל עִם הַכְּסִיל לְעוֹלָם is probably to be rendered
"as" or "like" here. "There is no remembering the wise man, (he is)
like the fool for ever". It has this meaning also in 7 11, and indeed elsewhere in the Old Testament. Thus עם is parallel with כ in the following
passages: I Chr 25 8 כקטן כגדול מבין עם־תלמיד (as the small so the great,
the teacher as the pupil), Job 9 26 חלפו עם־אניות אבה כנשר יטוש עלי־אכל
(they glide by as ships of reed, as an eagle swoops on its prey)[49]. We may
also compare the Ugaritic aššprk 'm b'l šnt 'm bn il tspr yrḫm (I will make
you number years like Baal, like the sons of El will you number
months)[50].

2 16b בְּשֶׁכְּבָר "for already". בש equals the classical באשר meaning
"for, because" (cf. Gen 39 23). So in Koh 7 2 and 8 4 באשר means "for"[51].
Zimmermann questions the grammatical consistency of the succeeding
words הַיָּמִים הַבָּאִים with בשכבר and thinks that the translator from the
Aramaic confused the tenses. For in translating the Aramaic participle

---

[45] Bibl 33 (1952), 205.

[46] Bibl 47 (1966), 268.

[47] A point which is not met by Joüon's emendation אז אין יותר, Bibl 11 (1930),
420. Cf. also Galling op. cit. 90.

[48] See Yadin, The Ben Sira Scroll from Masada, 20b.

[49] Cf. Gordis op. cit. 212; Held, JBL 84 (1964), 280 n. 36.

[50] Aqht II, VI 28-29 as UT 248b. See too Dahood, Bibl 47 (1966), 269.

[51] It may be noted that אשר too has the meaning "because" or "for"; cf. Koh 4 9
6 12 8 11. 13. 15 Gen 30 18 31 49. Cf. too under Koh 2 18.

אָתַיִן ("passing") by the corresponding Hebrew participle בָּאִים he over-looked the fact that, while an Aramaic participle may denote the past, the Hebrew participle denotes the present only. Hence, he says, a phrase which was natural in Aramaic ("because days *already have* passed and everything *was* forgotten") becomes peculiar in Hebrew ("for already the days are passing, everything is forgotten")[52].

2₁₆c וְאֵיךְ יָמוּת הֶחָכָם עִם הַכְּסִיל "And how (?) will the wise man die as the fool?". אֵיךְ is difficult here, and the emendation אַךְ (yea) has been suggested[53]. Zimmermann maintains that the Hebrew translator mis-understood the Aramaic particle הֵיכְדִין ("so"), and represented it as ("how")[54].

2₁₇ רַע עָלָי "Grievous unto me". Zimmermann notes that this ex-pression is equivalent to the Aramaic בְּאֵשׁ עַל (cf. Dan 6₁₅)[55]. The use of the preposition על with the pronominal suffix to express states of being in conjunction with a verb is, of course, common in Aramaic. For example, Dan 4₂₄ ישפר עליך (that it may please thee) and Dan 6₂₄ טאב עלוהי (he was glad). So in *Aḥiqar*, ls. 64–65, we find the phrase ויבאש עלוהי (and he grieves over him). We meet, however, with the same idiom in late Hebrew passages: for example, I Chr 13₂ אם־עליכם טוב (if it seems good to you); Est 3₉ אם־על המלך טוב (if it seems good to the king); Ps 16₆ שפרה עלי (it was pleasing to me). The usage is similarly found in the Mishna; יהי כבוד חברך חביב עליך כשלך (let the honour of thy friend be as dear to thee as thine own), Aboth 2₁₀.

2₁₈ אֲנִי עָמֵל. The vowel *a* in the second syllable of the third person singular of the verb עמל appears in 2₂₁, עָמַל. We accordingly recognise עָמֵל here as the stative participial form; compare 4₈c where עָמֵל serves the same function as the participle מְחַסֵּר, both being immediately govern-ed by the pronoun אני. This stative participial form of the verb עָמֵל is peculiar to Koheleth in the Old Testament[56], but we find it again in the Rabbinical literature (e.g. Aboth 2₂ Bero 28b)[57].

2₁₈ שֶׁאַנִּיחֶנּוּ "Because I will leave it". שׁ has here the force of "be-cause". Compare Cant 1₆ שאני שחרחרת (because I am swarthy); Gen 30₁₈ אשר־נתתי (because I gave) and 31₄₉ אשר אמר (because he said). So else-where in Koheleth (4₉ 8₁₅) אשר also means "because". The Hi. when

---

[52] JQR 36 (1945–46), 38–39.
[53] Winckler, Altorientalische Forschungen I (1896), 351.
[54] JQR 36 (1945–46), 39.
[55] Loc. cit. 20.
[56] עָמֵל in Prov 16₂₆ Job 3₂₀ 20₂₂ and in Judg 5₂₆ (pl.) appears to be a noun.
[57] See Jastrow II 1088b.

followed by the preposition ל as here (לאדם), means "bequeath" or
"leave"; so Greek ὅτι ἀφίω. Compare Ps 17₁₄ . . . והניחו יתרם ל (and
may they leave their remnant . . .). In Ben Sira 44₈ the Hiphil of נוח has
likewise the meaning "leave": "And there are some of them who have
left (הניחו) a name".

2₁₉ וְיִשְׁלַט. Apart from Ecclesiastes this verb is found in biblical
Hebrew only in late passages (Neh 5₁₅ Est 9₁ Ps 119₁₃₃). It occurs frequently, however, in the Aramaic section of the book of Daniel (e. g.
2₃₉ 3₂₇ 5₁₆ 6₂₅).

2₂₀ לְיָאֵשׁ, the Pi. infinitive of the root יאשׁ. BH³ points, as here,
on the basis of the most important MSS. Other MSS point לְיָאֵשׁ [58], with
compensating lengthening of the vowel before א (cf. בֵּאֵר Pi. pf., Deut
1₅). In לְיָאֵשׁ we must assume a virtual strengthening or doubling of א
as, for example, in בָּאֵר (Deut 27₈ Pi. inf. abs.) [59]. Apart from this instance in Koheleth, the root appears in biblical Hebrew only 5 times
(1 Sam 27₁ Isa 57₁₀ Jer 2₂₅ 18₁₂ Job 6₂₆), and on each occasion in the
Niphal. In rendering Koh 2₂₀ the Targum uses the Pi. infinitive לְיָאָשָׁא.
So in Rabbinical Hebrew we find the noun יֵאוּשׁ (Metz 21 b) in the form
of a derivative from the Pi.[60], and also the Hithp. תִּתְיָאֵשׁ (Aboth 1₇),
which presupposes the use of Pi. In the earlier biblical passages cited
above the verb has the meaning "to despair, give up", and the root has
a similar meaning in Rabbinical usage. But this hardly represents the
force of the term in Koheleth [61], nor are the renderings of the Septuagint
(ἀποτάξασθαι to bid farewell, renounce), the Vulgate (renunciavit renounce) and the Peshitta (ܡܫܬܒܩ to relax) adequate. In the mind of our
author יאשׁ seems to have the nuance "disillusion"; "and I turned to
disillusion my heart concerning . . .".

2₂₁ כִּשְׁרוֹן. The noun in this form is found only in Koheleth (2₂₁
4₄ 5₁₀). The verbal root כָּשֵׁר (Aram. כשר, Syriac ܟܫܪ), meaning "to
succeed, to prosper", appears in Koh 10₁₀ 11₆ and Est 8₅. A plural
nominal form כּוֹשָׁרוֹת is also found in Ps 68₇ with the meaning "prosperity". In Koheleth the noun has the force of "skill" or "industry"; so
the Septuagint ἐν ἀνδρείᾳ (in fortitude). We may compare the Ugaritic

---

[58] E. g. as the text of the British and Foreign Bible Society, edited by Snaith
1958.

[59] Cf. GK § 64e (170).

[60] See Jastrow I 560a.

[61] Although generally represented as "despair"; cf. e. g. Barton op. cit. 77;
Hertzberg op. cit. 77; Kroeber op. cit. 83; Strobel op. cit. 44.

epithet *kṯr* "skilled" applied to *Hyn*, the divine craftsman, and also *Kṯrt*, the women who were "skilled" in incantation and other rites[62].

2₂₂ הֹוֶה לְאָדָם. הֹוֶה is pointed as a Hebrew participle of the verb הָוָה "to be, to fall". הוה appears in Aramaic inscriptions from the·eighth century B.C. onwards[63], while we find the imperative הֱוֵה in Gen 27₂₉, and the participial form (הֹוֶה) in Neh 6₆. So in the Mishna הוה appears frequently as a form of the verb "to be" (e.g. Aboth 1₉. ₁₂. ₁₅). We would here render, "For what has (is there to) man?".

2₂₅ כִּי מִי יֹאכַל וּמִי יָחוּשׁ. The Septuagint, Theodotion and the Peshitta read ישתה (will drink) for יחוש, as in verse 24. So the Vulgate paraphrases *et deliciis áffluet ut ego* (and abound in delights as I). On the other hand, Aquila, Symmachus and Syro-Hexaplar (ܢܣܡܒ) presuppose יָחוּשׁ "to experience pain". So likewise the Targum reads חֲשָׁשָׁא, "feeling" or "anxiety". In Arabic again we have the verb حس "to feel, perceive", and according to BDB (301 f.) יחוש here is to be connected with this root. In the course of a lengthy consideration of our term, Ellermeier points out that the Akkadian *ḫâšu* means both "to hasten" and "to be worried". On the basis of this he concludes that we are to distinguish a Hebrew root חִישׁ "to hurry" and a related root חוּשׁ "to worry"[64]. Some scholars would not, however, regard "worry" as suitable to the context here in Koheleth. Thus Reider proposes a connection with the Arabic خوث "to be full of food" on the grounds that we would then have a suitable synonym for אָכַל[65]. So Rosenthal thought that יחוש is related to the Akkadian root *ḫšš* "to rejoice"[66], while Dahood would connect it with the Ugaritic root *ḫšt* which he thinks has the meaning of "joy" or "happiness"[67]. On the other hand, Gordis would associate the root with the Arabic حشى VI "abstain from, refrain"[68], and Du Plessis would agree with this view of the term[69].

---

[62] E.g. UT No. 761 (390) and Text 77₁₁. ₁₅ (UT 183a).

[63] E.g. *Zenzirli*, ls. 2–5, KAI I, 215 (39). *Carpentras*, ls. 3–4, KAI I, 269 (51). Cf. also Wagner, Die lexikalischen und grammatikalischen Aramaismen im alttestamentlichen Hebräisch, 1966, 72 (45).

[64] Ellermeier, ZAW 75 (1963), 197–217. So Müller, VT 18 (1968), 512, connects יחוש with חוש and regards it as "experiencing pain", while Castellino, CBQ 30 (1968), 27 n. 10, likewise thinks that the root means "to worry, fuss, feel agitation". Cf. too Driver, JTS 32, (1931), 253f., who associates יחיש of Isa 28₁₆ with חוש "to be agitated".

[65] VT 2 (1952), 129–130.

[66] Orientalia 16 (1947), 402.

[67] Bibl 39 (1958), 307f.

[68] Op. cit. 216f.

[69] De Fructu Oris Sui, Pretoria Oriental Series 9, 1971, 179.

Some uncertainty obtains, then, as to the identity and connotation of the root underlying יחוש in Koh 2₂₅. The meaning "rejoice" would certainly suit the context; but it is possible that חוּשׁ, which primarily seems to connote "worry", has a secondary meaning "to be concerned about, to reflect". Compare the Mandaic חשש, חוּשׁ "feel pain, to meditate"[70], and the Rabbinical חוּשׁ "to feel pain, consider"[71]. We might then possibly translate "For who eats and considers . . .".

2₂₅. חוּץ מִמֶּנִּי. חוּץ means "street" or "outside"[72]. Compare Deut 23₁₃ (יצא חוץ) where it has an adverbial force. Hence חוץ ממני signifies "outside of", or "apart from *me*" (*him*?, see below). חוץ with מן is found here only in biblical Hebrew, but it is frequently found in the Mishna: for example, חוץ מן היין חוץ מן הפת (except wine, except bread, Bera 6₁). The idiom corresponds to the Aramaic בר מן (Aram. בר = open field; cf. Dan 2₃₈), and Syriac ܠܒܲܪ ܡܸܢ.

Some MSS, the Syriac and Coptic Versions, read "apart from him", and commentators usually emend to מִמֶּנּוּ[73]. The emendation is unnecessary, however, for the form י as the third person masculine singular suffix occurs in Hebrew. In the Psalms alone we find more than one example. In 16₈ we have שויתי יהוה לְנֶגְדִּי תמיד כי מִימִינִי בל־אמוט (I will keep Yahweh continually before me, yea, from *his right hand* I will not depart). So in 42₅ we read אלה אזכרה ואשפכה עָלַי נפשי (These things I will remember and pour out *to him* my soul)[74]. This meaning of the suffix *y* also appears to obtain in Ugaritic. Thus in the text Baal II, viii, 12-13 we read *hmry mk ksu ṯbth* (but mire is the throne of his dwelling)[75], but in another context (Baal I, ii, 15-16) we find *hmry mk ksu ṯbty* where "his dwelling" is represented by *ṯbty* instead of *ṯbth*[76]. The suffix *y* as the form of the third person masculine is, of course, also found in Phoenician. For example ושכר אנך עָלַי מלך לאדני ל(רש)ף (for his lord, Rasif)[77]; אשר (and I hired against him the king of Assyria)[78].

---

[70] A Mandaic Dictionary, (Drower-Macuch), 138a.

[71] See Jastrow I 441a.

[72] KBL 283a.

[73] Cf. Barton, The Book of Ecclesiastes 1908, who mentions twelve scholars who read ממנו. Barton himself thought that ממני "gives no intelligible reading", 97. So also BH³, Zimmerli op. cit. 164; Hertzberg op. cit. 81; Kroeber op. cit. 82. Odeberg however (Qohaelaeth, 1929, 27) would accept the MT and translate as "except I", meaning the author himself.

[74] Cf. Dahood, Psalms, I 1966, 11.

[75] Text as Driver, CML 102a; UT 51 VII 12–13 (183b).

[76] Text as Driver, CML 104a; UT (178b).

[77] KAI I, 41₃ (9).

[78] KAI I, 24₈ (5). Cf. also Harris, Development of the Canaanite Dialects 1939, 54.

3₁ זְמָן "Season". In biblical Hebrew it appears only in late passages; here and Neh 2₆ Est 9₂₇. ₃₁. It occurs frequently in Aramaic (e.g. Ezr 5₃ Dan 2₁₆ 3₇. ₈ 4₃₃ 7₁₂, and is probably an Aramaic loan-word from Akkadian[1]. We also meet it in Ben Sira 43₇, זמני חוק (seasons of decree)[2], and again in the Mishna (e.g. Zeb 1₁ פסח בזמנו, a Passover at its appointed time).

3₁ לְכָל־חֵפֶץ "For every matter". The verb חָפֵץ primarily means "to delight in" (cf. Syriac ܚܦܨ Pa. "to urge"). Thus in early Hebrew passages both the verb and noun carry the notion of "desire, pleasure"; for example Judg 13₂₃ (verb), II Sam 23₅ (noun) and Isa 44₂₈ (noun). The noun also has this meaning in Koh 5₃ and 12₁. In an Aramaic inscription of the eighth century B.C. חפץ has, however, the force of "business": ואשלח מלאכי אלוה לשלום או לכל חפצי (when I send my ambassador to him for peace or for any of my business)[3]. So in later Hebrew חפץ has the meaning of "affair" or "matter". We detect the intermediate stage in such a passage as Isa 58₁₃ עשות חפצך ביום קדשי (doing thy pleasure [hence, *business*] on my holy day). The later connotation of the term as "affair, thing, object" is to be discerned here in Koh 3₁ and also in 3₁₇ 5₇ and 8₆. חפץ has likewise this meaning in post-biblical Hebrew. Thus in the Mishna (Metz 4₁₀) we read בכמה חפץ זה (how much is this thing?), and in the Talmud we find אדם מוכר חפץ לחברו (a man sells a thing to his fellow, Bera 5a).

Zimmermann thinks that the meaning of חפץ here in our text is "desire", and that it is a translation from the Aramaic צְבוּ "want, desire"[4]. But the meaning "matter" or "affair" suits the context better, since it serves as a comprehensive term for the list of activities and preoccupations mentioned in the immediate sequence.

---

[1] See Wagner, Die lexikalischen und grammatikalischen Aramaismen im alttestamentlichen Hebräisch, 1966, Nos. 77–79 (49).

[2] Text as Levi, The Hebrew Text of Ecclesiastes, 1951 (reprint), 56. See however, Yadin, The Ben Sira Scroll from Masada, 1965, 29, who thinks that חוק may be a mistake for חג "festival".

[3] Fitzmyer, The Aramaic Inscriptions of Sefire, 1967, 96.

[4] JQR 36 (1945–46), 19.

3₂ וְעֵת לַעֲקוֹר נָטוּעַ. This is the only instance in biblical Hebrew in which the root עקר is used in the Qal. Elsewhere it is used in the Ni. (Zeph 2₄) and Pi. (e.g. Jos 11₉ II Sam 8₄). לעקר is usually rendered "to pluck up", although some uncertainty attaches to its etymology[5]. In a Phoenician inscription from Karatepe the noun עקרת appears with the meaning "storehouses": ומלא אנך עקרת פער (and I filled the storehouses of Pa'r)[6]. Hence the meaning "to harvest" is more suggestive here in Koheleth than "to pluck up"[7]. We may compare too, with Dahood, the semantically related term אספים (storehouses) in I Chr 26₁₇, from the verb אָסַף "to gather"[8].

3₄ עֵת סְפוֹד וְעֵת רְקוֹד. This is the only line in verses 1–8 in which the infinitive is not preceded by the preposition ל. Dahood accordingly thinks that the preposition must be supplied from the previous line, and regards this as an example of "a double-duty preposition". In making this suggestion, he cites Ugaritic n'm lḥṭt b'n bm nr-ksmm (sweet to the wheat in the furrow, to the spelt in the tilth)[9]. It is true indeed that the preposition may serve a "double-duty" function[10]. But it is not necessary to assume this usage here. The construction is that of the infinitive construct with a gerundial meaning: "a time of weeping and a time of dancing". So in v. 8ᵇ we have the variation of עת with a following noun: עת מלחמה ועת שלום (a time of war and a time of peace).

3₁₁ᵇ הָעֹלָם: a difficult term. The Versions as a whole take it to mean "world" or "eternity". Thus the Septuagint reads αἰῶν and the Peshitta ܟܠܥܠܡܐ; so the Vulgate *mundum*, although in rendering the clause as *et mundum tradidit disputatione eorum* (he [God] has handed over the world to their contention) it presupposes לְרֻבָּם (√ריב, cf. Job 31₁₃ בְּרֻבָם) instead of the Massoretic בְּלִבָּם. Franz Delitzsch may be mentioned as representative of those older scholars who interpreted עלם in terms of "eternity"[11], and this is also the rendering of Hertzberg[12] and Zim-

---

[5] See KAI II, 40; cf. also DISO 220, ls. 42–44. עקר is found, however, in an Aramaic inscription from Sefire where it has the force of "offspring", and according to J. A. Fitzmyer the term literally denotes "the offshoot of a root", op. cit. 28.

[6] KAI I, No. 26₆ (5).

[7] So too Batten, ZAW 28 (1908), 190.

[8] Dahood, Bibl 47 (1966), 270.

[9] Ibid. Text UT 126: III 9–10 (193); Driver, CML 42b.

[10] See e.g. Dahood, Psalms I, 1965, 17. 201f.

[11] The Song of Songs and Ecclesiastes, 1885, 259f.

[12] Der Prediger 106f.

merli[13]. Rejecting this interpretation, Kroeber translates the term as *Welt*, and conceives of it as the coherence of the dynamic process of the events of life[14]. Jenni has again argued that עלם is to be explained as the extensive duration of time (*Zeitdauer*)[15], and this is broadly the view of Galling (*Dauer*)[16] and Hengel (*Zeitablauf*)[17]. Suggesting that Koheleth wished to emphasise the continuous nature of time, Ellermeier renders by "incessancy" (*Unaufhörlichkeit*)[18], and Barucq similarly interprets the term as denoting an indefinite duration of time, embracing past, present and future[19]. Strobel translates the term as "Ewigkeitssinn" and conceives of it as the actions of men which in divine providence can endure beyond the present[20]. Gordis again considers that the term is to be interpreted in the Mishnaic sense of the love of the world (Aboth. 4₇)[21]. But it is doubtful if any of these meanings suits the context here. Hence, both Macdonald and Kamenetzky proposed the emendation הָעָמֵל (the striving)[22], and this is still maintained by Ginsberg[23] and proposed in BH³. On the other hand, Hitzig would point הָעֵלֶם and claimed to discern in the term an etymological connection with the Arabic عِلْم "knowledge"[24]. Rashi had earlier taken the word to apply to the wisdom of the world, but it is significant that he thought it was written defectively because it signified what is hidden[25]. Among subsequent exegetes Graetz accepted this view of עלם and rendered it as "ignorance"[26]. That the root עלם may have this meaning may be seen from more than one biblical text. In Koh 12₁₄ it is used of "the hidden" (נֶעְלָם) works which God will judge. In Job 28₂₁ it is applied to wisdom being "hidden"

[13] Das Buch des Predigers Salomo 168–172.
[14] Der Prediger 116 and cf. also 134f.
[15] ZAW 65 (1953), 22–27.
[16] Der Prediger 93f., and cf. also his article in ZThK 58 (1961), 1–15.
[17] Hengel, Judentum und Hellenismus, 1973², 221. So Schmid, Wesen und Geschichte der Weisheit, 1966, 192, also renders as "Zeitablauf".
[18] Ellermeier, Qohelet, (Teil I, Abschnitt 1), 1967, 319f.
[19] Barucq, Ecclésiaste, 75. 81f.
[20] Das Buch Prediger (Kohelet) 55f.
[21] Gordis, Koheleth — The Man and his World, 222.
[22] Macdonald, JBL 18 (1899), 212; Kamenetzky, ZAW 24 (1904), 238.
[23] Ginsberg, The Quintessence of Koheleth, in: Biblical and other Essays, 1963, 50.
[24] Der Prediger Salomos, KEH, 1883², 229.
[25] See text as presented in Ginsburg, Coheleth, 309f. So it may be noted that the Targum concludes its lengthy treatment of the verse with a statement that God "hid" (כסי) from the Israelites the day of death.
[26] Kohélet oder der Salomonische Prediger, 1871, 70.

(נעלמה) from man, and again in Job 42₃ it is used of God "hiding (or darkening) counsel" (מעלים עצה). The meaning "darkness" or "ignorance" would agree with the burden (ענין) which according to the previous line "God gave to man to occupy him"[27]. This view of the term עלם is further supported by the appearance of the word *ǵlm* in Ugaritic with the meaning "darkness"[28].

3₁₁ᶜ מִבְּלִי אֲשֶׁר לֹא־יִמְצָא. בלי is a negative particle from the root בלה "to become old, worn". Hence מבלי means "from lack of, without, because of"[29]. Its use with a negative also appears elsewhere in biblical Hebrew. For example: Ex 14₁₁ הֲמִבְּלִי אֵין־קברים במצרים (Is it because there are no graves in Egypt?; IIReg 1₃ הֲמִבְּלִי אֵין־אלהים בישראל (Is it because there is not a God in Israel?). We may also note the Syriac usage ܡܛܠ ܕܠܝܬ (because there is not)[30]. V. 11 may then be rendered: ". . . even darkness he put into their heart, because of which man cannot discover the work which God did from the beginning even unto the end". Compare 8₁₇, "I have seen all the work of God, and indeed man is not able to discover the work which is done under the sun, for the sake of which man tries to seek but he does not discover it; and even if a wise man claims to know he is not able to discover it"[31].

3₁₁ᵉ וְעַד סוֹף. סוֹף (end) is a late word. Apart from Koh (3₁₁ 7₂ 12₁₃) it occurs only in Joel 2₂₀ (end, rear of enemy) and IIChr 20₁₆ (end of valley). סוף is found also in Aramaic (Dan 4₈. ₁₉ 7₂₈), while the expression עד סופא appears in Dan 6₂₇ and 7₂₆. The word occurs too in the Mishna; for example, Bera 1₁ עד סוף האשמורה הראשונה (unto the end of the first watch).

3₁₂ בָּם. Hertzberg defends this reading[32], although we should expect from בחייו (in his life) at the end of the line that the term should have a singular rather than a plural signification. Two Hebrew MSS[33] and the Targum read באדם, and this seems to be confirmed from 2₂₄ (אין

---

[27] The initial clause of verse 11, "The lot he made beautiful in his time", is either misplaced from the end of verse 8 or is an editorial insertion.

[28] *wǵlm* (and it grew dark). For text see UT 125₅₀ (192). *ǵlm* has also the meaning of "overwhelm": Keret I i 19, *ǵlm ym* (the sea overwhelmed). See G. R. Driver, CML 28. Cf. too the Phoenician Aḥiram Inscription (10th cent. B.C) שתה בעלם (I laid him in darkness-the grave), KAI I. 1₁ (1).

[29] Kamenetzky thinks, however, that מבלי should be deleted, as a dittography from the preceding בלבם. Loc. cit. 238.

[30] Thesaurus Syriacus I (Smith, 1879) 528 b.

[31] Cf. further below 150, 157.

[32] Op. cit. 100.

[33] Kennicott, Vetus Testamentum Hebraicum; Cum Variis Lectionibus II, 552.

טוב באדם). Accordingly Driver would explain the MT as a misreading of בם which was an early abbreviation for באדם [34].

וְלַעֲשׂוֹת טוֹב 3₁₂. The context suggests that the meaning here is that of experiencing a sense of well-being or success. Some scholars accordingly regard it as the equivalent of the Greek εὖ πράττειν [35]. This is denied by Barton and Gordis [36]; but it is nevertheless probable that there is a reflexion here of the Greek idiom "to succeed" or "fare well" [37].

כָּל־אֲשֶׁר יַעֲשֶׂה הָאֱלֹהִים הוּא יִהְיֶה לְעוֹלָם 3₁₄. Zimmermann thinks that יעשה should be in the Perfect, since "one cannot add to or subtract from that which is not made as yet". He regards the use of עָשָׂה later in the verse as another indication that the Perfect of the verb should be used throughout. The confusion arose, he explains, by the translator rendering the Aramaic participle עָבֵד as a future instead of a Perfect [38].

שֶׁיִּרְאוּ 3₁₄. שׁ here expresses purpose, "so that, in order that". So אשר has this meaning in earlier biblical texts. For example: Deut 4₁₀ אשר ילמדון ליראה אתי (so that they may learn to fear me); Deut 4₄₀ אשר ייטב לך (so that it may be well with you); I Reg 3₁₂ אשר כמוך לא־היה (so that there was not like you). The Aramaic די is also used in the same way: for example, Dan 4₃ די־פשר חלמא יהודעני (in order that they may make known to me the interpretation of the dream).

מַה־שֶּׁהָיָה כְּבָר הוּא . . . 3₁₅. Zimmermann thinks that the tenses are peculiar here. He thus contends that הָיָה is an example of a translator mistaking an Aramaic הוּא (it is, is) for הֲוָא (was, has been), and that conversely הוּא is a mistaking of an Aramaic הֲוָא for הוּא [39]. However, if we take כבר as signifying "of long ago", as in Rabbinic usage [40], the phrase is quite meaningful: "that which is, is of long ago . . .".

שם 3₁₇c כִּי עֵת לְכָל־חֵפֶץ וְעַל כָּל־הַמַּעֲשֶׂה שָׁם is obviously a difficulty here. With the Septuagint and Peshitta, many scholars accept, and attempt to justify, the meaning "there" [41]. But emendations have also been proposed. Thus Barton, Scott, Loretz, Strobel and Braun read שֹׂם

---

[34] Textus 4 (1964), 80.

[35] E.g. Wildeboer, Der Prediger, 1898, 134; Hertzberg op. cit. 100; Ranston who connects the Hebrew phrase with Theognis, Ecclesiastes and the Early Greek Wisdom Literature, 1925, 44.

[36] Barton, The Book of Ecclesiastes, 32; Gordis op. cit. 222.

[37] Cf. e.g. Herodotus 1₂₄. ₄₂; Plato, Alcibiades 1₁₁₆b.

[38] Loc. cit. 40.

[39] Loc. cit. 33–34.

[40] See Jastrow I 609b.

[41] E.g. Gordis op. cit. 225; Zimmerli op. cit. 175; Kroeber op. cit. 87; Galling op. cit. 96.

(appointed, decreed)[42]. Hertzberg proposes זְמָן (season)[43] and BH³ offers שָׁמֵר (observe). We would expect שם to contain a parallel to עת. Hence Dahood claims to recognise in it a noun meaning "place, proper place"[44]. He does this by equating שם with *samu*, in the Amarna text *ia-nu i(p)ru sa-mu ia-nu mi(ti)-ma* which, with S. A. B. Mercer, he translates as "place"[45]. But in this text *mi(ti)* is an uncertain reading, and *samu* may also mean "plant" (*sammu*)[46]. It will be noted that Barucq too renders "a proper place for every action"[47]. The Targum interprets the term as referring to the world to come, and this interpretation has been accepted by Ginsburg who also mentions משם in Gen 49 24[48]. But the reading שָׁם is there doubtful, and it is likely that in conformity with its context we should point as שֵׁם (name)[49]. Gordis likewise sees in our word a reference to the future world, and cites as supporting evidence Job 1 21 3 17. 19, where שם refers to the peaceful conditions of Sheol[50]. But the antecedent for שם as an adverb of place is not clear in Koh 3 17. Moreover, Koheleth himself conceives of Sheol as a place where "there is neither work (מעשה) nor reckoning nor thought nor knowledge" (9 10). Consequently for him the notion of Sheol as a place where "there is a time for every מעשה" would be meaningless. The Vulgate again renders שם as 'then' (*tunc*), but it has been rightly questioned if שם can have a temporal force at all[51]. Now it has been suggested that שם may have an interjectional force such as "lo, behold"[52]. And if this meaning

[42] Barton op. cit. 107, 111; Scott, Ecclesiastes, AB 18, 1965, 222; Loretz (who renders "wacht er", he watches over) op. cit. 256; Braun, Kohelet und die frühhellenistische Popularphilosophie, 89. 92. As Ginsburg notes (Coheleth, 1861, 315) many earlier commentators read שָׁם.

[43] Op. cit. 101.

[44] Bibl 47 (1966), 271.

[45] This text is to be found in Knudtzon, Die El-Amarna-Tafeln, I 1908, No. 155: 20–21 (634f.). Mercer's translation is in vol II, 505 of his The Tell El-Amarna Tablets, 1939. The Glossary to Knudtzon's work (vol II) by Weber-Ebeling also suggests "stelle?" (1511).

[46] This (*eine Pflanze*) is the rendering suggested by Knudtzon himself (vol. I 635).

[47] Op. cit. 84.   [48] Ibid.

[49] E. g. BH³, RSV, NEB.

[50] Op. cit. 225.

[51] See e.g. Driver-Gray, The Book of Job, 1921, Pt. II, 268; Powis Smith, Zephaniah, 1929, 40.

[52] Probably to be pronounced *sum* inasmuch as it is thought to be connected with the Amarna *Summa* "behold" which is regarded as deriving from the Akkadian demonstrative *su* plus the emphatic particle *-ma* (e. g. E. A. Speiser,

for שם is established, it is likely that it may also have the nuance "too, also"[53]. It is then possible that we are to recognise this asseverative particle here, and that accordingly we should render the line "for there is a time for everything and for every act too". But while this meaning for שם would suit the context, it must be admitted that the force of the term is still uncertain.

3₁₈. עַל־דִּבְרַת בְּנֵי־הָאָדָם. דברת is the construct of דִּבְרָה "manner, cause"; hence עַל־דברת denotes "because of, concerning". The expression also occurs in 8₂. Apart from Koheleth, עַל־דברת appears in biblical Hebrew only in Ps 110₄[54]. It corresponds to the earlier עַל־דְּבַר (e.g. Gen 12₁₇ 20₁₁ Ex 8₈), but it has a direct linguistic connection with the Aramaic עַל־דִּבְרַת (e.g. Dan 2₃₀). Dahood claims that in דברת we have an instance of Phoenician morphology in which certain prepositions end with ת: thus, he notes, we have the form עלת as well as על, and פנת in addition to לפן[55]. He suggests too that the Syriac rendering ܡܡܠܠܐ (talk, speech) betrays Phoenician influence, although he does not explain why[56]. The Peshitta ܥܠ ܡܡܠܠܐ here, however, is but a literal representation of the Hebrew עַל־דברת, and is no more exceptionable than the Greek περὶ λαλιᾶς, the literalness of which Dahood regards as "excusable".

3₁₈: לְבָרָם הָאֱלֹהִים וְלִרְאוֹת: An uncertain clause. Most scholars derive לברם from the root בָּרַר whose primary meaning is "to purify" (e.g. Ez 20₃₈ Job 33₃) but which in later Hebrew signified "to select, choose" (e.g. IChr 7₄₀ 9₂₂ Neh 5₁₈)[57]. In rendering διακρινεῖ the Septuagint seems to accept this secondary meaning of the root, while the Vulgate *probaret* (prove) and the Targum לנסאיהון ... למבחניהון (test ... try) show but slight variations from it. On the other hand, in reading ܒܪܐ the Peshitta took the root as ברא (create). In form לברם is regarded by many as the infinitive Qal (with the third plural masculine suffix), an analogy being drawn with the infinitive formation לרד (from רדד) in

---

JCS 1, 1947, 321–328; Haldar, JCS 4, 1950, 63–64, and Moran, JCS 7, 1953, 79f.). See Dahood's arguments in Bibl 38 (1957), 306f.; Psalms, I 1965, 81, and Psalms, III 1970, 410.

[53] See Whitley, Bibl 55 (1974), 394–398.

[54] Where, however, it has the form דברתי, the terminal *yodh* being probably an early genitive case ending. Cf. GK §§ 90k ff. (252f.).

[55] Bibl 33 (1952), 47.

[56] He merely writes: "The Greek literal transliteration περὶ λαλιᾶς is excusable, but the same leniency cannot be granted to the Syriac ܥܠ ܡܡܠܠܐ" (ibid).

[57] Cf. e.g. BDB 140f.; KBL 156a.

Is 45₁ and שַׁךְ (from שׂכך) in Jer 5₂₆ [58]. But on this interpretation the clause would lack a finite verb. Accordingly it has been suggested that the ל is an *Emphatic Lamedh* prefixed to the perfect of ברר [59]. A particle of this nature is common in other Semitic languages: thus the Arabic ل, the Akkadian and Ugaritic *lu* emphasise the word to which they are prefixed [60]. Such a usage is also recognised in Koh 9₄ כִּי־לְכֶלֶב חַי הוּא טוֹב (for indeed a living dog is better . . .) and in other biblical passages such as Ps 89₁₉ (כי ליהוה מגננו ולקדוש ישראל מלכנו, for *indeed* Yahweh is our shield, and *indeed* the Holy One of Israel our king) and Cant 1₃ (לְרֵיחַ שמניך, *how fragrant* are your anointing oils). If then we have an instance of the Emphatic Lamedh here in לברם it might be translated, "whom (God) indeed chose". The structure and meaning of the term, however, remain doubtful.

3₁₈ᵦ וְלִרְאוֹת. Many Versions (G S Sʰ V K) read the Hiphil לַרְאוֹת "to show", and some commentators accept this [61]. Syntactically it is taken as an infinitive consecutive, used in place of a finite verb, after לברם, with האלהים as subject (surely God has tested and shown) [62]. This is an acknowledged Hebrew usage [63], and is probably to be recognised here; but in view of the uncertainty attaching to לברם the syntax of ולראות is doubtful. Accepting the Massoretic Qal (so Targum) it might equally be construed with the earlier אמרתי, yielding a sense which accords with the context: "I considered in my heart concerning the sons of men . . . and saw that they are beasts". לברם האלהים would then be in the nature of a parenthesis, and may not even be original.

3₁₈ᵦ שְׁהֶם־בְּהֵמָה הֵמָּה לָהֶם: Again a difficult phrase. It is tempting to regard המה as a dittography of the last letters of בהמה [64]. The Septuagint too omits המה, although it erroneously takes להם with the following verse: καί γε αὐτοῖς συνάντημα (and even to them is the event) [65]. Driver suggests that the passage should be read as לראות משהם־בהם ההמה להם

---

[58] E. g. Barton op. cit. 111; McNeile, An Introduction to Ecclesiastes, 64; GK § 67 p (180).

[59] Gordis op. cit. 226; Eitan, REJ 74 (1922), 1–16; Jorge Megia, EstBib 22 (1963), 179–190.

[60] Nötscher, VT 3 (1953), 372f.; UT 76 (9₁₆).

[61] E. g. McNeile op. cit. 64; Barton op. cit. 112.

[62] So Gordis op. cit. 226f.

[63] See GK § 114 (351).

[64] So, for example, BH³ and Zimmerli op. cit. 175 n. 3.

[65] McNeile argues that this rendering of the LXX indicates that the Hebrew of v. 18 originally ended with גם להם, op. cit. 64. It would be difficult, however, on grounds of dittography to account for the particle גם.

(to see what they are in themselves, whether they are [true] to themselves)
or that בהמה is a mere dittography[66]. Montgomery thought the
difficulty of the passage would be resolved on a proper understanding of the nature of the term שהם. The element הם, he maintains, is a
conflation of the Aramaic הֵן and Hebrew אִם ("if"), while שׁ is the equivalent of the Aramaic דִּי: the combination as a whole was intended to
introduce the indirect question "whether". We may, he adds, compare
the Syriac ܗܢ [67]. But this sheds no light on הֵמָּה לָהֶם which constitute
the core of the problem. A solution may, however, be proposed on the
basis of the Septuagint. We observed that this Version omits המה, and
it is thus probably a late dittography. On the other hand, the Septuagint
testifies to the originality of להם, although misinterpreting its force
here. Rather it is probable that the term is to be recognized as an instance
of a pronominal element to which the Emphatic ל is prefixed. Compare,
for example, I Sam 26₁₁₋₁₂ where ונלכה לנו is to be rendered "Let us go,
we indeed", and וילכו להם as "They went, *they indeed*"[68]. So a literal
translation of our phrase here is "that they are beasts, *they indeed*". This
accords naturally with the sequel in which Koheleth declares that there
is little difference between the fate of man and beast.

---

[66] VT 4 (1954), 277.
[67] JBL 43 (1924), 241 f.
[68] See Whitley, JQR 65 (1975), 225–28.

4₁ₑ וּמִיַּד עֹשְׁקֵיהֶם כֹּחַ וְאֵין לָהֶם מְנַחֵם. Some scholars regard עשקים as syntactically difficult[1]. So Dahood thinks that, in accordance with Phoenician and possibly Ugaritic usage, we have here an intervention of the heavy pronominal suffix הם‑ between the *regens* and the genitive כח. He would then translate: "And from the grip of their powerful oppressors, they have none to free them"[2]. But it is doubtful if the construction is either applicable or necessary here. For Dahood's translation ignores the conjunction *waw* in וְאֵין, and we can hardly take it as an *emphatic waw*. Nor is it necessary to supply a verb for כח[3]. As the text stands we have a certain antithesis between the first and second parts of the line: "And from the hand of the oppressors (there is) power, but there is no one to deliver them".

In view of the occurrence of מנחם in the previous line (4₁ᵦ) its appearance here in 4₁ₑ is regarded as suspect. Various emendations have accordingly been proposed. Thus Horst and Scott would read מְנַקֵּם "avengeth"[4]. Offering a solution which would involve no change of consonants, Driver suggests מְנֻחָם (a shortened form of the Hithpael מִתְנַחֵם: cf. GK § 54, p. 149)[5]. Dahood again would point מַנְחֵם (the Hi.pt of נחה "to lead", followed by the 3 per. pl. suf., cf. Job 31₁₈ אַנְחֶנָּה) "who frees them"[6]. However, as Zimmerli points out we have a similar repetition of הָרֶשַׁע in 3₁₆, and therefore מְנַחֵם may have been intentional on the part of the author[7].

4₂ וְשַׁבֵּחַ אֲנִי. It is usual to take שבח as an infinitive absolute[8]. We find many examples of a subject following an infinitive absolute when it

---

[1] E.g. Gordis, Koheleth—The Man and his World, 1951, 228; McNeile, An Introduction to Ecclesiastes, 1904, 65.

[2] Bibl 47 (1966), 271f.   [3] As e.g. McNeile op. cit. 65.

[4] Horst, BH³, *ad loc.*; Scott, Ecclesiastes, AB 18, 1965, 222.

[5] VT 4 (1954), 227f.   [6] Bibl 47 (1966), 272; 48 (1967), 438.

[7] Das Buch des Predigers Salomo, 1962, 178 n. 1; cf. also Strobel, Das Buch Predigers (Kohelet), 1967, 69 n. 2, who notes that the root עשק is used 3 times in the verse.

[8] E.g. Barton, The Book of Ecclesiastes, 1908, 116f.; Gordis op. cit. 229; Hertzberg, Der Prediger, 1963², 102; Dahood, Bibl 33 (1952), 49f.; Galling, Der Prediger, 1969², 97.

takes the place of a finite verb (e. g. Lev 6₇ הַקְרֵב ... בְּנֵי־אַחֲרֹן, the sons of Aaron shall offer; Num 15₃₅ רָגוֹם ... כָּל־הָעֵדָה, all the congregation shall stone)[9]; but, apart from our text, an infinitive absolute followed by a personal pronoun occurs elsewhere in the Old Testament only in Est 9₁ וְנַהֲפוֹךְ הוּא (and which had been changed). Such a construction is thought however to appear in Phoenician. Thus in the *Kilamuwa* inscription we read ושכר אנך עלי מלך אשר (and I hired against him the king of Assyria), and in Azitawadd's inscription from Karatepe we find ועַן אנך ארצת עזת (and I subdued mighty lands)[10]. Moran, again, finds the infinitive absolute similarly used in certain Amarna documents, and regards Koh 4₂ as a "particularly pertinent" biblical example[11]. Driver has suggested, however, that שבח of Koh 4₂ and נהפוך of Est 9₁ should be vocalised as perfects[12]. So in a later publication he maintains that both Phoenician and Ugaritic exhibit a similar use of the perfect: such, he argues, is the force of פעל in the Phoenician ופעל אנך לשרש אדני נעם (and I showed favour to the issue of my Lord, *Karatepe*, L. 10) and *ngš* in the Ugaritic *ngš ank ảlèyn bᶜl* (I came upon the victor Baal, *Baal* III ii 23)[13]. Horst proposed in BH³ that שבחתי (as 8₁₅) should be read here for שבח, and Driver later commented that שבח may be an example of an abbreviation in which the pronominal affix is omitted[14].

It should be noted that the pointing שַׁבֵּחַ may be that of the infinitive absolute or infinitive construct (cf. שַׁלֵּחַ תְּשַׁלַּח, inf. abs., Deut 22₇; לְשַׁלֵּחַ inf. con. Ex 7₂₇), and further that in the Dead Sea Scrolls we have examples of an infinitive construct followed by a personal pronoun[15].

---

[9] See GK § 113 gg (347).

[10] Texts as KAI I: *Kilamuwa* 24 (5); *Karatepe*, 26; JA, 18 (5). See also Gordon, JNES 8 (1949), 112f.

[11] JCS 4 (1950), 169–172. See too Huesman, Bibl 37 (1956), 271ff., especially 285. Cf. also Jirku in: Von Jerusalem nach Ugarit, 1966, 363f., for a statement on the similar use of the Infinitive Absolute in Ugaritic.

[12] JBL 73 (1954), 130. It may also be noted that וְשַׁבֵּחַ is the reading found in the Babylonian—Yemenite MS studied by Ratzabi (Massoretic Variants to the Five Scrolls from a Babylonian-Yemenite MS) in Textus 5 (1965), 103.

[13] CML, 131. Cf. too Hammershaimb in: Hebrew and Semitic Studies Presented to G. R. Driver, 1963, 92f., who in accepting the Massoretic text of Koh 4₂ seems to regard the term as an infinitive absolute, but would explain it in terms of "a verbal regimen like the finite verbs in verbal clauses", 93. Cf. also the perceptive comments of Hoftijzer in a review of Hammershaimb's article, Bior 24 (1967), 29.

[14] Textus 4 (1964), 94.

[15] Gordis, Bibl 41 (1960), 399.

Thus in the Manual of Discipline vii 16 we read לְשַׁלֵּחַ הוּא מֵאִתָּם וְלֹא
יָשׁוּב עוֹד (he is to be sent away from them and not return again), and in
Damascus Document ix 1 we find בחוקי הגוים לְהָמִית הוּא (by the decrees
of the nations [Gentiles] he will be put to death). It is doubtful, of course,
if we have in these passages an exact parallel to our term in Koh 4₂,
since the waw prefixed to שבח indicates that ושבח serves a consecutive
verbal function. Nevertheless, their relevance lies in their testimony
to the use of the infinitive followed by a personal pronoun.

4₂ᵦ הַחַיִּים אֲשֶׁר הֵמָּה חַיִּים. המה is here a separate pronoun, repeating
and emphasising the subject of a relative clause. Another example occurs
in 7₂₆, הָאִשָּׁה אֲשֶׁר־הִיא מְצוֹדִים (a woman who is snares). Dahood remarks
that the construction appears in three Phoenician texts[16]. It is, however,
a common usage in biblical Hebrew[17]. For example: Deut 1₃₉ וּבְנֵיכֶם
אֲשֶׁר ... הֵמָּה יָבֹאוּ שָׁמָּה (and your sons who will come there); Neh 2₁₃
הוֹמַת יְרוּשָׁלִַם אֲשֶׁר הֵם פְּרוּצִים (the walls of Jerusalem which are destroyed)
and Ez 43₁₉ הַלְוִיִּם אֲשֶׁר הֵם ... הַקְּרֹבִים אֵלַי (the Levites who ... draw
near to me). Aramaic also exhibits the same use of the third personal
pronoun. For example: Dan 6₂₇ דִּי־הוּא אֱלָהָא חַיָּא (who is the living
God); Dan 7₁₇ דִּי אִנִּין אַרְבַּע (which are four). So in the Mishna
we find a similar usage; thus אֵלּוּ שֶׁהֵם צְרִיכִים (these that require)
Mik 10₄.

4₂ᵦ עֲדֶנָה. עדנה "hitherto" and עֲדֶן "still" (4₃) are thought to be
abbreviations from עַד־הֵנָּה and עַד־הֵן[18]. Dahood thinks that עדן is an
adverb deriving from the Ugaritic ʿdn (time) and that עדנה is the same
form with the terminative suffix, just as ʿlmh in Ugaritic denotes "to
eternity"[19]. However, it must be borne in mind that the words עדנה
"hitherto" and עדן "still" are distinctive in origin. עדנה derives from
a root עָדָה "up to, till, until", עדן from a root עָדַד "at the same time,
during, while, when"[20]. So, although ʿd means both "until" and "during" in Ugaritic, it is probable that in each respect the particle has a
different source. Thus in yšt (il y)n ʿd šbʿ trt ʿd škr (Il drinks wine *until*
he is sated, liquor until he is drunk)[21] ʿd may be compared with the
Hebrew root עדה (up to, until). On the other hand, in the phrase ʿd lḥm

---

[16] Bibl 33 (1952), 197.
[17] Cf. GK § 141 gh (453).
[18] So BDB 725b; KBL 684a; LHAVT 575b.
[19] Bibl 33 (1952), 48. Cf. also his Ugaritic-Hebrew Philology (1965), 36, where he
  regards עדנה as the same adverb as עדן followed by the -h *directionis temporale*.
[20] Driver, ZAW 78 (1966), 5f.
[21] UT No. 1813 (453b).

šty ʿelm (while the gods ate [and] drank) [22] *ʿd* seems to be cognate with *ʿdn* 'season' (cf. Aram. עֵדָן, Syriac ܥܶܕܳܢ, Arabic عِدَّان) [23].

4₃ אֵת אֲשֶׁר is hardly an accusative governed by וְשַׁבֵּחַ in v. 2 [24]. The Septuagint, ὅστις οὔπω ἐγένετο (whoever is not yet), and the Peshitta ܛ̇ܒ ... ܗ̣ܢܘܢ (better ... are they), take the Hebrew construction as a nominative, while the Vulgate supplies the verb *judicavi*. אֵת אֲשֶׁר is used in the sense of "if" in 1 Reg 8₃₁, but apart from Koh 4₃ it is doubtful if it appears elsewhere in biblical Hebrew in a nominative clause [25]. Ferdinand Hitzig cites Jer 38₁₆ and 6₁₈ as parallel instances [26]. But the *Qere* omits אֵת in 38₁₆, while in 6₁₈ אֵת־אֲשֶׁר is clearly an accusative after the imperative וּדְעִי. On the other hand, אֵת־שֶׁ often appears in a nominative clause in the Mishna. For example, Dem 2₅ אֵת־שֶׁדַּרְכּוֹ לְהִמַּדֵּד (whatever is measured) and Git 9₇ אֵת־שֶׁהָעֵדִים נִקְרִין עִמּוֹ כָּשֵׁר (the signatories which can be read together—that is legal).

4₆ חָפְנַיִם עָמָל טוֹב מְלֹא כַף נַחַת מִמְּלֹא. חָפְנַיִם is pointed as a dual absolute, and as such its syntactical relationship with עָמָל is problematic. BH³ would solve the difficulty by inserting ו before עָמָל. We would expect, however, that, like the previous clause, we should have a construct chain here, as indeed in the Septuagint (ὑπὲρ πληρώματα δύο δρακῶν μόχθου, than the fill of two fists of trouble). If, then, the מ of חָפְנַיִם is original, it is probable that we must recognise it as the *Mem Encliticum* [27]. This is a particle which is found elsewhere in biblical Hebrew. Thus in Deut 33₁₁ מָחַץ מָתְנַיִם קָמָיו (crush the loins of his adversaries) an enclitic Mem follows the construct dual. So in Gen 14₆ the Massoretic בְּהַרְרָם שֵׂעִיר should probably be read as בְּהַרְרֵי־ם שֵׂעִיר (in the mountains

---

[22] Driver loc. cit. 6.

[23] UT No. 1823 (454a).

[24] Against, e.g. Siegfried, Prediger und Hoheslied, 1898, 45; Wright, The Book of Koheleth, 349. Barton op. cit. 117, also took אֵת here as the sign of the accusative.

[25] The Particle אֵת is, of course, frequently used in a nominative clause. For a recent treatment of the particle see Hoftijzer, Oud Stud 14 (1966), 1–99, and the literature cited there (1 n. 1). Hoftijzer himself believes that originally the particle was used with pronominal suffixes, but on the disappearance of the case endings it became connected with nominal forms (95). It may be noted that Saydon, VT 14 (1964), 193–210, regards Koh 4₃ as an instance cf. "an apparent erroneous use of the particle" (208), and thinks that the verb "to be" should be understood in rendering it (209).

[26] Der Prediger Salomo's, 1883², 235.

[27] So Dahood, Bibl 43 (1962), 355, and also 49 (1958), 89f. The original force of this particle seems to have been that of emphasis or indefiniteness. In poetry it was sometimes used as a balancing element. See Hummel, JBL 76 (1957), 86. 90, and Freedman, ZAW 72 (1960), 103f.

of Seir) with the Versions. Similarly an enclitic Mem is to be discerned in בְּיָדָם זעמי (in the hand of my rage) in Isa 10₅[28]. The phenomenon of the enclitic Mem also occurs in other Semitic languages. Thus in a Phoenician text of the third century B.C. we have אלם נרגל (the god Nergal)[29], while, according to Gordon, an enclitic Mem is to be seen in the two words ending with מ in the phrase ירדם ישבם אנך (I brought down, I settled) of the *Karatepe* inscription[30]. So in *ḥtnm bˤl* (O, son-in-law of Baal) and *bnm il* (son of Il)[31] we have Ugaritic examples in which the enclitic Mem is interposed between a construct and a genitive, as in our text חׇפְנַיִם עמל[32]. It may be noted that עמל has here, as in 2₁₈, the force of "wealth": "Better one handful of peace than two handfuls of wealth . . .".

4₁₀ אִם יִפְּלוּ הָאֶחָד יָקִים אֶת־חֲבֵרוֹ. Some scholars would read יפל instead of יִפְּלוּ[33]. יפלו may, however, be taken partitively[34]. Compare Gen 11₃ and Judg 6₂₉ ויאמרו איש אל רעהו (and a man said to his neighbour); Isa 47₁₅ איש לעברו תעו (they err, each according to his way).

4₁₀ᵦ וְאִילוֹ "and woe to him", a combination of the two words אִי. וְאִי לוֹ is in place of the older אוֹי as, for example, אוֹי־לִי in Isa 6₅ and Jer 5₁₀. אוֹי לו is found in the Mishna (e.g. Yeb 3₅), but the shortened form אִי לו also occurs; for example, אי לו על אשתו וְאִי לו על אשת אחיו (woe to him on the loss of his wife, and woe to him on the loss of his brother's wife, Yeb 13₇). So in the Jerusalem Targum we find אִי מה בִּישִׁין (Ah, how evil, Lev 26₂₉). The Targum (Babylonian) takes אִילוֹ here in Koheleth as אִלוֹ (אִם לוֹ) "if"[35], but the Septuagint (οὐαὶ αὐτῷ), the Peshitta (ܘܳܝ) and the Vulgate (*vae*) read as אִילוֹ. So in Koh 10₁₆ we have אִי־לָךְ ארץ (woe to thee O land). Dahood suggests that אי is a defective writing of the classical אוֹי[36]. But there is little need to postu-

---

[28] See further Hummel loc. cit. 92 ff.

[29] KAI I No. 59₂ (13).

[30] Gordon, JNES 8 (1949), 114, regards ירדם and ישבם as causative adverbial infinitives followed by the enclitic element מ. It could hardly, he adds, be the suffix "them" which in this text is נם, as in the previous word ענתנם (I humbled them).

[31] UT 129, § 13. 101.

[32] For remnants of the enclitic MEM in Arabic, Aramaic and Canaanite Amarna, see Hummel loc. cit. 88 ff.

[33] See Hertzberg op. cit. 102. So Dahood, Bibl 49 (1968), 243. BH³, however, would insert השנים before יפלו.

[34] Cf. Gordis op. cit. 232.

[35] Cf. Koh 6₆ where אִלוֹ "if" naturally occurs.

[36] Bibl 33 (1952), 38.

late this in view of the appearance of the form אי in the Mishna and Jerusalem Targum. We may compare also the form הי in Ez 2₁₀.

4₁₂ וְאִם־יִתְקְפוֹ הָאֶחָד. The subject of the verb יתקף is impersonal, while the verbal suffix anticipates the following (objective) noun האחד. On this latter construction we may compare Koh 2²¹ יִתְּנֶנּוּ חֶלְקוֹ (he will give it as his portion), Ex 2₆ וַתִּפְתַּח וַתִּרְאֵהוּ אֶת־הַיֶּלֶד (and she opened and saw him [viz.] the child), and Ex 35₅ יְבִיאֶהָ אֵת תְּרוּמַת יהוה (and bring it [viz.] the offering of Yahweh). האחד serves a similar appositional function in v. 10, וְאִילוֹ הָאֶחָד (and woe to him [viz.] the one). The root תקף appears in Hebrew only in late passages (Job 14₂₀ 15₂₄), but we find it frequently in Aramaic (e. g. Dan 4₈. ₁₇ 5₂₀) and in the Mishna (e. g. Aboth 3₈ אפילו תָּקְפָה עליו מִשְׁנָתוֹ even if his study is too difficult for him).

4₁₃ מִסְכֵּן. This word occurs in the Old Testament only in the book of Koheleth (4₁₃ 9₁₅₋₁₆), although it is also found in Ben Sira (4₃ 30₁₄) and again in the Talmud[37]. We, however, find the noun מִסְכֵּנוּת with the meaning "scarcity" in Deut 8₉; and, according to Gordis, מִסְכָּן in Isa 40₂₀ is a misvocalisation of מְסֻכָּן[38]. Podechard thought that the appearance of מסכן in Koheleth is due to Aramaic influence[39], and it is true that the word is known in that language[40]. However, we already meet the term *muškēnu* in the Old Akkadian period with the meaning "dependent"[42], and it also appears in the Amarna Letters[41] and in Ugaritic literature[43] with reference to an inferior or poor person. We may compare too Arabic مسكين, Syriac ܡܣܟܺܢܳܐ and Mandaic מסכינא (*miskina*)[44] all of which denote "poor" or "beggarly". The meaning of the word in Koheleth would likewise seem to be that of "poor". מסכן appears twice as a proper name in Phoenician, and Dahood implies that we have here another link between the author of Koheleth and the Phoenician language[45]. But in view of the widespread use of the term there is little certainty of this.

---

[37] Jastrow II 807.

[38] Op. cit. 233.

[39] E. Podechard, L'Ecclésiaste, 1912, 46.

[40] E.g. Targum on Koh 4₁₃ (מסכין), and 4₁₄ (מסכינא); Deut 15₁₁ (למסכנך).

[41] See Speiser, JCS 6 (1952), 91; cf. also Driver-Miles, The Babylonian Laws, II 1955, 152 (No. 65).

[42] Knudtzon, Die El-Amarna Tafeln, II 1915, 1475.

[43] Virolleaud, Palais Royal d'Ugarit, III 1955, 234.

[44] A Mandaic Dictionary (Drower-Macuch) 268b.

[45] Bibl 33 (1952), 206.

4₁₃ לְהִזָּהֵר. In the Niphal, as here and in 12₁₂, זהר denotes "take care" or "be advised". It has likewise this meaning in Aramaic (Ezr 4₂₂ זהרין), Ben Sira (42₈ זהיר) and the Mishna (e. g. Aboth 1₉ זהיר).

4₁₄ כִּי־מִבֵּית הָסוּרִים יָצָא לִמְלֹךְ. The majority of scholars regard הָסוּרִים as the passive participle masculine plural, with the article, of אסר "to imprison"[46]. It is thus assumed that the Qames under the ה implies the elision of the א, and that therefore הָסוּרִים is the equivalent of הָאֲסוּרִים as attested by some MSS[47]: compare אֲרַמִּים in II Reg 8₂₈ with הָרַמִּים in the later text of II Chr 22₅. מבית הסורים is then generally interpreted as "from the house of prison". Yet it is doubtful if this view of the phrase is suitable to the context. It is significant that Rashbam, the medieval Jewish exegete, thought that the words referred to the maternal womb from whence the old and foolish king came[48]. Some support for this interpretation may be seen in the reading סוֹר הָעֶרְוָה (the filth of the genitals) instead of סוֹד־הערוה in Hodayot 1₂₂[49]. It is thus possible to take סורים of our text as the plural of סוֹר. The etymology of the term, however, remains doubtful. Dahood mentions the Ugaritic mssr ʿsr which means something like "the entrails of a bird", and thinks that a root srr underlies סורים[50]. We may compare too the Hebrew שֹׁר "navel-string, navel" (Ez 16₄ Prov 3₈ Cant 7₃), Aramaic שׁוּרָא (Targ. Ez 16₄) and the Arabic سِرّة "the navel"[51]. Dahood translates "to go from between the entrails", taking בֵּית as "between" as in Ez 41₉ Job 8₁₇ and elsewhere[52]. But this is unnecessary if we regard בית־הסורים as denoting "the maternal womb". In the Hodayot 1₂₂ we find the term כּוּר "crucible" signifying "womb"[53], and therefore a term like "house" would not be surprising here. More suggestive is Dahood's proposal that למלך should be vocalised לִמְלֹךְ, the Lamedh being regarded as Emphatic[54]. We may then translate our line as: "for from the womb

---

[46] Gordis op. cit. 234; Galling op. cit. 99; Hertzberg op. cit. 103; Zimmerli op. cit. 78; Barucq, Ecclésiaste, 96.

[47] BH³. So also Bodl 2333. All the Versions, except the Targum which offers a free and expansive text, likewise take the root as אסר.

[48] Ginsburg, Qoheleth, 332.

[49] With Yadin, JBL 74 (1955), 42. Mansoor, The Thanksgiving Hymns, 1961, 101 n. 2, would argue that סוד = יסוד "foundation". Yet the reading סוֹר (filth) would equally accord with the following clause מקור־הנדה (the fountain of menstruation). מקור is also used in Rabbinical literature with reference to the interior of the womb (Jastrow II 830a).

[50] Bibl 43 (1962), 356f. See too UT No. 1798 (452a).

[51] Lane I iv, 1338 (col. 3).   [52] Loc. cit. 357.

[53] Mansoor op. cit. 101 n. 4.   [54] Ibid.

even a king goes forth". This interpretation of מבית־הסורים corresponds
with נולד רָשׁ in the following line: "for despite his royalty he was born
poor" [55]. A passage of similar purport appears in 5 13-14: "a son is born
and there is not anything in his hand; as he came from the womb of
his mother (יָצָא מִבֶּטֶן אִמּוֹ) naked will he return as he came".

4 15 b עִם הַיֶּלֶד הַשֵּׁנִי אֲשֶׁר יַעֲמֹד תַּחְתָּיו. Zimmermann regards הַשֵּׁנִי as an
indication of an Aramaic original; for he thinks that while the Aramaic
תִּנְיָנָא means "second", it may also have the more special meaning "second
in command" even "viceroy, general". The word here then, he argues,
would have the meaning of "crown prince" [56]. But apart from the
question of interpretation, it is doubtful if this line is original here. For
a reference to "the second lad" is scarcely intelligible without some
mention of another lad. Hence the line seems to belong to the material
of vv. 10 and 12 which has a comment on a "second" (שֵׁנִי) lad helping "the
one" (הָאֶחָד) in a struggle with an assailant. This is the more likely since
the order of the text in vv. 10-12 is uncertain; and it is probable that originally the line עִם הילד השני ... תחתיו stood in close proximity to הַשְּׁנִים
יעמדו גדו (v. 12) [57] or else is a disconnected passage from a proverbial
source relating to the same theme.

Zimmermann further maintains that אשר היה in v. 16a (... אֵין־קֵץ
לְכֹל אֲשֶׁר הָיָה לִפְנֵיהֶם) is a mistranslation of an Aramaic דְהוּא (which he)
which the translator took as דַהֲוָא (which was). The rendering, then,
should have been: "There is no end to the people before whom he
stands" [58]. Zimmermann thus takes לפניהם in a spatial sense. But, as the
contrasting הָאַחֲרֹנִים (those who are hereafter) in the following line
indicates, לפניהם has here a temporal force. We may compare Koh 1 10
אשר היה מִלְּפָנֵנוּ ... "already it was in the age which was before us".

4 16b לֹא יִשְׂמְחוּ־בוֹ. With all the Versions, בו is normally interpreted
as referring to the "second lad" mentioned in v. 15 b. But even if 15 b
were original to its context the theme introduced in v. 16 is so different
that it is difficult to connect בו with an antecedent in 15 b. On the other
hand, 15a, together with 16a-b, constitute a separate and independent
unit; its burden is the number of people who inhabit the earth. 16 a

---

[55] Schunck, VT 9 (1959), 195 ff., however, argues that רשׁ is but an abbreviation for
ראשׁ, and would render "Familienhaupt" (Head of a family). The reference, he
thinks, is to Seleucus II.

[56] JQR 36 (1945/46), 34-35.

[57] V. 11 is clearly misplaced in its present context. Cf. too the reconstruction offered
by Torrey, VT 2 (1952), 175-177.

[58] Loc. cit. 34-35.

mentions that there is no end—אֵין קֵץ—to such numbers, but as this
is a feature common to all ages, future generations will see nothing in
it at which to rejoice. קֵץ (masc. noun) accordingly appears to be the
antecedent of בו.

4₁₇ כִּי־אֵינָם יוֹדְעִים לַעֲשׂוֹת רָע. לעשות is awkward here, and Driver
suggests that the Massoretic Text is a misreading of an original abbreviated text אינם יודע׳ מלעשות רע "knowing not otherwise than to do
evil"[59]. Such a mistake, however, could equally be an example of haplography due to the preceding word יודעים ending with מ.

---

[59] Textus 4 (1964), 79.

5₁ אַל־תְּבַהֵל "Do not hasten". In early biblical books the root בהל appears in the Niphal with the force of "dismay" or "alarm" (e.g. Gen 45₃ Judg 20₄₁ I Sam 28₂₁), although it is also found in later books in the Piel with the same force (e.g. Job 22₁₀ Ps 83₁₆ Dan 11₄₄). However, בהל in the Piel with the meaning "hasten" is confined to a few late passages; Koh 5₁ 7₉ II Chr 35₂₁ and Est 2₉[1].

5₁ᵦ מְעַטִּים "Few". The plural occurs elsewhere only in Ps 109₈ where it is again used adjectively, יהיו־ימיו מעטים.

5₃ כַּאֲשֶׁר תִּדֹּר נֶדֶר לֵאלֹהִים ... לְשַׁלְּמוֹ. We have here substantially the same text as Deut 23₂₂ₐ, כי־תדר נדר ליהוה אלהיך לא תאחר לשלמו. Characteristically the word יהוה is omitted in Koheleth.

5₅ₐ אַל־תִּתֵּן. נתן has here the sense of "allow, permit". Compare Gen 20₆ לֹא־נְתַתִּיךָ לִנְגֹּעַ אֵלֶיהָ (I did not allow you to draw near to her); Ex 3₁₉ לֹא־יִתֵּן אֶתְכֶם מֶלֶךְ (the king will not allow you).

5₅ₐ לַחֲטִיא אֶת־בְּשָׂרֶךָ "To cause thy flesh to sin". The characteristic ה of the Hiphil infinitive is sometimes elided in biblical Hebrew; for example, לַצְבֹּות and לַנְפֹּל in Num 5₂₂, and לַסְתִּיר in Isa 29₁₅[2]. Zimmermann suggests that we have here a mechanical translation from an Aramaic לְחַיָּבָא לְבִשְׂרָךְ and that the Hebrew should have been לְחַיֵּב אֶת־בְּשָׂרֶךָ, thus more correctly representing the force of the Aramaic root חוב (חב) "to condemn". However, we have a similar causative use of חָטָא in Deut 24₄ ... וְלֹא תַחֲטִיא and also in Isa 29₂₁ מַחֲטִיאֵי־אָדָם. Moreover, according to Deut 23₂₂, sin is incurred by failing to fulfil a vow (והיה בך חטא); and there is probably an allusion to this passage here in Koheleth.

5₅ₐ וְאַל־תֹּאמַר לִפְנֵי־הַמַּלְאָךְ. Some Versions (G S Sʰ K) read "God" instead of "messenger"; and it is likely that אלהים was the original reading[3]. For if מלאך were original, there is no reason why these Versions should read "God". On the other hand, the editors of the Hebrew

---

[1] So the Pual מבהלים in Est 8₁₄, and cf. Qere (Pual) מבהלים for Kethib מבחלת in Prov 20₂₁.

[2] Cf. GK § 53q (148). This is also a feature of the Dead Sea Scrolls; see, e.g. Goshen-Gottstein, in: Scripta Hierosolymitana, IV 1965, 109.

[3] Cf. McNeile, An Introduction to Ecclesiastes, 68; Barton, Ecclesiastes (ICC), 125.

text would be tempted to soften the anthropomorphism in accordance with the notion of מלאך as the messenger or representative of God (e. g. Gen 16₇ 19₁ Isa 42₁₉).

Zimmermann considers מלאך "impossible in the present context", and explains its presence as a faithful reproduction of the Aramaic שְׁלִיחָא. This, he thinks, denoted the messenger sent to collect the pledges for the house of God[4]. Dahood's latest interpretation of לִפְנֵי-הַמְּלַאךְ is that the Massoretic pointing is a mistake for לְפְנֵי-הִמָּלֵאךְ, Niphal infinitive construct of מָלֵא, followed by the dative suffix. He would translate: "before you have fulfilled it". However, מלא with the meaning "fulfil" is usually found in the Piel, and indeed that is the form of the verb in the examples cited by Dahood (IReg 2₂₇ 8₁₅. ₂₄ IIChr 36₂₁ Ps 20₅₋₆ Jer 44₂₅)[5]. Perles earlier pronounced הַמַּלְאָךְ "wholly unintelligible", but his proposed מַלָּאָךְ "thou fillest" is based on the Piel form of the verb[6].

5₅ᵇ לָמָה is here probably to be rendered "lest", as also in 7₁₆₋₁₇, and is the equivalent of the classical פֶּן. Dahood notes that the Phoenician לם is used in this sense[7]; but so is לְמָה in both biblical (Ezr 4₂₂ 7₂₃) and Egyptian Aramaic[8].

5₆ כִּי בְרֹב חֲלֹמוֹת וַהֲבָלִים וּדְבָרִים הַרְבֵּה: A difficult line syntactically, since it has no expressed verb. It is reproduced literally by the Septuagint, and the only change in the Peshitta is the addition of ܘܠܚܒܠ (of error) after הרבה. The Vulgate, however, presents a freer translation: *Ubi multa sunt somnia, plurimae sunt vanitates, et sermones innumeri* (Where there are many dreams there are many vanities, and words without number). Most commentators regard the line as corrupt, and in varying ways emend the Hebrew text[9]. Zimmermann maintains that the difficulties of

---

[4] Loc. cit. 32–33.

[5] Bibl 47 (1966), 282. Cf. also his earlier statement in Bibl 33 (1952), 207, where, from the appearance of מלאך in two Phoenician inscriptions, he argued for Phoenician influence on Koheleth.

[6] JQR 2 (1911–1912), 130.   [7] Bibl 33 (1952), 195.

[8] See Driver, Aramaic Documents of the Fifth Century B.C., Letter 12 (35) and 83 n. 7.

[9] E.g. BH³ which emends the text on the basis of v. 2, reading עִנְיָן after ברב and בדברים as ודברים; so Zimmerli, Das Buch des Predigers Salomo, 189 n. 1; Strobel, Das Buch Prediger (Kohelet), 84, would delete כי as a dittography, and regards the rest of the line as continuing the note of interrogation introduced by למה at the beginning of the previous line: "Why ... in a multitude of dreams and vanities and many words". Both Barton op. cit. 125 and Galling, Der Prediger, 101, interpret the line as a gloss. Cf. also the comments of Hertzberg, Der Prediger, 120, and Kroeber, Der Prediger, 117.

the line spring from a mistranslation of an Aramaic דבשגיאותה דחלמין והבלין ומלין שָׁגִין דִי לאלהא דחל "Because in the multitude of dreams, vanities and talk, persons err; have reverence for that which belongs to the God". Thus he assumes that the translator took שגין as שַׁגִין "many" instead of שָׁגִין "they err", and accordingly rendered by the Hebrew הַרְבֵּה[10]. Gordis defends the Massoretic text on the grounds that ב in ברב is to be taken as "asseverative". He thus translates: "In spite of all the dreams, follies and idle chatter, indeed, fear God"[11]. But the syntax of this rendering, whereby the line in question is interpreted as a circumstantial clause, depends on the following phrase כי את־האלהים יְרָא which is itself probably a late addition.

The syntactical difficulty of our passage disappears if we recognise that *waw* may have an asseverative or emphatic function. Thus in II Sam 3₃₈ הֲלוֹא תדעו כי־שׂר וְגָדוֹל נפל, the *waw* prefixed to גדול is emphatic: "surely you know that a *truly* great prince has fallen". In Ps 49₂₁ the *waw* before לא is similarly used: אדם ביקר וְלֹא יבין נמשׁל כבהמות נדמו "Man in *Yekar* will *certainly* not understand; he is like the beasts that perish"[12]. Again in Ps 90₂ the *waw* before מעולם has a similar function: בטרם הרים ילדו ... וּמֵעוֹלָם עד־עוֹלָם אתה אל "Before the mountains were created ... *yea* from eternity to eternity thou art God"[13]. This emphatic use of the *waw* is likewise found in Ugaritic. For example, in the passage *št alp qdmh mra wtk pnh* the *waw* prefixed to *tk* serves such a purpose: "set an ox before him, a fatling *right* in front of him"[14]. So here in Koh 5₆ we may render: "for in a multitude of dreams and vanities there are *indeed* many words (ודברים הרבה)".

5₈ וְיִתְרוֹן אֶרֶץ בַּכֹּל הִיא מֶלֶךְ לְשָׂדֶה נֶעֱבָד. This line has been termed "an insuperable crux"[15]. The first half may be rendered: "But the advantage of land pertains to all"[16]. The second half is, however, more enigmatic. The Niphal of עבד is found only in Deut 21₄ and Ez 36₉. ₃₄, and in each instance it is used of "tilled" land. So, it is in the sense of

---

[10] Loc. cit. 27f.

[11] Koheleth—The Man and His World 239–40.

[12] *Yekar* here probably means "Mansion" another name for Sheol. See Dahood, Psalms I, AB, 1965, 303 and also 274.

[13] Cf. Prijs, BZ 8 (1964), 105–109.

[14] Text as UT 51 V 10₇–10₈ (172a). See Dahood, Psalms I, 24. Cf. too Aistleitner, WUS 94 (3), and Pope, JAOS 73 (1953), 95–98.

[15] Gordis op. cit. 240.

[16] The interpretation "in all respects" as בכל in Gen 24₁ (Wright, The Book of Koheleth, 365) is hardly acceptable, as we are here in Koheleth clearly dealing with people.

cultivated land that both the Septuagint (τοῦ ἀγροῦ εἰργασμένου) and the Peshitta (ܟܣܡܠ ܡܬܟ) render לשדה נעבד [17]. Yet it is doubtful if נעבד is to be construed with שדה. Rather it would seem that it should be construed with מלך. Zimmermann claims that נעבד is a faulty translation of an Aramaic מִשְׁתַּעֲבַד and that the rendering of the original should be "... even a king is dependent on a field" [18]. But we should expect that יתרון "advantage, benefit" in the first part of the line should have some balancing element in the second part. Now, in Mishnaic usage the Niphal may have a Middle signification [19]. It is thus possible that נעבד may have the meaning "is served, benefits". Further, the ל prefixed to שדה could have the force of "from", as, for example, לבקר לבקר (from morning to morning) in I Chr 9₂₇, and יהוה לַמַּבּוּל ישב וישב יהוה מלך לְעוֹלם (Yahweh has sat enthroned from the flood, and Yahweh has sat enthroned as king from eternity) in Ps 29₁₀ [20]. We may then translate Koh 5₈: "but the advantage of land pertains to all, a king benefits from a field" [21].

5₉b וּמִי־אֹהֵב בֶּהָמוֹן לֹא תְבוּאָה. לֹא תבואה is a difficult clause, although some commentators accept it by supplying יִשְׂבַּע from the previous line [22]. On the basis of the Peshitta ܠ ܢܩܢܝܘܗܝ (he will not acquire it) Gordis argues that תבואה should be a verb pointed תְבוּאֶהוּ = תְבוֹאֵהוּ, and translates "it will not come to him" [23]. However, the point of the proverb seems to be that a man already has such wealth (המון) but derives no satisfaction from it. The Greek Version, though no clearer than the Massoretic, seems to presuppose a לוֹ in the original, and in the Targum again we find לֵית לֵיהּ (it is not to him). It would appear therefore that the original text read לֹא לוֹ תְבוּאָה (cf. לֹא לוֹ, Hab 2₆; מִבְּלִי לוֹ, Job 18₁₅), and that לוֹ was omitted through homonymy. We may then translate: "He who loves riches has no gain". The ב before המון is probably to be regarded as a dittography from the preceding אהב.

5₁₀b לִבְעָלֶיהָ "to its owner". בעל is used with the plural form of the pronominal suffix, although the meaning is clearly singular. The plural

---

[17] The Vulgate reads: *et insuper universae terrae rex imperat servienti* (and, moreover, a king reigns over all the land subject to him).
[18] Loc. cit. 37f.
[19] See Segal, A Grammar of Mishnaic Hebrew, 1927, 59.
[20] See Whitley, JQR 73 (1972), 199–206, especially 205f.
[21] The line is, of course, variously rendered. E.g. Galling op. cit. 100, renders interrogatively: "What advantage should it mean for the land, if a king is there only for the tilled land?".
[22] E.g. Ginsberg, Coheleth, 348; Zimmerli op. cit. 192; cf. too Hertzberg op. cit. 130.
[23] Op. cit. 241.

form also appears in verse 12b, where again the meaning is singular. But the usage also occurs in earlier Hebrew; for example, Ex 21₂₉ וְהוּעַד בִּבְעָלָיו וְלֹא יִשְׁמְרֶנּוּ (and its owner is warned, but he did not guard it) and Ex 22₁₀ בְּעָלָיו וְלֹא יְשַׁלֵּם וְלָקַח (and its owner shall accept [the oath] and not make restitution).

5₁₂ רָעָה חוֹלָה "a grievous evil". חוֹלָה is the Qal feminine participle used as an adjective. Compare also the use of the Niphal feminine participle in such passages as Jer 10₁₉ נַחְלָה מַכָּתִי (my wound is grievous) and 14₁₇ מַכָּה נַחְלָה (a grievous blow). We likewise find חֳלִי רָע (an evil affliction) in Koh 6₂. Zimmermann, however, suggests that both רעה חולא and חלי רע are renderings of an Aramaic בִּישָׁה בִּישָׁה (evil, evil). It was, he explains, an Aramaic characteristic to repeat a word for the sake of emphasis. Hence, thinking the repetition pointless, the translator offers the present Hebrew text[24]. But there is no reason why a Hebrew translator should have been embarrassed by בישה בישה. We find עָמֹק עָמֹק (deep, deep) in Koh 7₂₄, while repetition was also a Hebrew literary device; for example, מאד מאד (Num 14₇), צדק צדק (Deut 16₂₀), טוב טוב (Judg 11₂₅), גבהה גבהה (I Sam 2₃).

5₁₄ בַּעֲמָלוֹ. The Septuagint and Peshitta represent the ב by the preposition "in", while the Vulgate renders it by *de*. Commentators generally regard it as the ב of "instrumentality"[25] or of "price"[26]. It is likely, however, that ב here has the force of מִן "from". The interchange of ב and מ obtains in many instances in the Old Testament. Thus in II Sam 22₁₄ we have יִרְעַם מִן־שָׁמַיִם יהוה (Yahweh will roar from heaven), but in the parallel passage in Ps 18₁₄ we find וַיַּרְעֵם בַּשָּׁמַיִם. Similarly in II Reg 14₁₃ we find בְּשַׁעַר אפרים עד־שַׁעַר הַפִּנָּה (from the Gate Ephraim to the Corner Gate), but the corresponding passage in II Chr 25₂₃ is . . . מִשַּׁעַר[27]. The use of the preposition ב with the meaning "from" is also known in Phoenician. Thus in the *Abibaal* Inscription we read מלך גבל במצרם (the king Gebal from Egypt)[28], and in Azitawadd's Inscription we read ואל יעמסן במשכב ז עלת משכב שני (and may he not carry me from this resting-place unto another resting-place)[29].

---

[24] Loc. cit. 28–29.

[25] E. g. Barton op. cit. 132; McNeile op. cit. 70.

[26] So Gordis op. cit. 243. Cf. too Hertzberg's translation "davon für seine Mühen", op. cit. 126; Kroeber's "für seine Mühe davon", op. cit. 93, and Zimmerli "für seine Mühe", op. cit. 193.

[27] See Sarna, JBL 78 (1959), 310f.

[28] Text as KAI I, 5₂ (1). For discussion see vol. II, 8.

[29] Text as KAI I, 14₅₋₆ (3).

In Ugaritic, *b* is likewise used in the sense of "from". For example, *b bt mlk* (from the house of the king)[30], and *tbᶜ bbth* (they departed from his house)[31]. In the light of such evidence, then, it would seem that בַּעֲמָלוֹ should be rendered "from his work"[32].

5₁₅. עמת in כָּל־עֻמַּת שֶׁבָּא seems to be derived from a feminine noun עֻמָּה meaning "nearness, juxtaposition". Normally it is preceded by the particle ל and has the force of a preposition or adverb. For example, Ex 25₂₇ לְעֻמַּת המסגרת (near the frame). But לעמת also developed the meaning "after the manner of, according to". Thus יפילו . . . לְעֻמַּת אחיהם (they will cast lots . . . after the manner of their brethren, I Chr 24₃₁), and לְעֻמַּת כקטן כגדול (according to the small, so the great, I Chr 25₈). So in Koh 7₁₄ we find לעמת־זה (together with this). In our phrase in 5₁₅ כל is a combination of ל and כ which were in turn prefixed to עמת. It is thus probable that the original form of כל־עמת was כְּלְעֻמַּת; compare the form מֻלְעֻמַּת (beside) in I Reg 7₂₀[33]. It is also likely that כל־עמת שֶׁ has a structural affinity with the Aramaic כָּל־קֳבֵל דִּי (e.g. Dan 2₄₀); for כל־קבל is a composite of כ and לקבל. קֳבֵל is primarily a noun with the meaning "front". Preceded by the particle ל, it becomes the preposition לקבל "before, in front of" (e.g. לקבל צלמא "before the image", Dan 3₃) and also the adverb "because of" (e.g. לקבל דנה "because of this", Ezr 4₁₆) and "according to" (Ezr 6₁₃ לקבל די, Egyptian Aramaic לקבל זי)[34]. In this modal sense לקבל is often augmented with כ (כלקבל) and assumes the form כָּל־קֳבֵל (e.g. Dan 2₈. ₁₂, and Targ. here on Koh 5₁₅). It would thus appear that an original Hebrew כְּלְעֻמַּת became, under the influence of Aramaic usage, כָּל־עֻמַּת.

---

[30] UT No. 1107₆₋₇ (236a).

[31] 2 Aqht II: 39, UT 248a. See also 95, § 105.

[32] Cf. Dahood, Bibl 33 (1952), 191. Barr has expressed caution in accepting the meaning "from" for Ugaritic *b* on the grounds that the Ugaritic particle may be equally rendered by another preposition. Thus, citing *štym bkrpnm yn bks ḥrṣ dmᶜsm* which Gordon (UT 59) translates as "drink wine from jars, the blood of vines from cups of gold", Barr remarks (Comparative Philology and the Text of the Old Testament, 1968, 177) "one may drink 'in' or 'with' a cup, as well as 'from' one". However, in a recently published text we find the phrase *dšn bḫbr kṭr tbm* in which, as the context shows, *b* unequivocally means "from": "Koshar pours spirits *from* the vat" (Margulis, JBL 89 (1970), 292–293. 295). Cf. too Brekelmans, UF 1 (1969), 5–14, who concludes a study of the particle *b* with the remark that "*b from* does occur in the Hebrew Book of Psalms", 14.

[33] Cf. McNeile op. cit. 70f.; Gordis op. cit. 243.

[34] Cf. Driver, Aramaic Documents of the Fifth Century B.C., 104. So also in the Bilingual (Ludian-Aramaic) Inscription (5th–4th cent. B.C.) from Sardes we find לקבל זי, KAI I, No. 260 (B) 5 (50).

5₁₆ₐ גַּם כָּל־יָמָיו בַּחֹשֶׁךְ יֹאכֵל. This part of the verse is intelligible as
it is, although the Septuagint, Syro-Hexaplar and Coptic Versions read
וְאֵבֶל (and grief) for יֹאכֵל. Some difficulty, however, attaches to the
second part of the verse, וְכָעַס הַרְבֵּה וְחָלְיוֹ וָקָצֶף, since the verb כָּעַס and
the pronominal form וחליו yield little sense in their contexts. Accordingly
כעס is usually read as the noun כַּעַס and the final ו of וחליו regarded as a
dittography for וָחֳלִי[35]. But, as the line would then lack a verb, the
question of its syntactical relationship with the preceding line remains.

Zimmermann thinks that in the verse as a whole we have a mistranslation from an original Aramaic

אף כל יומוהי בקבלא אכל
ורגז שגיא וביׁשה וקצפא

(Because all his days he eats in complaint, much annoyance, malaise and
anger). Thus the translator took קְבְלָא as "darkness" instead of its other
meaning "complaint". וביׁשה was again wrongly interpreted as וּבִישָׁה
(and his sickness) instead of וּבִישָׁה (and malaise)[36]. It is true that this
last suggestion would account for the Hebrew וחליו instead of וְחֳלִי,
but the substitution of "complaint" for "darkness" would not improve
the sense of the passage.

Dahood takes the consonants יאכל as the Aphel imperfect of כָּלָה
(to be complete, spent) which in the Piel and Hiphil means "to complete,
spend". He suggests that the same Aphel form is to be discerned in the
Ugaritic *yakl ktr whss* (Let Kothar and Hasis complete it)[37]. But however
this may be[38], the Aphel does not occur in Hebrew[39]. Nor would a
causative form of כלה with the meaning "spend" necessarily improve
the sense of our passage. For Koheleth largely judges life by the circumstances in which a man may "eat and drink". Wealth, properly used,
can enable a man "to eat and drink" with pleasure, and view life with
satisfaction (2₂₄ 3₁₃ 5₁₇). Here in the context of 5₁₆ a miserly man hoards
wealth, only to lose it through some disaster. Such a man "toils for

---

[35] See e.g. Galling, Der Prediger (op. cit. 102); Hertzberg op. cit. 129. Driver too
would read the noun כַּעַס, but prefixes ולו on the assumption that it has fallen
out by haplography (VT 4, 1954, 229).

[36] Loc. cit. 29–30.

[37] Bibl 47 (1966), 272f. (text as UT 51 V 103).

[38] *S* is, of course, the normal causative element in Ugaritic (UT 83, 9₃₈). Cf. Merrill,
JNSL 3 (1974), 40–49, who is sceptical of the existence of the Aphel in Ugaritic.

[39] Forms such as אשכים (Jer 25₃) and האזניהו (Isa 19₆) are to be regarded as mere
scribal errors; see GK§ 53k and p (146f.).

the wind" (5₁₅), and Koheleth characteristically (cf. 2₁₄ 6₄) refers to him as one "who eats in darkness — בחשך יאכל—...".

The Versions offer considerable help in our understanding of the second part of the verse. For וְכָעַס הרבה the Septuagint reads καὶ θυμῷ πολλῷ, the Peshitta ‎ܘܒܪܘܓܙܐ ܣܓܝܐܐ‎ (and in much anger) and the Vulgate *in curis multis* (in many cares). It is therefore likely that the preposition ב of בחשך should be regarded as applying elliptically to the following nouns[40]. Gordis objects that Hebrew usage would demand the repetition of the preposition—בכעס בחלי ובקצף—, and cites certain passages in Deuteronomy chapter 28 in support of his view[41]. But while this usage is understandable in the verbose and explicit prose of Deuteronomy, it is not always the case in Hebrew poetry. Thus in Job 12₁₂ we read בִּישִׁישִׁים חכמה וְאֹרֶךְ ימים תבונה (with the aged is wisdom, and *in* length of days understanding). So in Jon 2₄ we find that the force of the preposition ב in בִּלְבַב is anticipated in מְצוּלָה: מְצוּלָה בלבב ימים תשליכני (thou hast cast me into the deep, into the heart of the seas)[42]. We may again follow the Versions in reading וָחֳלִי instead of וחליו. The verse as a whole may then be rendered: "for all his days he eats in darkness, and in much sorrow and anxiety and anger".

5₁₇ טוב אשר יפה. הִנֵּה אֲשֶׁר־רָאִיתִי אָנִי טוֹב אֲשֶׁר־יָפֶה לֶאֱכוֹל־וְלִשְׁתּוֹת, is difficult, and it seems that, contrary to the Massoretic accentuation, we must construe טוב with the first part of the line[43]. We might thus render: "Behold that which I have discovered is good, that it is becoming to eat and drink". Some scholars have seen the Greek καλὸς κἀγαθός underlying טוב אשר יפה[44]. But we would then expect the order ... יפה טוב, and יפה has the meaning "becoming, proper" in Rabbinical litera-

---

[40] Barton op. cit. 133.

[41] Op. cit. 244. Gordis would accept the MT here.

[42] For Ugaritic usage cf. Dahood (Bibl 47, 1966, 273) who cites *al tkl bnqr ʿnk my* (UT reads *mḫ*, sap) *rišk udmʿt* (Do not waste with flowing your eyes, the waters of your head with tears) where the preposition *b* of *bnqr* applies to the parallel *udmʿt* (UT 125 ₂₆₋₂₈). See also Pope, JCS 5 (1951), 123–128, for a discussion of the particle in Ugaritic. We might also mention Isa 48₁₄ יעשה חפצו בבבל וזרעו כשדים, where the preposition ב in בבבל seems to apply to כשדים.

[43] As some commentators; e.g. Barton op. cit. 133; Hertzberg op. cit. 129; Kroeber op. cit. 93. So it may be observed that while the LXX is faithful to the MT, the Vulgate paraphrases *Hoc itaque visum est mihi bonum ut comedat quis, et bibat* (This therefore has seemed good to me, that he who eats and drinks).

[44] E.g. Graetz, Kohélet oder Salomonische Prediger, 1871, 87; Wildeboer, Der Prediger, 1898, 141; Ranston, Ecclesiastes and the Early Greek Wisdom Literature, 1925, 33.

ture (e.g. יָפֶה שְׁתִיקָה לַחֲכָמִים silence is becoming to the wise, Pes 99a). However, as Koheleth uses טוב as well as יפה it is possible that, though not consciously reproducing the language of the Greek idiom, he nonetheless, reflects the influence of Greek thought. Zimmermann argues that הִנֵּה is a mistranslation of the Aramaic הָא "this", and that the original was, ... הָא דַחֲזָא אֲנָה דְטָב (This is what I have seen to be good ...)[45]. But since he too takes טוב with the preceding words, his Aramaic reconstruction is not materially different from our interpretation of the passage.

5₁₈ וְהִשְׁלִיטוֹ. The Hiphil of שלט also occurs in 6₂. But it appears elsewhere in biblical Hebrew only in Ps 119₁₃₃ (תַשְׁלֶט-). The verb is likewise used in the causative (Haphel) in Dan 2₃₈. ₄₈.

5₁₉ מַעֲנֶה. It is probable that with the Versions as a whole we should read מענה as מַעֲנֶה (= מַעֲנֵהוּ). Gordis contends that ענה has here the meaning "to answer"[46], but it is likely that it has the second meaning of the root which is "to occupy with" as in 1₁₃ and 3₁₀ where it is likewise followed by the preposition בְּ[47]. The following words בְּשִׂמְחַת לִבּוֹ may perhaps be rendered "with contentment of heart"[48].

---

[45] Loc. cit. 26.

[46] Op. cit. 246.

[47] Cf. Schmid, Wesen und Geschichte der Weisheit, 1966, 193 and n. 256.

[48] Cf. Greenfield, HUCA 30 (1959), 11f. for the various nuances of שׂמח and its derivatives.

6₂ מִמֶּנּוּ . . . וְאֵינֶנּוּ חָסֵר לְנַפְשׁוֹ . . . אִישׁ אֲשֶׁר, *"A man to whom* God gives riches and wealth and honour *and he does not lack for himself* from all which he desires, but God does not enable him to eat *from it*". Zimmermann contends that there is an inconsistency here, arising from a misrepresentation of an Aramaic phrase וְלָא חָשֵׁךְ לְנַפְשֵׁהּ (and he does not *withhold* from himself) by the Hebrew ואיננו חסר לנפשו. He observes that the Aramaic חֲשַׁךְ has two meanings, (1) "diminish" and (2) "stint, withhold". The translator wrongly chose the first meaning. He should rather, says Zimmermann, have used the Piel of חסר as in 4₈ וּמְחַסֵּר אֶת־נַפְשִׁי מְטוֹבָט (and deprive myself of the good)[1]. The contexts are, however, different. In 4₈ the author is referring to the pointlessness of a man without an heir toiling to amass wealth, thereby depriving himself of pleasure. The man here in 6₂ does not, on the contrary, strive, since God endows him richly with goods. He lacks nothing, but ironically God does not enable him to enjoy his wealth. The Hebrew text ואיננו חסר לנפשו accords therefore more naturally with the context than an alleged Aramaic ולא חשך לנפשה. חָסֵר is pointed either as a verb or as an adjective. It is likely, however, that it is to be considered as parallel to יִתְאַוֶּה (he desires) later in the verse, and therefore construed as a verb[2].

6₃ᵦ וְגַם קְבוּרָה לֹא־הָיְתָה לּוֹ. This has little logical connection with the previous clause. It is therefore preferable with some scholars to place it after וְלֹא יָדַע of verse 5[3]. Gordis would retain the passage in its present position but would vocalise לא as לָא "if"[4], and in this he is followed by Kroeber[5]. But if לָא were original to the text we should expect that it would immediately follow וגם; compare וגם אם "and even if", 8₁₇. On the other hand, it is obvious that the still-born would not have a proper burial; but even so, Koheleth maintains that even with this mark of

---

[1] JQR 36 (1945/46), 24–25.
[2] Against Franz Delitzsch, The Song of Songs and Ecclesiastes, 305, and Barton, The Book of Ecclesiastes, 134, who regard it as an adjective. It is interesting that the reading of *MS. Bodl. 2333* is חֹסֶר Textus 5 (1966), 104.
[3] So e.g. Zimmerli, Das Buch des Predigers Salomo, 196.
[4] See Gordis, Koheleth—The Man and His World, 249.
[5] Der Prediger 94–95.

dishonour (cf. e.g. Deut 28 26 II Reg 9 10 Jer 14 16) the fate of the still-born is better than that of the man who, though living long, derives no enjoyment from life.

6 5b‎. נַחַת לָזֶה מִזֶּה‎. נחת‎ has here the force of "better", "satisfaction", "pleasure"; compare 4 6 ... טוֹב מְלֹא כַף נַחַת מִמְּלֹא‎ "better the fullness of the hand of pleasure than the fullness of...". The idiom נחת ל־מ‎ is again evident in such Rabbinical passages as Erub 13b נוֹחַ לוֹ לאדם‎ שלא נברא משנברא‎ "It is better for man not to have been created than to have been created"[6].

6 6‎. וְאִלּוּ‎. אִלּוּ‎ (if) is a combination of אם‎ and לוּ‎. Compare ואם לוא‎ in the Qumran Scroll[7], and אִם לא‎ (which should read אִם לוּ‎) in Ez 3 6. The form אִלּוּ‎ is likewise to be compared with the Syriac ܐܠܘ‎ and Aramaic אִילוּ‎. Apart from this passage in Koheleth, אלו‎ appears in biblical Hebrew only in Est 7 4. It is, however, often found in the Mishna; for example, אִלּוּ הָיִינוּ בסנהדרין‎ (If we had been in the Sanhedrin, Mak 1 10) and ... אִילוּ הָיִיתִי יוֹדֵעַ‎ (If I had known..., Ned 9 2).

6 7‎. אֶל־מָקוֹם אֶחָד‎. It has been suggested that מקום‎ here means Sheol, and, moreover, that it is the antecedent of לְפִיהוּ‎ and הַנֶּפֶשׁ‎ in verse 7[8]. But while it is probable that מקום‎ does mean Sheol in verse 6[9], it is questionable if it is the antecedent of לפיהו‎ and הנפש‎. 6 7 recalls the theme of verse 3, וְנַפְשׁוֹ לֹא תִשְׂבָּע‎, but it is more specifically based on the thought and language of Prov 16 26, נפש עָמֵל עמלה לו כי אכף עליו פיהו‎ "the appetite of the labourer works for him, for his mouth urges him on". In this proverb נפש‎ and פיהו‎ clearly refer to עָמֵל‎. So here in Koh 6 7 both פיהו‎ and נפש‎ relate to הָאָדָם‎ [10]. The proposal to render נפש‎ as "throat"[11] is, again, unnecessary, since "appetite" or "hunger" accords better with the verse as a whole; compare Isa 5 14 and 29 8 where נפש‎ has the meaning

---

[6] See Gordis ibid.; Jastrow II 886b. It may be noted that the Qumran Scroll reads נוחת‎ for נחת‎; see Facsimile in Muilenburg, BASOR 135 (1954), 25.

[7] Muilenburg loc. cit. 22.

[8] Ackroyd, ASTI 5 (1966/67), 85; Dahood, Bibl 49 (1968), 368.

[9] Cf. 3 20 where the context suggests that אל מקום אחד‎ means Sheol.

[10] Ackroyd renders הנפש‎ by "(its) appetite", ibid.; but Dahood ibid. rightly observes that "its" need not be in brackets, since the article with נפש‎ balances the pronominal element of פיהו‎.

[11] Dahood ibid.; Strobel, Das Buch Prediger (Koheleth), 100; Ellermeier, Qohelet, Abschnitt I, 249f. It will not, of course, be denied that the word may have this meaning; see Murtonen, STOr 23 (1958), 63ff. Yet Murtonen emphasises that the main meaning in all Semitic languages is the "soul, vital principle", 68. The LXX renders by ψυχή, but as Bertram observes, ZAW 64 (1952), 28f., this is theologically motivated.

of "appetite". It is likewise used in this sense in the Mishna; for example, נֶפֶשׁ הַיָּפָה "a good appetite" (Hul 4₇).

מַה־לֶּעָנִי. מַה־לֶּעָנִי יוֹדֵעַ לַהֲלֹךְ נֶגֶד הַחַיִּים. The first part of the line, יוֹדֵעַ, is difficult. The Versions and many commentators interpret לֶעָנִי as "poor"[12]. But emendations have also been offered. Thus Karl Budde proposed לֶעָשִׁיר מִן־הֶעָנִי (to the rich over the poor)[13], Hertzberg מֵהֶעָנִי לַיּוֹדֵעַ (over the poor man who understands it)[14], while both Ellermeier and Galling would read לָמָה אֲנִי יוֹדֵעַ (why do I understand?)[15]. Burkitt, again, regarded מה יענ as a corruption of מבלעדי "except", and rendered "except that he knows how to walk (i.e. behave) before his contemporaries"[16]. This would take the line 8b as qualificatory of 8a, but the presence of מה suggests that it contains an independent parallel thought. Kroeber indeed observes that לעני is parallel with לחכם in the previous line. He thus thinks the term means "to the reserved" (der Zurückhaltende) and connects it with the root עָנָה "to be humble"[17]. It is probable, however, that we should rather connect the root with עָנָה "to answer". In Job 9₁₄₋₁₅ ענה is used in the sense of "answering effectively" or "justifying oneself": אַף כִּי־אָנֹכִי אֶעֱנֶנּוּ אֶבְחֲרָה דְבָרַי עִמּוֹ: אֲשֶׁר אִם צָדַקְתִּי לֹא אֶעֱנֶה (Would that I could answer him effectively, that I could choose my words with him; though I am innocent, I cannot express myself). So in Ben Sira 9₁₄ ענה occurs in the sense of giving an intelligent answer: ככחך ענה רעך ועם חכמים הסתייד (according to thy ability answer thy neighbour, but with the wise seek counsel). It would thus appear that in Koh 6₈ עני conceals some such term as עָנֶה "a shrewd or intelligent speaker", which serves as a parallel to חכם. We may therefore render the verse as a whole: "What advantage is there to the wise man over the fool; what to the intelligent man who knows how to conduct himself before his fellows?"

טוֹב מַרְאֵה עֵינַיִם מֵהֲלָךְ־נֶפֶשׁ 6₉. Apart from the primary meaning "to see", ראה has other meanings in Koheleth. Thus in passages such as 2₃ and 5₁₇ it means "to perceive, to discern". In 2₁ רְאֵה בְטוֹב means "enjoy the good" (cf. 6₆), and in 2₁₂ לִרְאוֹת חָכְמָה means "to experience wisdom". Here in 6₉ מַרְאֵה עֵינַיִם connotes both experiencing and enjoying, hence, "attaining pleasure". This expression has a similar conno-

---

[12] See Gordis op. cit. 250f.; Zimmerli op. cit. 197; Strobel op. cit. 100; Barucq, Ecclésiaste, 110.

[13] So Hertzberg, Der Prediger, 130.

[14] Ibid. and 128.

[15] Ellermeier, ZThK 60 (1963), 12; Galling, Der Prediger, 104.

[16] JTS 23 (1922), 25.   [17] Op. cit. 118.

tation in Talmudic Hebrew; for example, מראה־עינים באשה "the pleasure of looking at one's wife" (Yoma 74b). So we may note that in 11₉ מַרְאֵי־עֵינֶיךָ similarly conveys the notion of experiencing and enjoying pleasure.

It is usual to render מְהַלָּךְ־נֶפֶשׁ as "the wandering of desire"[18]. However, Galling notes that in certain passages in Koheleth (3₂₀ 5₁₄ 6₄ 9₁₀) הלך means "to go hence (to death)"[19], and we may compare Ps 39₁₄ אלך ואיננו "I go and am not". We may then perhaps render the line as a whole, "better the pleasure of the moment than the departing of life".

6₁₀   מַה־שֶּׁהָיָה כְּבָר נִקְרָא שְׁמוֹ וְנוֹדָע אֲשֶׁר־הוּא
אָדָם וְלֹא־יוּכַל לָדִין עִם שֶׁהַתַּקִּיף מִמֶּנּוּ

If הָיָה is to be taken as meaning "what was"[20], the tenses of the first line scarcely accord with one another. Thus, as in 3₁₅, Zimmermann argues that שהיה is due to a translator taking an Aramaic דהוא as דַּהֲוָא (which was) instead of דְּהוּא (which is)[21]. It will further be observed that in the Massoretic Punctuation אדם is construed with the preceding clause. The Septuagint (καὶ ἐγνώσθη ὅ ἐστιν ἄνθρωπος), Vulgate (et scitur quod homo est), and many commentators accept this[22]. However, "and it is known what man is" is an abrupt and largely meaningless phrase in the context. Zimmermann ascribes the awkwardness of the passage to the word נודע. This, he notes, is the equivalent of the Aramaic חֲכִים (pass. part. of חֲכַם "to know"); and it was in taking חכים of his Aramaic text as חֲכִים rather than חַכִּים, "a wise man", that the translator made a mistake. The original accordingly read: "... and a wise man, because he is man, cannot contend with that which is mightier than he"[23]. But this reconstruction does not improve the sense of the verse.

Dahood proposes that instead of the Massoretic אשר הוא we should read אַשְׁרֵהוּ, which, with נוֹדַע, might be rendered "and its destiny was known". In support of this he cites אֶשֶׁר "luck" in Gen 30₁₃, and further suggests that the expression in our text is to be connected with the

[18] So RSV; cf. NEB "give rein to desire". So too Gordis op. cit. 251; Hertzberg op. cit. 128; Zimmerli op. cit. 197; Kroeber op. cit. 95; McNeile, An Introduction to the Book of Ecclesiastes, 41, again quoted Marcus Aurelius iii 15, ὁρμὴ τῆς ψυχῆς.
[19] Op. cit. 104. Strobel points to the use of הלך נפש in II Sam 23₁₇ and I Reg 19₃ and would render "risky adventure of life", op. cit. 100.
[20] So Gordis op. cit. 223, who also notes Mishnaic usage. Compare too Ex 32₁.₂₃. מה היה לו "What has happened to him?".
[21] Loc. cit. 35.
[22] E.g. Barton op. cit. 136; Gordis op. cit. 253; Hertzberg op. cit. 135. 138; Zimmerli op. cit. 200; Kroeber op. cit. 95; Strobel op. cit. 102.
[23] Ibid.

Ugaritic *aṭryt* (2 Aqht VI: 36), phonetically equivalent to אֲשֶׁר, and which has the meaning "destiny or fortune"[24]. In this proposal Dahood takes אדם with the following words, but he would delete the ו of ולא. Moreover, apart from the necessity of changing אשר הוא to אֲשֶׁרֵהוּ, "destiny" is scarcely a suitable term for the cosmic phenomenon as a whole which the author has in mind here.

We can, however, accept the Hebrew text as it is, although rejecting the Massoretic punctuation. The first line logically ends with הוא: "that which is, was already called by name, and it is known what it is". The subject of the next line naturally begins with אדם, and the ו of ולא may be regarded as asseverative[25]. We would then render: "man cannot indeed argue with one that is stronger than himself". שֶׁהִתַּקִּיף is thought by some scholars to be a conflation of שתקיף, which is the reading of the *Qere* and some MSS, and a variant הַתַּקִּיף[26]. However, it is possible that the MT could be an abbreviation of an original שהוא תקיף[27]. The adjective תקיף appears here only in biblical Hebrew, but it is found frequently in biblical Aramaic (Dan 2₄₀. ₄₂ 3₃₃ 7₇ Est 4₂₀). It is likely that the root תקף is of Aramaic provenance[28].

6₁₂ וְיַעֲשֵׂם. עָשָׂה has here the force of "spending time". The verb has this meaning nowhere else in biblical Hebrew. Gordis indeed thinks that it may be discerned in Ruth 2₁₉[29], but the context rather suggests that it means "to work". עשה is, however, used of "spending time" in post-biblical Hebrew: for example, עָשָׂה במערה "he lives in a cave" (Midrash Tillim on Ps 17₄), לַעֲשׂוֹת שם "to live there" (Midrash Rabba Genesis, sec. 91)[30]. It is, moreover, probable that we are to recognise Greek influence here on Koheleth. For the Greek verb ποιέω is frequently used of "time", and especially in Hellenistic Greek. Thus in the Septuagint version of Prov 13₂₃ we read Δίκαιοι ποιήσουσιν ἐν πλούτῳ ἔτη πολλά (The righteous shall *spend* many years in wealth). So in Tobit we find ποιῆσαι αὐτὸν ἐκεῖ (that he should spend there, 10₇), and again ποιήσασα ... μῆνας τέσσαρας (having spent ... four months) in Josephus (Antiq VI, 1₄)[31].

---

[24] Bibl 33 (1952), 208.   [25] Cf. above under 5₆.

[26] E.g. Gordis op. cit. 253; Hertzberg op. cit. 138. It may be noted that the *Qere* is the reading of Bodl 2333 (Textus 5, 1966, 104).

[27] So Driver, Textus 4 (1965), 79.

[28] Cf. Wagner, Die lexikalischen und grammatikalischen Aramaismen im alttestamentlichen Hebräisch, 120.

[29] Op. cit. 254.   [30] See Jastrow II, 1125a.

[31] For earlier usage, cf. Thucydides VII, 28 τὴν νύκτα ἐφ᾽ ὅπλοις ποιεῖσθαι (to spend the night under arms).

7₅ גַּעֲרַת חָכָם . . . שִׁיר כְּסִילִים. Zimmermann observes here that שִׁיר, "song", does not provide a fitting parallel to גערת, "rebuke". Rather, the term required is "praise". Hence, he thinks it is likely that the Aramaic תּוּשְׁבַּחְתָּא or שְׁבָחָא, meaning both "song" and "praise", proved ambiguous to the Hebrew translator[1]. However, there is but little difference between the notion of "song" and "praise" in Hebrew. Thus in Ps 149₁ and Isa 42₁₀ we find שִׁיר and תְּהִלָּה used synonymously: . . . שִׁירוּ ליהוה שיר חדש תהלתו (sing to Yahweh a new song, his praise...). So in Jer 20₁₃ שִׁירוּ has the connotation of "praise": שירו ליהוה הללו אֶת־יהוה[2].

7₇ כִּי הָעֹשֶׁק יְהוֹלֵל חָכָם וִיאַבֵּד אֶת־לֵב מַתָּנָה[3]. "Oppression"[3] is the normal meaning of עשק, but some scholars think it is not a parallel to מתנה regarded as "gift" or "bribe". Thus, Seidel considers עָשָׁק as a root which yields the contrasted meanings "oppress" and "help", and accordingly interprets as a "bribe" or "gift"[4]. But it is probably misleading to interpret this line in terms of parallelism. For while the second stich ויאבד אֶת־לב מתנה is usually rendered "and a bribe corrupts the understanding" (RSV)[5], it is a rendering which is open to question. We note that the gender of the verb does not accord with that of the noun, although a masculine form of the verb preceding a feminine noun is known in

---

[1] JQR 36 (1945/46), 24.

[2] It may also be noted that in the ancient Jewish prayer *Yistabah* we find a similarity of meaning in the following terms: שיר ושבחה הלל וזמרה (song and praise, hymn and psalm. Hertz, The Authorised Daily Prayer Book, 1942, 422).

[3] Both the LXX (συκυφαντία) and the Vulgate *calumnia* render עשק here by "scandal". However, it is also by this term that these Versions render עשקים in Koh 4₁ where the meaning appears to be "oppression" rather than "slander". It is true that Syriac ܟܣܐ may have the force of "accuse" (cf. Brockelmann, Lexicon Syriacum, 552b, and van der Ploeg, Oud Stud 5, 1948, 142f.) but in Koh 4₁ the Peshitta renders עשקים by ܕܟܣܝܐ (oppressed), and here in 7₁ its rendering is ܟܣܘܣܐ.

[4] See Gordis, Koheleth—The Man and His World, 260, who cites Seidel (Debir 1, 1923, 34).

[5] So cf. Zimmerli, Das Buch des Predigers Salomo, 203; Kroeber, Der Prediger, 97; Galling, Der Prediger, 105; Strobel, Das Buch Prediger (Kohelet), 106; Barucq, Ecclésiaste, 120.

biblical Hebrew[6]. However, if מתנה were the subject of the clause we should expect that the Waw should be attached to it rather than to the verb. The fact that it is attached to the verb suggests that the subject is continued from the preceding stich, and that ויאבד[7] governs את־לב מתנה. It is significant that the Septuagint (BC, καὶ ἀπόλλυσι τὴν καρδίαν εὐγενείας αὐτοῦ), Aquila and Theodotion (τὴν εὐτονίαν τῆς καρδίας αὐτοῦ, the durability of his heart)[8] take it as the object of the clause. The Vulgate similarly renders *et perdet robur cordis illius* (and shall destroy the strength of his heart). That we also may see in מתנה a root מתן meaning "strength" is attested by the Mishnaic הוו מתונים בדין) מתונים, be firm in judgement, Aboth 1₁) and the Arabic مَتُنَ "be strong"[9]. It is thus likely that we must regard the ה as the archaic third person singular masculine suffix attached to the noun מֹתֶן (מׇתְנַיִם loins; cf. אֹזֶן, אׇזְנַיִם). The Massoretic מתנה should thus be pointed מׇתְנֹה[10]. The line may then be rendered: "for oppression stupefies the wise man, and destroys his strong heart" (cf. Jer 4₉ (וׇאׇבַד לֵב־חׇמֶלֶךְ)[11].

7⁸ אֶרֶךְ־רוּחַ "Length of spirit, patience". אֶרֶךְ, the construct of an unused absolute אׇרֵךְ (cf. כׇּתֵף cons. כֶּתֶף), is an adjective. This is the only instance of its occurrence with רוח in the Old Testament, although it is often used with אַפַּיִם (e. g. Ex 34₆ Num 14₁₈ Ps 86₁₅ 103₈), and a few manuscripts actually read אַפַּיִם here in Koheleth[12]. Dahood equates the term ארך־רוח with the name ארכרח found in a Phoenician inscription, and suggests that it is another indication of Phoenician influence on Koheleth[13]. However, the opposite phrase ק(צר) רוח (shortness of spirit, impatience) is likewise probably to be discerned in Phoenician[14], but

---

[6] See GK § 145 (465).

[7] Instead of ויאבד the Qumran Scroll reads ויענה (to pervert, as, for example, Jer 3₂₁ Prov 12₈), but this does not affect the syntax of the line.

[8] Cf. McNeile, An Introduction to Ecclesiastes, 161.

[9] Freytag, IV 148a.

[10] Cf. Driver, VT 4 (1954), 229f. So for example in Gen 49₁₁ we find עירה (his colt) *Kethib*, but עירו *Qere*; again in II Reg 19₂₃ we have קצה (his border) but in the parallel text in Isa 37₂₄ קצו. See Sperber, A Historical Grammar of Biblical Hebrew, 1966, 265.

[11] Some commentators have thought that a line is missing at the beginning of v.7 (see e. g. Franz Delitzsch, Commentary on the Song of Songs and Ecclesiastes, 317; Kroeber op. cit. 97 and 145), and Muilenburg, BASOR 135 (1954), 26, considers that space for such a line can be detected in the fragmentary MS discovered at Qumran.

[12] De Rossi, Variae Lectiones Veteris Testamenti III, 255b. So also MS Bodl 2333.

[13] Bibl 33 (1952), 109f.

[14] CIS Part I i, No. 100b (121).

it is also found more than once in biblical Hebrew (e.g. Ex 6₉ Job 21₄
Prov 14₂₉ Mic 2₇). Moreover, Koheleth uses the term אֶרֶךְ־רוּחַ as a
contrast to the following גֹּבַהּ־רוּחַ (haughtiness of spirit), and as such
it is more effective than אֶרֶךְ־אַפַּיִם.

7₁₀ מֶה הָיָה שֶׁהַיָּמִים הָרִאשֹׁנִים הָיוּ טוֹבִים מֵאֵלֶּה "How was it that the
former days were better than these?". Zimmermann thinks that in מה
היה we have a misrepresentation of an Aramaic מָה הוּא, "How is it . . .?".
The translator, he explains, took the Aramaic הוּא "he is" as the verb
הֲוָא (הוה) "was"[15]. The present tense "is" would perhaps be a more
facile rendering, although in the context "was" is quite intelligible:
"How *was* it that the former days *were* . . .?". However, in certain instances Koheleth seems to use הָיָה in the sense of "is". Compare 7₂₄
רָחוֹק מַה־שֶּׁהָיָה where, as the context shows, היה has the force of "is": "and
it is far from me, remote is that which *exists* . . .".

7₁₀b שָׁאַלְתָּ עַל־. For the idiom compare Neh 1₂ וָאֶשְׁאָלֵם עַל־. The
earlier form was שָׁאַל לְ; for example, Gen 43₇ שָׁאַל . . . לָנוּ.

7₁₁ טוֹבָה חָכְמָה עִם־נַחֲלָה. עם is translated by the Septuagint (μετά),
Vulgate (*cum*), and Targum (עם) as "with". And this is a common interpretation of the particle[16]. The Peshitta again renders עם by ܡܢ (wisdom
is better *than* weapons of war)[17], and some translators emend the Massoretic עם to מֵעַם; "wisdom is better than . . ."[18]. But the insertion of
a comparative מ before עם is unnecessary, since the particle has here,
as in 2₁₆, the force of "as"[19]; "wisdom is as good as an inheritance".

7₁₂ כִּי בְּצֵל הַחָכְמָה בְּצֵל הַכָּסֶף: A difficult line, due to the uncertainty
attaching to the meaning of בצל. The Versions differ in their rendering
of the term. Thus, some (G Sʰ K) read בְּצֵל in the first half of the line,
while others (Sym S V) read כְּצֵל in both instances. It has accordingly
been argued that כצל . . . כצל was the original reading[20]. But, apart
from offering the כ of comparison, כצל does not necessarily yield an
easier text. Zimmermann contends that the solution to the problem lies

---

[15] Loc. cit. 35.
[16] So RSV; McNeile op. cit. 104; Barton, The Book of Ecclesiastes, 139 and 149;
Franz Delitzsch op. cit. 320; Gordis op. cit. 166 and 262f.
[17] The translator seems to have mistaken נחלה for נחילה "instrument" (so Ginsburg,
Coheleth, 376) and also seems to have been influenced by 9₁₈, "wisdom is better
מכלי קרב—than weapons of war".
[18] So Hertzberg, Der Prediger, 136 and 139; Galling op. cit. 106; and NEB "Wisdom
is better than possessions".
[19] As rightly recognised by Zimmerli op. cit. 206; Kroeber op. cit. 97 and 118, and
Barucq op. cit. 120.
[20] E.g. McNeile op. cit. 75; Barton op. cit. 143.

in an Aramaic original דְּבָטְלָהֿ חוּכְמְתָא בָּטֵל כַּסְפָּא (where there is no intelligence, there is no money). The translator thus associated both participles with טְלָא (shadow), preceded by the preposition בּ, and in each case wrote the Hebrew בצל (in the shadow of)[21]. Dahood would delete the second בּ as a scribal error, and, regarding the first as a *Beth Essentiae*, translates: "The sheen of silver is the protection of wisdom"[22]. But even this scarcely offers a reading which is logically compelling. Torczyner (Tur Sinai) proposed that both instances of בצל should be displaced by the verb בָּעַל "to possess": "he who possesses wisdom possesses money"[23]. This yields an acceptable reading, and, as we shall see, accords suitably with the sequel.

The second line of v. 12 is equally difficult: וְיִתְרוֹן דַּעַת הַחָכְמָה תְּחַיֶּה בְעָלֶיהָ. Both the Septuagint and Peshitta take דעת and חכמה as a double genitive following יתרון (and the superfluity of the knowledge of wisdom), while the Vulgate reads *hoc autem plus habet eruditio et sapientia* (but learning and wisdom excel in this). Continuing his Aramaic reconstruction, Zimmermann argues that the original was וְיִּתְרָן מַנְדַּע דְחוּכְמְתָא תְּקַיֵּם לְמָרֵהּ (But an advantage is knowledge because wisdom sustains its possessor). Thus, the translator took the particle ד as a genitive relation instead of a subordinating conjunction, and further took the words יותרן מנדע as constructs, producing the peculiar דעת החכמה[24].

But while Zimmermann's reconstruction is linguistically plausible, it is doubtful whether the phrase ויתרון דעת is original to the Hebrew text. Its presence constitutes the real difficulty in the line, and the verse as a whole is concerned with wisdom (חכמה) rather than knowledge (דעת). It is therefore probable that ויתרון דעת should be transferred to verse 11 where it should replace וְיֹתֵר. ויתר is hardly suitable there, since we should expect a parallel to the previous hemistich, and ויתרון דעת would provide such a parallel. ויתר may, moreover, be explained as an incomplete writing of ויתרון דעת. V. 12 would then as a whole read: "He who possesses wisdom possesses money, for wisdom sustains its possessor".

---

[21] Loc. cit. 30. So Ginsberg, Studies in Qoheleth, 22.
[22] Bibl 33 (1952), 209f. The phrase *ẓl ksp* occurs in Ugaritic where it seems to mean "work, or spendour of silver" (Baal II ii 25 as Driver, CML 92 and 93; Gordon, UT 25 II 27, 170). But it is doubtful if it has any significance for our text in Koheleth.
[23] "Dunkle Bibelstellen", in: Vom Alten Testament, Karl Marti zum siebzigsten Geburtstage gewidmet, 1925, 280.
[24] Loc. cit. 30.

7₁₄c ... עַל־דִּבְרַת שׁ. In Koh 3₁₈ and 8₂ we find עַל־דִּבְרַת with the function of a preposition ("concerning"), and in Ps 110₄ we meet the form עַל־דִּבְרָתִי which appears to have an adverbial force ("after the manner of"). But שׁ עַל־דִּבְרַת occurs here only in biblical Hebrew. It is the equivalent of the Aramaic עַל דְּבְרַת דִּי (Dan 2₃₀ 4₁₄), and, like that expression, serves as the conjunction "in order that".

7₁₄c ... לֹא יִמְצָא הָאָדָם אַחֲרָיו מְאוּמָה. The Septuagint represents this clause literally: ἵνα μὴ εὕρῃ ὁ ἄνθρωπος ὀπίσω αὐτοῦ οὐδέν (that man should not find anything after him). But this rendering offers little meaning in the context, although, with varying interpretations, it is accepted by most commentators[25]. The Vulgate renders *ut non inveniat homo contra eum iustas querimonias* (that man may not find just complaint against him). It may be that the Vulgate associates מְאוּמָה (anything) with מאום (מוּם) "blemish" (cf. Job 31₇ Dan 1₄). It is similar, however, to the Version of Symmachus, τοῦ μὴ εὕρειν ανθρωπον κατ᾽ αὐτοῦ μέμψιν (that man may not find complaint against him). Now this rendering corresponds to the Syriac idiom ܟܐܢ "to find something after", that is, "to find fault with". We may note the Peshitta Version of John 19₄ ܘܠܐ ܡܫܟܚ ܐܢܐ ܒܗ ܟܐܢܐ (I find no fault with him) and of Acts 28₁₈ ܟܐܢܐ (and they did not find fault with me). So the Peshitta Version of Koh 7₁₄c is naturally ܕܠܐ ܢܫܟܚ ܒܪܢܫܐ ܡܕܡ ܟܐܢܐ (that a man will not find anything after him). Interpreted in accordance with this Syriac idiom, our text yields the sense: "so that man does not find any fault with him (God)"[26].

7₁₆ לָמָּה תִּשּׁוֹמֵם. תשומם is probably a shortened form of the Hithpoel, from the root שָׁמַם "to destroy, astound". Here perhaps it has the sense of "embarrassed". So in Ben Sira 43₂₄ נִשְׁתּוֹמֵם carries the meaning "surprised". Felix Perles thought תשומם "peculiar both in form and sense", and on the basis of Ben Sira 11₃₃ למה מום עולם תשא, would here read לָמָּה תִשָּׂא מוּם, "why should you incur blame?"[27].

7₁₇ בְּלֹא עִתֶּךָ. Compare Job 22₁₆ קֻמְּטוּ וְלֹא־עֵת (they were snatched away before their time), *Aḥiqar* 102 ותהך בלא ביומיך (and thou goest away before thy time), and the Phoenician *Eshmunazar* inscription בל עתי (not at my time)[28].

7₁₈b יֵצֵא אֶת־כֻּלָּם. The Septuagint, Targum, Symmachus and Syro-Hexaplar take יצא in the basic sense of "going forth, proceeding". The

[25] E.g. Hertzberg op. cit. 141; Gordis op. cit. 265; Zimmerli op. cit. 97 and 119.
[26] Cf. Burkitt, JTS 23 (1922), 24; Driver, VT 4 (1954), 230.
[27] JQR NS 2 (1911/12), 130f.
[28] KAI I, No. 14₃. ₁₂ (3).

Peshitta reads ܢܩܦ "to adhere", but this is clearly a scribal error for ܢܦܩ "to go out". It is, however, questionable if the usual biblical meaning of יצא is satisfactory here. Accordingly some scholars interpret it as escaping or avoiding the issue[29]. But this interpretation seems to be too negative to suit the context. It is to be noted that יצא connotes "what is due" in Ben Sira; for example ושית אבלו כיוצא בו (and arrange his mourning as his due, 38₁₇; cf. also 10₂₇). So in Mishnaic Hebrew the verb conveys the sense of "fulfilling one's duty": thus אם כיוּן לבו יָצָא (If he directs his mind (to the Shema) he fulfils his obligation, Bera 2₁). Hence, we may render here: "he gives due attention to both of them"[30]. In rendering *nihil negligit* the Vulgate appears to testify to this interpretation.

7₁₉ הַחָכְמָה תָּעֹז לֶחָכָם. תעז derives from the root עָזַז "to be strong", but in reading βοηθήσει the Septuagint presupposes תַּעֲזֹר (עזר/) "strengthens", and this is also the reading of the Syro-Hexaplar Version and the Qumran Scroll[31]. Modern commentators as a whole likewise prefer the reading תעזר[32]. Objection to תעז rests on the ground that עזז is normally used intransitively (e. g. Judg 3₁₀ 6₂), whereas the passage here requires a transitive function of the verb. Gordis, however, argues that תעז in our passage is used transitively, and cites Ps 68₂₉, עוּזָּה אלהים זו פעלת לנו (strengthen O God that which thou hast wrought in us) and Prov 8₂₈ בְּאַמְּצוֹ שׁקחים ... בַּעֲזוֹז עינות (when he established the skies ... when he made fast the fountains) as parallels[33]. BDB again accepts the Massoretic Text and translates, "Wisdom is strong for the wise"[34]; but this is hardly suitable. If we accept תעז we must render transitively, "Wisdom strengthens the wise". On this view the ל prefixed to חכם would denote the object (cf. e. g. Lev 19₁₈ Dan 11₃₈) rather than the dative. Dahood suggests that we have here in Koheleth an example of a *Comparative Lamedh*, and translates: "Wisdom is stronger than the wise man"[35].

---

[29] E. g. Hertzberg op. cit. 137; Zimmerli op. cit. 209; Barucq op. cit. 129 and 132f. Cf. too BDB 423a.

[30] Cf. Gordis op. cit. 267f. So both Galling op. cit. 107 and Kroeber op. cit. 97, render "tut beidem Genüge" (does satisfaction to both), while Strobel op. cit. 112 renders "does the one and the other". It is also to be noted that Bodl 2333 reads the Hiphil יוציא ad loc. which may have the meaning "fulfills".

[31] Muilenburg states (loc. cit. 27) that 14 Kennicott MSS read תעזר; but in fact the reading of these MSS noted by Kennicott (Vetus Testamentum Hebraicum; Cum Variis Lectionibus II, 556) is תעוז, an orthographical variant of תעז.

[32] E. g. Kroeber op. cit. 98; Galling op. cit. 107; Strobel op. cit. 112.

[33] Op. cit. 269.   [34] 738b.   [35] Bibl 47 (1966).

7₂₀ כִּי אָדָם אֵין צַדִּיק בָּאָרֶץ אֲשֶׁר יַעֲשֶׂה־טּוֹב וְלֹא יֶחֱטָא. Zimmermann regards this as a difficult sentence, and attributes the difficulty to the word צַדִּיק. A translator, he argues, took the Aramaic זכי as זַכַּי "righteous" instead of זָכֵי "succeeds". The original accordingly read: "No man *succeeds* (זָכֵי) on earth in doing good without evil"[36]. But there is no particular difficulty about צדיק. Such a person is one who "does good and does not sin", a phrase which seems to be based on I Reg 8₄₆ כי אין אדם אשר לא־יחטא. The text of the Hebrew is thus as meaningful as that proposed by Zimmermann.

7₂₁ אֲשֶׁר לֹא־תִשְׁמַע. אשר לא "lest". Compare Gen 11₇ אשר לא ישמעו, I Reg 22₁₆ אשר לא־תדבר. We may compare also the Aramaic דִּי לָא as in Dan 2₁₈ די לא יהובדון (lest they perish).

7₂₅ חָכְמָה וְחֶשְׁבּוֹן "Wisdom and knowledge". חשבון denotes "reckoning" made on the basis of knowledge. The term also has the meaning "reckoning" in Ben Sira (e.g. 42₃), and it has likewise the force of "calculation" in Talmudic literature (e.g. חשבונות, Shab 150a). חשבון occurs again in Koh 7₂₇ and 9₁₀ where its meaning is similar to that here in 7₂₅.

7₂₆ מוֹצֵא. The Hiphil participle of יָצָא, the second vowel of which being that of the ל״ה verbs[37]. Compare also חוֹטֵא (חטא) in 2₂₆ 8₁₂ 9₂. ₁₈. This vocalisation appears occasionally in earlier biblical books (e.g. I Sam 22₂ נֹשֶׁא, Isa 65₂₀ חוֹטֶא), but it is frequent in Mishnaic Hebrew[38].

7₂₆ מַר מִמָּוֶת. מר is generally taken as the adjective "bitter", from the root מָרַר "to be bitter"[39]. Similarly, the Septuagint renders πικρό-τερον and the Vulgate *amariorem*. Dahood, however, argues that the meaning required here is "stronger", and points to an Aramaic text in which מרירא is used of a chain, איסורא[40]. It will be observed that the Arabic مرير also denotes "strong"[41], while in the Ugaritic text Aqht I the root *mrr* has the meaning "strengthen": *ltbrkn alk brkt tmrn alkn mrrt*, "Do bless me and I shall go forth blessed; strengthen me and I shall go forth strengthened"[42]. It is again to be noted, with Dahood[43],

---

[36] Loc. cit. 25–26.
[37] See GK § 7500 (216).
[38] See Segal op. cit. 90.
[39] Cf. BDB 600; KBL 569.
[40] Bibl 39 (1958), 308f.
[41] Freytag iv, 164b.
[42] Ls. 194–195, UT 247a.
[43] Ibid. 309f.

that the word מַר in Ez 3₁₄ has the force of "strong" rather than "bitter":
ואלך מַר בחמת רוחי "and I went forth *strong* in the fervour of my spirit".

7₂₆ אֲשֶׁר־הִיא מְצוֹדִים וַחֲרָמִים לִבָּהּ. The Massoretic accentuation indicates that מצודים and וחרמים are to be construed together. And most
commentators accept this view of the passage. היא is thus regarded as
resuming and emphasising the subject אשר and introducing two instances of *casus pendens*: "her heart is full of traps and snares"[44]. Nevertheless, אשר היא is an awkward expression, as Perles recognised when
he proposed the suggestive reading אֲשֻׁרֶיהָ (her steps, feet) in agreement
with לִבָּהּ ... יָדֶיהָ (her heart ... her hands)[45]. Rejecting this emendation,
Dahood suggests that the consonantal text אשר הא would yield a vocalised
text אֲשֻׁרֵי־הִיא (the feet of her). He compares this construction with the
Ugaritic *diy ḥyt* (the wings of her), in which *diy* is a plural construct, and
ḥyt an independent feminine singular pronoun in the genitive case[46]. But
such a construction would be strange in a line in which the pronominal
suffix is used in expressing the other parts of the body, לבה ... ידיה.
Even the biblical example to which Dahood appeals contains the pronominal suffix construction: לִבּוֹ ... אֲשֻׁרָיו (Ps 37₃₁).

7₂₇ רְאֵה זֶה מָצָאתִי. Exegetes usually take זה as a demonstrative
pronoun referring to what follows[47]. Dahood, however, equates זה with
the Phoenician ז which may have the force of a relative as, for example,
in בת ז בני יחמלך—the building *which* Yhmlk built[48]. He would then
translate: "See what I have found"[49]. But since זה can apply logically
only to the sequel, it makes no syntactical difference whether we construe it as a demonstrative pronoun or as a relative pronoun. That it
is more natural to take it as a demonstrative pronoun may be seen,
however, from verse 29 ראה־זֶה מצאתי אשר—see, this I have found,
that ...

7₂₇ אָמְרָה קֹהֶלֶת. The Versions of the Septuagint and Coptic, and
most moderns read as 12₈, אמר הַקֹהֶלֶת[50]. Dahood nevertheless contends

---

[44] So Gordis op. cit. 273 and translation 170. Cf. too Hertzberg op. cit. 142; Zim-
    merli op. cit. 212.
[45] Loc. cit. 131.
[46] Bibl 47 (1966), 275f.
[47] See, e.g. Hertzberg op. cit. 143; Kroeber op. cit. 99.
[48] Text as KAI I, No. 4₁ (1). Cf. also Friedrich-Röllig, Phönizisch-Punische Gram-
    matik, 1970, § 293 (149).
[49] Ibid. 276f.
[50] E.g. Gordis op. cit. 129; Hertzberg op. cit. 143; Zimmerli op. cit. 212; Kroeber
    op. cit. 98.

that we have here in 7₂₇ an example of an archaic third person masculine singular of the Canaanite *Qatala* form as in Ugaritic. In support of his argument he cites, among other instances, Ps 11₅ אהב חמס שָׂנְאָה נפשׁו (who loves injustice hates himself)[51].

7₂₉ לְבַד. Composed of בַּד "separation", and the particle ל. It has thus the force of "only" as here. Elsewhere, however, it is either used with a suffix (e.g. הָאדם לְבַדּו היות, man being alone, Gen 2₁₈) or refers to a preceding or following noun (e.g. הוא לְבַדּו, he only, Gen 42₃₈; לְבַד־בך, only in thee, Isa 26₁₃). This reference in Koheleth is the only instance in biblical Hebrew where it is used absolutely. The Mishnaic בִּלְבַד "alone" seems to be a development from this. Thus, חוץ מזו בלבד (except this alone, Yoma 3₃).

7₂₉ b וְהֵמָּה בִקְשׁוּ חָשְּׁבֹנות רַבִּים. BDB regards חשבנות as the plural of a singular noun חֶשְּׁבֹון meaning "device, invention"[52]. Gordis considers it unnecessary to assume the existence of a distinct noun חֶשְּׁבֹון in order to account for השבנות. Rather it derives from חשׁבֹּון which is but another form of חֶשְׁבֹון. Like many commentators, he thinks that חשבנות has in Koheleth, as in IIChr 26₁₅, the meaning "devices"[53]. But while such a secondary meaning would be suitable in the text of Chronicles, it would have no relevance in Koheleth. Zimmermann proposes that an Aramaic וְאִינוּן תבעו חוּשְׁבְּנִין שָׁגִין (They have sought out erring schemes) underlies the Hebrew[54]. But this only differs from the Massoretic text in reading "erring" for "many". The Septuagint reads λογισμοὺς πολλοὺς (many arguments) and the Vulgate *infinitis . . . quaestionibus* (with many questions), and in doing so take חשבנות in its primary sense of "calculation" or "questioning". It will be observed that the author states that God made man יָשָׁר, a word which means "straight, right, pleasing". But the context implies that חשבנות represents a contrast to ישר; hence, "what is devious, irregular, questionable"[55]. We may accordingly render our passage: "but they pursued many *questionable things*".

---

[51] Psalms I, AB, 1965, 26.

[52] 364a.

[53] Op. cit. 170 for translation, 271 for discussion. Cf. too Barton op. cit. 148f.; Rankin, IB 5, 68.

[54] Loc. cit. 28.

[55] Hertzberg op. cit. 138, Zimmerli op. cit. 212, and KBL³ 347a, render "arts"; Kroeber op. cit. 99 by "crooked ways"; and Barucq op. cit. 130 and 139 by "complications".

8₁ פֵּשֶׁר "Interpretation, solution". The word occurs here only in biblical Hebrew, but it is common in biblical Aramaic (פְּשַׁר, e. g. Dan 2₄₅ 4₃ 5₁₅). So in Egyptian Aramaic we find הפשר which is probably an Aphel form of the verb, meaning "to settle an account"[1]. פְּשַׁר is again the word used in the Targum to translate פתרון, its *phonemic* equivalent, in Genesis (e. g. 40₅. ₈).

8₁ פָּנָיו יְשָׁנֵּא (אני). יְשָׁנֵּא (changed) derives from the root שנה (Aramaic שְׁנָא, Syriac ܫܢܐ) "to change", and is the equivalent of יְשַׁנֶּה , which is indeed the reading of many MSS[2]. Dahood thinks that this confusion between ישנא and ישנה arose from a dittography of א in an original Phoenician orthography (ישנאן (ישנא אני)[3]. But the interchange of Lamedh He and Lamedh Aleph verbs obtains elsewhere in late biblical Hebrew. Thus in Jer 52₃₃ we find וְשִׁנָּה את בגדי כלאו (and he changed his prison clothes) while the parallel text in IIReg 25₂₉ is וְשִׁנָּא .... Similarly, the Massoretic text of Lam 4₁ is יְשְׁנֶא, but many MSS read ישנה[4]. In IReg 22₂₅ we have להחבה but in the parallel phrase in IIChr 18₂₄ להחבא[5]. Again in Job 14₂₀ we find משנה פניו but in Ben Sira 13₂₄ ישנא פניו. So in Mishnaic Hebrew Lamedh He and Lamedh Aleph verbs frequently interchange both in form and vocalisation (cf. 7₂₆)[6].

8₂ אֲנִי פִּי־מֶלֶךְ שְׁמוֹר. The Hebrew text is unintelligible, and, as we know from the Versions and Commentaries, proved an embarrassment to both ancient and modern interpreters. In *Aḥiqar*, however, we find the line על אנפי מלך אלתקום ... אשתמר לך (in the presence of the king do not stand (delay) ... take heed to thyself)[7]. It is thus clear that אנפי מלך underlies אני פי־מלך in our text. In an Aramaic inscription of the fifth century B. C. we also find the expression מן אנפי תימא (from the

---

[1] Cowley, Aramaic Papyri in the Fifth Century B.C., 1923, 167, No. 63₁₄.

[2] De Rossi, Variae Lectiones Veteris Testamenti III, 256b.

[3] Bibl 33 (1952), 41.

[4] BH³.

[5] See Sperber, A Historical Grammar of Biblical Hebrew, 246.

[6] See Segal, A Grammar of Mishnaic Hebrew, 90f.

[7] Cowley op. cit. 215, l 101.

face of Tema)[8]. Dahood admits that אנפי מלך is the correct reading, but contends that the present text arose only because the original was written in Phoenician orthography, אנפמלכ[9]. But there is no need for such an assumption when the form אנפי תימא already existed in the Aramaic of the fifth century B. C. The corrupted element is אני, and this is doubtless a scribal confusion of the initial letters of אנפי with the familiar personal pronoun[10]. אנפי מלך must therefore be regarded as an Aramaism in our text, and the clause as a whole rendered: "Take heed in the presence of a king". Compare Prov 25₆ . . . אל־תתהדר לפני־מלך (Do not put your-self forward in the king's presence . . .).

8₄ שִׁלְטוֹן. Compare Arabic سلطان "ruler"[11]. Apart from 8₈ the word appears nowhere else in biblical Hebrew, but we meet it in Ben Sira 4₇ in the sense of "governor", and in Dan 3₂₋₃ we find the cons. pl. שלטני־ with the meaning "authorities". It also appears in the Mishna; for example, אדבר עליך לַשִּׁלְטוֹן (I will speak to the ruler for you, Kidd 3₆). Although a nominal form, the word is used here and in 8₈ in an adjectival capacity, "powerful". Compare, however, the phrase אני שָׁלוֹם "I am peaceful" in Ps 120₇.

8₄ מַה־תַּעֲשֶׂה. וּמִי יֹאמַר־לוֹ Compare Job 9₁₂ מה־תעשה אליו מי יאמר and Dan 4₃₂ ויאמר לה מה עבדת (and say to him, What doest thou?).

8₈ שַׁלִּיט בָּרוּחַ. שליט occurs in 7₁₉ (pl.), 10₅ (השליט) and Gen 42₆ (השליט) with the force of a noun. Followed by ב, it has here in 8₈ the function of an adjective; and this is the only instance in biblical Hebrew where it is so used[12]. But we find an identical use of שַׁלִּיט in biblical Aramaic; for example, דִּי־שַׁלִּיט . . . במלכות (that powerful . . . in the king-dom, Dan 4₁₄. ₂₂. ₂₉.

8₈ᵇ וְאֵין מִשְׁלַחַת בַּמִּלְחָמָה. משלחת occurs elsewhere in biblical Hebrew only in Ps 78₄₉ where it has the meaning of "company" or "detachment". But that meaning is inappropriate here, and it is commonly thought that the context suggests "discharge": "and there is no discharge in battle".

---

[8] KAI I, No. 228₁₄f. (46).

[9] Bibl 39 (1958), 311.

[10] אני is, of course, omitted by the Versions and deleted by some modern critics (e.g. Irwin, JNES 4, 1945, 130f.), or else we have an emendation such as את־פי המלך (e.g. Galling op. cit. 110).

[11] Freytag ii 341a.

[12] Wagner lists 7₁₉ 8₈ and 10₅ as denoting "Machthaber" (ruler, plenipotentiary), thereby ignoring the adjectival use of שליט in 8₈. He draws attention, however, to the widespread use of the root in Aramaic sources: Die lexikalischen und gram-matikalischen Aramaismen im alttestamentlichen Hebräisch, 114.

The Septuagint similarly renders by ἀποστολή, and the Peshitta by ܦܘܠܛܐ
(escape). The Vulgate paraphrases as *nec sinitur quiescere ingruento bello*
(neither is he suffered to rest when war is at hand), while the Targum
freely interprets ולית כלי זינא מְסַיְעָן בקרבא (and weapons of war do not
help in battle). On the basis of מִשְׁלוֹחַ ידם in Isa 11 14 Gordis suggests
that משלחת means "control"[13]. But while משלוח ידם may be so interpreted, it is doubtful if משלחת could. Zimmermann claims that in suggesting "discharge", משלחת conveys the wrong meaning in our text, since
"furloughs" or "discharges" are not inevitable in war. He points out
that the root שְׁלַח in Aramaic has the force of "strip" or "peel", and that
it is used with זֵינָא (military outfit) in the sense of putting away one's
armour. He accordingly maintains that some form of "to strip, divest"
was present in the original Aramaic version[14]. Dahood accepts משלחת
as "deliverance", but takes exception to במלחמה. He suggests that the
final letter should be dropped. מלחם might then be equated with the
Ugaritic *mlḥ* which has the meaning "sharp". This, he argues, is similar
to the Arabic *maliḥ* which has the force of "cleverness". Hence, he would
render: "and there is no deliverance in cleverness"[15].

But there can be no serious objection to the Massoretic מִשְׁלַחַת
and to the meaning "discharge". In Deut 20 8 we find an injunction that
anyone who is fainthearted before the battle should retire then, in case
his timidity should affect the prowess of others. The principle seems,
therefore, to have been established that, once the enemy is engaged, there
is no withdrawing from the battle.

8 8b וְלֹא־יְמַלֵּט רֶשַׁע אֶת־בְּעָלָיו. The literal rendering "and wickedness
does not deliver its possessor" yields little sense. The reading is indeed
improved if we read עֹשֶׁר "riches" instead of רֶשַׁע "wickedness", with
some critics[16]. Dahood again suggests that בָּעַל is here dialectical for
פָּעַל, and means "to work"[17]. However, *bʿl* may have the meaning "to
work" or "to make" in Ugaritic[18], and it is thus likely that בעל here in
Koheleth has a similar force. So בָּעַל seems to have this meaning in

[13] Koheleth—The Man and his World, 281.
[14] JQR 36 (1945/46), 42. More suggestive is Ginsberg's contention (VTS 3, 1955,
144) that the Aramaic original was קברא "grave" which the translator misread
as קרבא "battle".
[15] Bibl 33 (1952), 211.
[16] E.g. BH³; Zimmerli, Das Buch des Predigers Salomo, 216; Barucq, Ecclésiaste,
141. 149; Galling, Der Prediger, 110.
[17] Bibl 44 (1963), 303.
[18] UT No. 494 (375).

Prov 1₁₉ אֶת־נֶפֶשׁ בְּעָלָיו יִקָּח . . . . (the life of his workers he claims) and 3₂₇ אַל־תִּמְנַע־טוֹב מִבְּעָלָיו ("do not withhold good from him who produces it", pointing מִבְּעָלָיו-participle)[19].

8₉ רָאִיתִי וְנָתוֹן. וְנָתוֹן is the infinitive absolute consecutive, continuing the thought from the preceding verb. We find the same usage in 9₁₁ שַׁבְתִּי וְרָאֹה. Compare also Gen 41₄₃ וְנָתוֹן אֹתוֹ, Neh 9₈ וְכָרוֹת עִמּוֹ, Est 2₃ וְנָתוֹן . . . [20].

8₉ᵇ עֵת אֲשֶׁר. Some Versions (G S Sʰ K) read אֵת for עֵת. The Massoretic text has, however, a natural adverbial force (acc. of time) denoting "while", and is to be compared with מְקוֹם שֶׁ־ (= where) in 1₇. We may note also the use of עֵת in Jer 51₃₃, עֵת הַדְרִיכָה עוֹד מְעַט (when it is trodden a little while).

8₁₀   וּבְכֵן רָאִיתִי רְשָׁעִים קְבֻרִים וָבָאוּ
וּמִמְּקוֹם קָדוֹשׁ יְהַלֵּכוּ וְיִשְׁתַּכְּחוּ בָעִיר אֲשֶׁר כֵּן עָשׂוּ.

בכן means "thus, then". Besides here it occurs in the Old Testament only in Est 4₁₆. But we frequently find it in the Targum; for example בְּכֵן "thus", II Sam 22₄₇; בְּכֵן "then", Isa 16₅. But while בכן presents no difficulty, the verse as a whole is obscure and uncertain, and is variously rendered by both ancient translators and modern exegetes. In reading ασεβεῖς εἰς τάφους εἰσαχθέντας the Septuagint seems to presuppose קְבָרִים מוּבָאִים (the wicked carried to their tombs) instead of קְבֻרִים וָבָאוּ, and the Syro-Hexaplar and Coptic Versions agree with the Septuagint. On the other hand, the Peshitta (ܡܬܩܒܪܝܢ), Targum (אתקברו) and Vulgate (*sepultos*) represent the Massoretic קְבָרִים (buried). On the basis of the Septuagint, Gordis would render the verse: "I have seen the wicked brought to their grave with pomp, and when men walk from the holy place, they are praised in the city where they thus acted"[21]. So other scholars, such as Barton, Kroeber and Strobel have regarded the Septuagint as fundamental to an understanding of the Hebrew text[22]. Burkitt suggested, however, that קְבָרִים should read קְרֵבִים (coming near)[23], and for the Massoretic קברים ובאו, G. R. Driver would read קְרֵבִים וּבָאִים

---

[19] Cf: here too Dahood ibid. It is grammatically possible to translate "from the producers of it", but, as we noted above under 5₁₀ᵇ, the singular בַּעַל may take a plural form of the suffix.

[20] See GK 113, 4a (345), and Rubinstein, VT 2 (1952), 362ff.

[21] Op. cit. 285.

[22] Barton, The Book of Ecclesiastes, 155; Kroeber, Der Prediger, 100; Strobel, Das Buch Prediger (Kohelet), 131.

[23] JTS 23 (1922), 25f.

(approaching and entering)[24]. Galling has recently accepted this reading, while Hertzberg was prepared to countenance it[25]. Again Zimmerli would accept the Massoretic קְבָרִים, but would read וּבָאִים מָקוֹם for the Massoretic וּבָאוּ וּמִמְּקוֹם[26]. וישתכחו in the second line is further regarded as uncertain. The Septuagint, Syro-Hexaplar, Aquila, Symmachus, Theodotion, Jerome and some Hebrew MSS read וְיִשְׁתַּבְּחוּ (and were praised), and many scholars would accept this reading[27]. Moreover, some scholars would take the whole verse as applying to the wicked and his arrogance[28], while others regard only the first part as applying to the wicked, and the second half as referring to the righteous[29].

Again וּמִמְּקוֹם קָדוֹשׁ[30] has been variously construed by different exegetes. Some connect it with the first part of the verse[31], others with the second part[32]. The meaning of the phrase is, further, uncertain. Scholars generally take it literally as "holy place" or "temple"[33], although the significance of such a meaning is not clear here. Gordis thinks that the expression may be a euphemism for "cemetery" and compares בית עולם in 12₅[34]. Humbert, however, seems to be more suggestive in his contention that we have here an allusion to the "embalming place" (w^cb.t, literally "pure place") mentioned in Egyptian Wisdom literature[35]. Thus in the Admonitions of Ipuwer, for example, we read of "the lords of the embalming place being thrown upon the ground" while "he that could not make a coffin . . ."[36]. It may, then, be this "place of embalming" which Koheleth had in mind when he used the phrase מקום קדוש and

[24] VT 4 (1954), 230. Driver renders the verse as a whole: "And then I have seen wicked men, approaching and entering the holy place, walk about and boast in the city that they have done right", ibid.
[25] Galling op. cit. 111; Hertzberg, Der Prediger, 170.
[26] Op. cit. 219.
[27] E. g. McNeile, An Introduction to Ecclesiastes, 77, 106. Barton op. cit. 155; Gordis op. cit. 285; Burkitt loc. cit. 26; Driver loc. cit. 230.
[28] E. g. Barton op. cit. 153; Gordis ibid.; Burkitt ibid.; Driver ibid.
[29] E. g. Zimmerli op. cit. 219; Kroeber op. cit. 101; Strobel, op. cit. 131; Galling op. cit. 111.
[30] מקוֹם pointed with *Qames* as many MSS.
[31] E. g. McNeile op. cit. 106; Barton ibid.; Burkitt ibid.; Driver ibid.
[32] E. g. Zimmerli ibid.; Kroeber ibid.; Strobel ibid.; Galling ibid.
[33] See e. g. Kroeber op. cit. 119.
[34] Op. cit. 285f.
[35] Recherches sur les sources égyptiennes de la littérature sapientale d'Israël, 1929, 120.
[36] Erman, Die Literatur der Ägypter, 1923, 141.

which for his purpose seemed to represent "decent burial"[37]. Certainly it would suit the context, since it would offer a parallel to "graves" (with LXX) in the previous line, while a parallelism between "the wicked" and, "the righteous" (אֲשֶׁר כֵּן־עָשׂוּ, so Sym. ὡς δίκαια πράξαντες) is already discernible. Accordingly we may render the verse: "And then I saw the wicked brought to their graves, while the righteous depart life (יְהַלִּכוּ)[38] without (מִן) decent burial, and are forgotten by the community (בָּעִיר)".

8₁₁ פִּתְגָם. The word denotes "decree" or "judgement". Elsewhere in biblical Hebrew it is found only in Est 1₂₀. It is, however, found in the Aramaic portions of Ezra (e.g. 4₁₇ 6₁₁) and Daniel (e.g. 3₁₆ 4₁₄), and again in Egyptian Aramaic[39]. It likewise appears in the Targum; for example, פתגמיא האלין (these commandments, Ex 34₂₇). It is likely that פתגם is of Persian origin, and that it appears in Hebrew through the medium of Aramaic[40].

8₁₄c כְּמַעֲשֵׂה הַצַּדִּיקִים. מעשה has here the force of "reward" or "recompense". Compare Isa 32₁₇ מעשה הצדקה (the reward of righteousness).

8₁₅ וְהוּא יִלְוֶנּוּ בַעֲמָלוֹ. "And it (joy) accompanies him in his work". ילונו is the Qal imperfect of the root לָוָה, with the meaning here of "accompany". There is another root לָוָה which is used in the Qal and Hiphil, and means "to borrow"[41]. But the root here in Koheleth is used in this instance only in the Qal. Elsewhere it is used in the Niphal in the sense of "join" (e.g. Isa 14₁ Est 9₂₇). Zimmermann regards the presence of לוה here as "very strange", because "accompany . . . is employed almost exclusively in connection with human beings". He therefore thinks that the translator would have done better to retain the original Aramaic יְחַבְּרְנַהּ ("and he combine it (joy) in his work")[42]. But לָוָה is used in Ben Sira 41₁₂ (Hiphil ילוך) in the sense of a name accompanying one,

[37] Cf. Zimmerli op. cit. 220, who entertains Humbert's suggestion, but translates מקום קדוש by "heilige Ort", 219.

[38] Accepting the consonantal text, but pointing Qal (e.g. Job 41₁₁) in accordance with the other instances (e.g. 3₂₀ 6₄ 9₁₀ 12₅) of Koheleth's use of this verb to denote "departure" from the world.

[39] See Driver, Aramaic Documents of the Fifth Century B.C., 25, Letter 4.

[40] See Driver op. cit. 50; Rosenthal, A Grammar of Biblical Aramaic, 58–59. Cf., however, Rabinowitz who suggests that פתגם is but a transliteration of the Greek ἐπίταγμα (command), Bibl 39 (1958), 82 n. 2.

[41] BDB, 531a; KBL³, 476.

[42] Loc. cit. 38. Ginsberg (Studies in Koheleth, 4) thinks, however, that ילונו is but a mutilated חלקו "his portion".

while it is again used in the Mishna (Aboth 6₉ מְלַוִּים, Piel part.) of pearls and precious stones not "accompanying" one to the grave.

8₁₆c שֵׁנָה בְּעֵינָיו אֵינֶנּוּ רֹאֶה "Sleep in his eyes he does not see". The idiom "seeing sleep" appears here only in the Old Testament. Elsewhere we hear of sleep "fleeing from the eyes" (Gen 31₄₀), and of sleep not being "given to the eyes" (Ps 132₄ Prov 6₄). Gordis notes that the expression לא היינו רואין שינה (we did not see sleep) occurs in Tosephta Sukkah 45 [43], but this may depend on Koheleth. We find the idiom however in Latin writers. Thus the poet Terence (Publius Terentius Afer, c. 195–159 B. C.) wrote *somnum hercle ego hac nocte oculis non vidi meis* [44]. So later still we hear Cicero (c. 106–43 B.C.) using the expression *somnum non vidit* [45].

8₁₇c בְּשֶׁל אֲשֶׁר "on account of which". בשל appears in the late passages Jon 1₇ (בשלמי on account of whom), and 1₁₂ (בשלי on account of me). The expression בשל אשר corresponds to the Aramaic בְּדִיל ד; for example, the Targum on Gen 6₃ בשרא בדיל דאנון (because that they are flesh). The element של may be the equivalent of an earlier זו ל as in Ps 12₈ מן הדור זו לעולם (from the generation which is to eternity).

8₁₇c וְגַם אִם־יֹאמַר הֶחָכָם לָדַעַת "and even if the wise man claims to know". Compare the same idiom in IIChr 13₈ ועתה אתם אמרים להתחזק (and now do you claim to withstand . . .?).

---

[43] Op. cit. 288.
[44] Heauton Timorumenos III i 82.
[45] Epistulae Ad Familiares VII, xxx.

9₁ וְלָבוּר. If this is from the root בּוּר "to clear up, explain"[1], it occurs here only in the Old Testament. It is possible, however, that the term is to be identified with the verb בָּקַר (as in 3₁₈) "to search out" on the grounds that its form is that of the Ayin Waw rather than that of the more common Double Ayin formulation; compare יָגֵד from גָּדַד (Gen 49₁₉), יָרוּן from רָנַן (Prov 29₆). Gordis accepts this view, and regards לָבוּר as an infinitive consecutive with the force of a finite verb[2]. Yet the state of the text remains doubtful. In place of the Massoretic וְלִבִּי רָאָה אֶת־כָּל־זֶה many Versions (G S Sʰ K) presuppose וְלָבוּר אֶת־כָּל־זֶה (and my heart saw all this)[3]. And, if we interpret רָאָה in the sense of "perceive", this is a likely reading[4]. Dahood suggests that these different readings can be explained on the basis of the original orthography and quotes Friedrich Delitzsch as maintaining that they derive from a consonantal text ולבראתכלו[5].

9₁ᵦ עֲבָדֵיהֶם "their works". Apparently from a singular form עֲבָד and presupposed here only in the Old Testament. The retention of *Qames* under the second syllable in a plural noun with a heavy suffix is an indication of the Aramaic provenance of the word. Compare, for example, כְּנָת, כְּנָוָתְהוֹן (colleague, their colleagues) Ezr 4₁₇, and Targumic עוֹבָד, עוֹבָדֵיהוֹן (work, their works) on Koh 8₁₁[6].

9₁ᵧ הַכֹּל לִפְנֵיהֶם "all is before them". Compare the Septuagint τὰ πάντα πρὸ προσώπου αὐτῶν, and the Vulgate *sed omnia in futurum servantur incerta* (but all things are kept uncertain for the time to come). The Peshitta

---

[1] BDB 101b.

[2] Koheleth — The Man and His World, 289.

[3] Cf. McNeile, An Introduction to Ecclesiastes, 148.

[4] So e.g. Zimmerli, Das Buch des Predigers Salomo, 223; Kroeber, Der Prediger, 102; Galling, Der Prediger, 113.

[5] Bibl 33 (1952), 41 (Delitzsch, Die Lese- und Schreibfehler des Alten Testaments, 1920, 19). Cf. too Driver, Textus 4 (1964), 92 who suggests that ולבור conceals an original ולבי בר (and my heart [mind] explored . . .), which, written in the abbreviated form ולב׳בר, was misread as ולבור.

[6] Cf. also Stevenson, Grammar of Palestinian Jewish Aramaic, 1924, who notes that the vocalisation of disyllabic words like שָׁלָם remain unchanged with the addition of terminations (28, D nouns) and inflections (32, D nouns).

presents a rather different text, ܟܠ ܒܡܥܕܘܬܗܘ ܗܒܠ. Thus instead
of לפניהם it reads the singular ܡܥܕܘܗܝ which, unlike the Hebrew,
agrees with the antecedent האדם. It also takes the first Hebrew word of
verse 2, הַכֹּל, which it reads as הֶבֶל, with the end of verse 1. In its next
clause— ܟܠ̈ܡܝ ܒܠܚܘ —it, however, represents the Massoretic הַכֹּל
כַּאֲשֶׁר לַכֹּל. It will be noticed that the Septuagint renders the first part
of verse 2 as ματαιότης ἐν τοῖς πᾶσιν.

Zimmermann contends that the Massoretic text arose from a
mistranslation of the original Aramaic כלא קדמיהם כלא. The translator
took כלא as כְּלָא "all" in both instances, whereas he should have read
the first word as כְּלָא "as nought". His Hebrew translation should,
therefore, have been כְּאֵין לִפְנֵיהֶם הַכֹּל "as nought before them is everything"[7].

9₃ זֶה רָע. Dahood claims that the article is required before רע,
and rejects the possibility that it may be due to haplography. Rather,
he argues, in Phoenician spelling זהרע is equivalent to the Hebrew
זה הרע[8].

9₃ᵦ וְהוֹלֵלוֹת בִּלְבָבָם בְּחַיֵּיהֶם וְאַחֲרָיו אֶל־הַמֵּתִים (and madness is in their
hearts while they are alive, and afterwards(?) to the dead). Zimmermann
remarks that the last three words are unusual from the point of view
of grammar and sequence of thought: we would expect אַחֲרִית instead
of אחריו, and לְמֶוֶת or לָמוּת instead of אֶל־הַמֵּתים. The peculiarity of the
Hebrew is therefore, he thinks, to be explained from the ambiguity of
the original Aramaic which read וַאֲחֹרוֹהִי לְמֵיתַיָא "and his back is turned
to the events to come". The translator thus failed to recognise למיתיא
as לְמֵיתַיָא (root אתא), taking it instead as לְמִיתַיָא "to the dead"[9]. But
this alleged original is scarcely more acceptable than the Hebrew. As
for אחריו, many explanations are forthcoming. The Septuagint and
Peshitta take it as the plural אַחֲרֵיהֶם (after them). Symmachus and the
Targum, and some moderns[10], take it as אַחֲרִיתָם (their end), while again
many commentators accept it as "afterwards"[11]. But however we inter-

---

[7] JQR 36 (1945/46), 30f.
[8] Bibl 33 (1952), 41. Many scholars (e. g. BH3; Kroeber op. cit. 102; Galling op. cit.
113) insert the article before רע, although Zimmerli notes that it is omitted elsewhere in the book as denoting a "neutral evil", op. cit. 223 n. 4.
[9] Loc. cit. 41f.
[10] E.g. BH³; Galling op. cit. 113; Barucq, Ecclésiaste, 154.
[11] E.g. Barton, The Book of Ecclesiastes, 160; Gordis op. cit. 291; Hertzberg, Der
Prediger, 172; Zimmerli op. cit. 223; Kroeber op. cit. 103; Strobel, Das Buch
Prediger (Kohelet), 135.

pret אחריו, the originality of הַמֵּתִים is suggested by the contrasting term בְּחַיֵּיהֶם; and this is a contrast maintained in the sequence, especially in v. 5: "for *the living*, הַחַיִּים, know that they will die, but the dead, המתים, do not know".

9 4 בִּטָּחוֹן. We meet the word in II Reg 18 19 (= Isa 36 4) in the sense of "trust, confidence". Here the meaning is rather "hope" as in Talmudic literature; for example, יש להם בִּטָּחוֹן (there is hope for them, Y. Bera ix, 13) [12].

9 4 b לְכֶלֶב. As we noted under לברם in 3 18, the *Lamedh* is that of emphasis. Here we observe that it is parallel to the article in the following stich, הָאַרְיֵה הַמֵּת (the dead lion).

9 5 אֵין. וְהַמֵּתִים אֵינָם יוֹדְעִים with the pronominal suffix ם repeats the subject המתים: literally, "and the dead, *they* do not know". This usage is characteristic of Mishnaic Hebrew; thus, אֵלּוּ שֶׁהֵם צְרִיכִים, these that require (Miq 10 4).

9 9 עִם־אִשָּׁה. In common with many exegetes, Dahood thinks that "wife" rather than "woman" must be intended here, and therefore comments that we would expect the use of the article. He would thus explain its omission on the grounds that in Phoenician אשת, even without the article, meant "wife" [13]. There are, however, no strong reasons for assuming that Koheleth was referring to "wife" here; but if he were, there are many instances in biblical Hebrew in which אִשָּׁה, without the article, is used of "wife"; for example, Gen 21 21 24 3. 37 Lev 20 14.

9 10 כֹּל אֲשֶׁר תִּמְצָא יָדְךָ "All which thy hand finds", Compare I Sam 10 7 and Judg 9 33 אשר תמצא ידך.

9 11 שַׁבְתִּי וְרָאֹה. BH[3] suggests the reading וָאֶרְאֶה on the basis of 4 1. 7 [14]. רָאֹה is, however, an infinitive absolute form (cf. Ex 3 7 רָאֹה רָאִיתִי), and may accordingly be an infinitive absolute here [15].

9 11 a פֶּגַע appears elsewhere in the Old Testament only in I Reg 5 18 where it has the force of "mischance, misfortune". Here it means "event, happening".

9 12 b הָאֲחֻזוֹת. Probably a passive participle, feminine plural, from אָחַז "to hold". This form of the verb has normally the vowel וּ (*Sureq*) instead of ֻ (*Qibbus*) followed by *Daghes Forte*: compare the forms עֲמֻקָּה

---

[12] See Jastrow I, 156 b, who also mentions "faith" as a meaning of the term.

[13] Bibl 33 (1952), 211.

[14] Cf. too Zimmerli op. cit. 228 n. 1; Galling op. cit. 114.

[15] Cf. Rubinstein, VT 2 (1952), 364, and Kroeber op. cit. 120.

(Prov 22₁₄) and עֲמוּקָה (Prov 23₂₇)[16]. The noun אֲחֻזָּה "possession" is, however, similarly formed (e. g. Gen 47₁₁).

9₁₂c כָּהֵם יוּקָשִׁים בְּנֵי הָאָדָם. כָּהֵם is found in II Sam 24₃ (= I Chr 21₃) and II Chron 9₁₁ with the force of "as these". The Peshitta, however, reads ܗܟܢܐ = כה (thus). This would connect the מ with the following word to read מִיוּקָשִׁים, and might be regarded as the Pual participle from יָקֹשׁ "to ensnare"[17]. But it is possible to accept the present text on the view that the מ of the Pual Participle is sometimes dropped; for example, אֻכָּל (Ex 3₂), הַיֻּלָּד (Judg 13₈)[18]. We might then render "like these are ensnared the sons of men . . .".

9₁₃ וּגְדוֹלָה הִיא אֵלָי. גְּדוֹלָה is used in Jon 1₄ of a "great" wind. It would seem, however, that the word must have some such connotation as "significant" here. Hence, Driver suggests the emendation דְּגוּלָה "remarkable" on the basis of Cant 5₁₀ דָּגוּל מרבבה (more admirable than myriads)[19]. Yet גָּדוֹל is applied to people like Moses (Ex 11₃) and Mordecai (Est 9₄) in the sense of "outstanding" or "distinguished". It will further be observed that גדול is used of "king" and גדולים of "siegeworks"[20] in the immediate sequel (v. 14), and it is thus likely that the author intentionally uses גְּדוֹלָה here in v. 13.

9₁₅ וּמָצָא בָה אִישׁ. The Septuagint regards "king" in v. 14 as subject of the verb, and thus takes מצא as a Qal perfect: καὶ εὕρῃ ἐν αὐτῇ ἄνδρα . . . (and should find in it a man . . .). But this misinterprets the adversative force of the passage. The Peshitta renders מצא as passive, ܘܐܫܬܟܚ, and some moderns read נִמְצָא, Niphal[21]. Hertzberg regards the verb as impersonal, and so does Gordis who cites Gen 48₁₋₂, וַיַּגֵּד . . . וַיֹּאמֶר לְיוֹסֵף לְיעקב (and one said to Joseph . . . and one told Jacob)[22]. Again, Driver proposes מָצָא (= מָצוּא) and thinks that it anticipates the familiar post-biblical מָצוּי "found" in the sense of "present"[23]. However, we find מצא

---

[16] See, however, Sperber, A Historical Grammar of Biblical Hebrew, 439, who shows that Qibbus (ֻ) and Sureq (וּ) are interchangeable, and that Sureq is even followed by Daghes.

[17] Cf. e. g. Wright, The Book of Koheleth, 414; Hertzberg op. cit. 182; Galling op. cit. 114; GK § 52 rem. 6 (143).

[18] For the possibility that forms like אפל are perfect participles of earlier passives of Qal see GK, ibid., and § 52e (140f.). Cf. too our remarks on מצא 9₁₅ below.

[19] VT 4 (1954), 231.

[20] So Gordis who defends the text מצודים (op. cit. 300f.). Some versions (G S Σ V A) and 2 MSS read מצורים, and so would BH³; Kroeber op. cit. 104; and Galling op. cit. 115.

[21] E. g. BH³; Kroeber (ibid. 115) and Galling (ibid.).

[22] Hertzberg op. cit. 182–183; Gordis op. cit. 301; cf. too Barton op. cit. 167.

[23] Loc. cit. 231.

in Gen 2₂₀ (‏וּלְאָדָם לֹא־מָצָא‎, but there is not found for man) where it is used in a capacity similar to that in our text, and where it is thought to be a Qal passive[24]. It is therefore probable that ‏מצא‎ here in Koheleth should be pointed ‏מֻצָא‎ and similarly explained[25].

9₁₈ ‏מִכְּלֵי קְרָב‎ "than weapons of war". ‏קְרָב‎ is an Aramaic word found in Hebrew only in late passages (e. g. Ps 55₂₂ Zech 14₃). It appears again in Dan 7₂₁ (‏קְרָב‎) and often in the Targum (e. g. Gen 14₂ Lev 5₂₁). BH[3] suggests the reading ‏מִכְּלֵי יְקָר‎ (than precious jewels), but this is unnecessary. The Massoretic text accords with its context, which is concerned to emphasise the superiority of wisdom over war.

---

[24] See Freedman, ZAW 64 (1952), 191. Cf. also Chomsky, JQR 35 (1943–44), 284.
[25] See Bergsträsser, "Passiv Kal" in: Hebräische Grammatik (Part II, second half) 1929, 87–89, who cites, among other examples, ‏תֻּקַח‎ (Gen 12₁₅) and ‏יֻתַּן‎ (Lev 11₃₈). Gordon considers that internal passives are also to be found in Ugaritic. He further remarks that Qal passives are preserved in the Massorah only when the consonantal orthography requires them. There is no passive Qal in Mishnaic Hebrew, and, where the consonantal text permitted, the Massoretes changed the form into a conjugation found in the Mishna. UT 9₁₃ (73f.).

10₁ₐ יָבִיעַ (√נבע "to bubble") is regarded by some scholars as a dittography[1], while others again defend it[2]. It is clear, however, that both verbs are singular, and therefore we would expect זְבוּב "fly" rather than זבובי (cons. pl.). The singular "fly" would again more suitably counterbalance סִכְלוּת מְעָט (a little foolishness) in the next line. Dahood contends that the present Massoretic text arose from an original זבבמת, which a scribe could take in three ways; זבוב מות, זבובי מת, and זבוב מת. He bases this on the assumption that the only Canaanite orthography which did not employ vowel letters at this time (4–3 cents. B.C.) was Phoenician[3]. שמן רוקח (the oil of the perfumer) may be compared with Ugaritic šmn rqḥ[4].

10₁ᵦ יָקָר "Precious". The word appears in earlier biblical passages (e.g. ISam 3₁ IISam 12₃₀), but it is probably an Aramaism. Compare Dan 2₁₁ יקירה "weighty". We also find the root יָקָר in *Aḥiqar* and in other Aramaic documents[5]. So we meet יקר in the Targum; for example, מלין דיקר (words of honour), Ps 87₃.

10₂ᵦ לִשְׂמֹאלוֹ "to his left". שְׂמֹאל (Ugar. *šmal*[6], Aram. שמאל, Syriac ܣܡܠܐ) is probably, by metathesis, a compound of שאם and ל[7]. Compare Arabic الشأم "north"[8], that is, what is on the north as one looks towards the east, hence "left" (cf. ימין "right" = south). Again Arabic شأم

---

[1] E.g. BH³; Barton, The Book of Ecclesiastes, 168; Zimmerli, Das Buch des Predigers Salomo, 229; Galling, Der Prediger, 116; Strobel, Das Buch Prediger (Kohelet), 148. The word is also omitted in Symmachus and the Vulgate, while both the LXX (σκευασίαν preparation) and the Peshitta (ܡܐܢܐ vessel) read a noun instead of it.

[2] E.g. Kroeber, Der Prediger, 107; Driver, VT 4 (1954), 232. Gordis, Koheleth — The Man and His World, 305, retains the term, but, like the Peshitta, he regards it as a noun with the meaning "vessel" or "container".

[3] Bibl 33 (1952), 42f.

[4] UT 120₅ (191a). Cf. also Dahood, Bibl 47 (1966), 278.

[5] See Cowley, Aramaic Papyri of the Fifth Century B.C., 291a, and DISO 110, Ls. 26–48.

[6] UT 491.

[7] So BDB 969b.

[8] Lane I iv, 1490, col. 2, although the form الشمال is also used (1491 col. 1).

primarily means "to be unlucky"[9]. And it is in this sense of "misfortune" or "error" that שְׂמֹאל is used here in Koheleth. The term has likewise a moral connotation in Talmudic Hebrew; for example, לְמַשְׂמְאִילִים בֹּה (to those who make the wrong use of it, Shab 63a).

10₃ כְּשֶׁהַסָּכָל. This form is normally regarded as a conflation of the *Qere* כְּשֶׁסָּכָל and a variant כְּהַסָּכָל[10]. However, the *Kethib* which embodies the article seems peferable. In verses 12-13 we have a generalisation concerning the words of a wise man and a fool, but in the immediate sequel (v. 14) pertaining to the fool we have the use of the article, הַסָּכָל[11].

10₃b וְאָמַר לַכֹּל סָכָל הוּא "And he declares to everyone that he is a fool". So this passage is usually rendered[13]; and Prov 12₂₃ וְלֵב כְּסִילִים יִקְרָא אִוֶּלֶת (but the heart of fools proclaims folly) and 13₁₆ וּכְסִיל יִפְרֹשׂ אִוֶּלֶת (but the fool flaunts his folly) may be cited in its favour. The Septuagint and Peshitta, however, interpret אמר לכל in the sense of the fool regarding *all* but himself as foolish. So the Vulgate renders *omnes stultos aestimat*. McNeile accepted this view of the phrase and thought that לכל should be rendered as הַכֹּל[13], while Barton took לכל as "concerning all"[14]. Dahood argues that ל is the *Lamedh* of Reinforcement, and accordingly holds that כל means "every man" (and he says every man is a fool)[15]. But as an interpretation, this is substantially no different from taking ל as the preposition "concerning" (concerning all).

10₄ מְקוֹמְךָ אַל־תַּנַּח. "Do not leave your place". תַּנַּח is the Hiphil jussive (2 m.s.) of נוּחַ as in 7₁₈ and 11₆. For the meaning "abandon, leave" compare Jer 14₉ אַל־תַּנִּחֵנוּ (do not abandon us) and Ps 119₁₂₁ בַּל־תַּנִּיחֵנִי (do not abandon me).

10₄b מַרְפֵּא. From the root רָפָא "to heal". The meaning required here, however, is that of "submissiveness, deference", suggesting the root רָפָה "to sink, relax": "if the anger of the ruler turns upon you, do not leave your place, submissiveness mollifies great (serious) omissions (errors)". Conversely in Jer 8₁₅ we have the form מרפה with the connotation "healing": ". . . for a time of healing, but behold terror". Thus, in late Hebrew there was not only a tendency for ה"ל and א"ל verbs to

---

[9] Lane, op. cit. 1490, col. 2.

[10] E. g. BH³.

[11] So in MS Bodl 2333 we have the *Kethib* (Textus 5, 1966, 106).

[12] E.g. RSV; Gordis op.cit. 308; Hertzberg, der Prediger, 183–184 and 181; Zimmerli op.cit. 230.

[13] An Introduction to Ecclesiastes, 151 and 165. Cf. also Kroeber, Der Prediger, 107; Galling op.cit. 115. Strobel op.cit. 148 renders "he says to each".

[14] The Book of Ecclesiastes 169.

[15] Bibl 33 (1952), 192–193.

coalesce into the same forms, but also, apparently, to confuse the original meaning of the different roots. So in the Aramaic of *Aḥiqar* (100) we have the word רפאה, commonly translated "healing"[16], but which rather connotes "deference": ... אל תכבה מלת מלך רפאה תהוי "Do not suppress the word of a king, let there be deference to...". So here in Koh 10₄ we recognise the original רפא "heal", with the connotation of "sink, defer". Thus through interchange of form there was also, eventually, an obscuring of the original meanings of the two roots[17].

10₅ כְּשְׁגָגָה שֶׁיֹצָא מִלִּפְנֵי הַשַּׁלִּיט. This is an independent clause, bearing no relation to what follows. כ is thus probably to be regarded as "asseverative" rather than "comparative" and rendered "indeed" or "yea": "yea an error which derives from the presence of the ruler". Compare, for example, Ex 3₁₂ ויאמר כִּי־אהיה עמך "and he said, indeed I will be with you", and Neh 7₂ כי הוא כָאִישׁ אמת "for he is indeed a man of 'truth'"[18]. יֹצָא is the feminine participle for יֹצְאָה (m. יֹצֵא), and is another example of a ל"א verb assuming the vowel form of a ל"ה verb[19]; compare גֹּלָה fem. sing. part. of גָּלָה (mas. part. גֹּלֶה).

10₆ נִתַּן הַסֶּכֶל בַּמְּרוֹמִים רַבִּים וַעֲשִׁירִים בַּשֵּׁפֶל יֵשֵׁבוּ. נתן in the Niphal has the force of "set, place". Compare Ez 32₂₃ ... אשר נִתְּנוּ קברתיה "whose graves are set...". סֶכֶל appears here only in the Old Testament, and is thought to have the meaning "folly". סָכָל, however, occurs frequently in the book (2₁₉ 7₁₇ 10₃. ₁₄), and the Versions accordingly render "fool" here. It is usual to follow the Versions in taking רַבִּים as an adjective qualifying בַּמְּרוֹמִים[20]. Unlike במרומים it lacks the article, but Jer 2₂₁ הַגֶּפֶן נכריה (a wild vine) and Ez 39₂₇ הַגּוֹיִם רבים (many nations) are among the passages quoted as parallels[21]. However, it is probable that רבים is to be construed with the following word ועשירים and rendered "the aged". Both nouns would not have the article, but taken together may be rendered "the aged and the rich". Dahood accepts this view of the passage, but

---

[16] E. g. Cowley op. cit. 223; H. L. Ginsberg in ANET 428 b.

[17] The interchange of ל"ה and ל"א forms is, of course, frequently found in Aramaic (see, e. g. Stevenson, Grammar of Palestinian Jewish Aramaic, 1924, 73 f.), and is still more frequent in Mishnaic Hebrew (see Segal, A Grammar of Mishnaic Hebrew, 90 f.).

[18] Cf. Muilenburg, HUCA 32 (1961), 135–160, and Vriezen, in: Von Ugarit nach Qumran, 1958, 266–273. See too Gordon, UT 9₁₈ (76), for the use of the Emphatic *K* in Ugaritic.

[19] Cf. GK 75 qq (216).

[20] E. g. Hertzberg op. cit. 182; Zimmerli op. cit. 233; Kroeber op. cit. 107; Galling op. cit. 115; Strobel op. cit. 150.

[21] See, e. g. Gordis op. cit. 310.

suggests that it is an indication that Koheleth lived in a Phoenician city where the rule of the king was limited by "a gerontocratic assembly selected from among the wealthy merchants". As philological evidence he cites the Ugaritic text *rbt ilm lḥkmt šbt dqnk ltsrk* (You are aged, El, and truly wise; the greyness of your beard has truly instructed you)[22]. But this interpretation of רבים may be supported directly from Hebrew literature. For example, Job 32₉ where רבים parallels זקנים (old) and means "aged", and Job 4₃ where רבים balances ידים רפות (faltering hands) and connotes "aged". So in the Manual of Discipline (IQS) רבים is a designation of the senior members of the group[23].

10₈ גוּמָץ. An Aramaic word, appearing here only in biblical Hebrew. The Targum uses גומצא (Syriac ܓܘܡܨܐ) to translate שׁוּחָה "pit" in Prov 22₁₄ and 23₂₇, and again to translate שַׁחַת "pit" in Prov 26₂₇ כרה שַׁחַת בה יפל (he who digs a pit falls into it).

10₉ יִסָּכֶן. Niphal of סכן "to be in danger", a root which is found here only in the Old Testament. We meet it, however, in the Mishna (e.g. סְכַנְתִּי בעצמי, I was in danger, Ber 1₃) and again in the Targum (e.g. נפשי מסתכנא my soul is endangered, Ps 119₁₀₉).

10₁₀b וְיִתְרוֹן הַכְשֵׁיר חָכְמָה. The text is doubtful[24], but הַכְשֵׁיר, which occurs here only in biblical Hebrew, seems to be the Hiphil infinitive construct of כָּשֵׁר. This verb appears in Koheleth 11₆ in the sense of "succeed", but in Est 8₅ it rather denotes "what is proper". It is found again in Talmudic Hebrew in the Aphel with the meaning "to improve, grow better"[25]. Hence our phrase here may have some such meaning as "but the development of skill is an advantage".

10₁₁ בְּלוֹא לָחַשׁ. "Without a charm" in the sense of "before a charm". Compare Koh 7₁₇ בלא עתך and Job 15₃₂ בלא־יוֹמוֹ.

10₁₂ תְּבַלְּעֶנּוּ. The feminine singular of the verb בלע (to overwhelm) is used here, although we would expect the plural form (cf. GSV) in agreement with the plural noun שפתות (lips). However, a feminine singular form of the verb appears with a plural noun elsewhere: for example, Prov 1₂₀ חָכְמוֹת . . . . בָּרְחֹבוֹת תִּתֵּן קוֹלָהּ (wisdom uttereth her voice in the broad places), Job 27₂₀ תַּשִּׂיגֵהוּ כמים בלהות (terrors as water overtake him).

10₁₅ עֲמַל הַכְּסִילִים תְּיַגְּעֶנּוּ. Hertzberg regards these words as "unintelligible" and accepts the reading עמל הכסיל מתי יַגְּעֶנּוּ (the work of

---

[22] Bibl 47 (1966), 278–279.

[23] E.g. vi 7. 8ff. See Pope, Job, AB, 1965, 212f., in his discussion of Job 32₉.

[24] Cf. BH3. So Galling op.cit. 116, proposes הכשרון ויתרון (Is there, then, a gain and an advantage from wisdom?)

[25] Jastrow I, 679b.

the fool finally wearies him) proposed in BH³ and elsewhere²⁶. Objection to the Massoretic text rests on the assumption that it offends the rules of concord. Thus עָמָל which is masculine elsewhere in the book (e.g. 2₁₀ 3₁₃ 4₆ 6₇ 8₁₅) is here thought to be feminine. The suffix נו of the verb is, again, singular, whereas the antecedent הכסילים is seemingly masculine plural. Zimmermann too draws attention to the difficulties of the text, and considers that they can be explained in terms of an Aramaic original. His arguments are, however, complex, and we will quote him at length: "The restored Aramaic shows up the difficulty and gives the solution . . . טַרְחוּטָא דְּשַׁטְיָא תְּשַׁלְהִינֵּהּ דְּלָא יְדַע (the labour of the fool wearies him so that he does not know . . .). The translator, in rendering the translation with עָמָל, forgot for the moment that he put down a masculine noun, and when he came to the feminine תשלהינה transcribed mechanically with the feminine. On looking at דשטיא he lapsed in thinking it plural דְּשַׁטְיָא . . ."²⁷. Thus according to Zimmermann, the translator suffered from many misconceptions, and made at least three mistakes in producing the present text.

It may be, however, that we can justify the reading of the Massoretic text. In the Ugaritic third masculine imperfect plural, preformative *y* is often represented by *t*²⁸. For example, *ilm nʿmm ttlkn šd* (the good gods walk the field, UT 52₆₇₋₆₈) and *ilm tġrk tšlmk* (may the gods guard thee (and) give thee peace, UT 117₇₋₈). So in biblical Hebrew we have instances of the masculine plural subject with a verb whose preformative element is ת. Thus in Ez 37₇, וַתִּקְרְבוּ עֲצָמוֹת עֶצֶם אֶל עַצְמוֹ וְרָאִיתִי וְהִנֵּה עֲלֵיהֶם גִּדִים (and the bones drew near, bone unto his bone, and I looked and behold sinews were upon them), the verbal ending ו and the suffix ending הם of the preposition על indicate that ותקרבו serves a plural masculine function. So in Job 19₁₅ גָּרֵי בֵיתִי וְאַמְהֹתַי לְזָר תַּחְשְׁבֻנִי נָכְרִי הָיִיתִי בְעֵינֵיהֶם (the sojourners of my house and my maids regarded me as a stranger, although I was innocent in their eyes) the verbal ו and the suffix הֶם of עֵינֵי show that תַּחְשָׁב is masculine plural²⁹. It is again possible that preformative *t* with the force of a third masculine singular exists in Ugaritic. *Wtkms hd* (and Hadad was prostrate, UT 75 II₅₅) and *tmẓʿ kst*

---

²⁶ Hertzberg op. cit. 193; cf. Kroeber op. cit. 121; Galling op. cit. 116.

²⁷ JQR 36 (1945–46), 40–41.

²⁸ C. H. Gordon UT 74–75.

²⁹ Van Dijk offers a suggestive article on this question, VT 19 (1969), 440–447. His claim that ותקרבון in Deut 5₂₃ and ותאמרו in Deut 5₂₄ have as antecedents 3rd masc. pls. is, however, doubtful. The contexts suggest that these forms are 2nd masc. pls.

dnil (Danel tears his garb, IAqht 36, UT p. 245a) are thought to be instances[30].

From these considerations it may be argued that some problematical singular Hebrew verbs with preformative ת find their explanation in the view that they are examples of **Taqtul* third masculine singular formations. Thus the textual problems of Isa 42₂₀, רבות ולא (*Qere* רָאוֹת) רָאִיתָ, תִּשְׁמֹר פָּקוֹחַ אָזְנַיִם וְלֹא יִשְׁמָע, would be solved if we regard תִּשְׁמֹר as third masculine singular: "he sees many things but he does not observe, his ears are open but he does not hear"[31]. Similarly ... תְּשׁוּר in Job 20₉ וְלֹא עוֹד תְּשׁוּרֶנּוּ מְקֹמוֹ is probably to be regarded as third masculine singular in agreement with מְקֹמוֹ: "and his place will not behold him any more"[32].

It is, then, possible that we are to recognise in the preformative ת of תְּיַגְּעֶנּוּ a third masculine singular of the **Taqtul* type. עָמָל would thus retain its masculine gender, and הַכְּסִילִים could be construed as a combination of הַכְּסִיל with the old genitive case-ending י[33], and the enclitic מ[34]. It is noticeable that "the fool" is always referred to in the singular in chapter 10, while הַכְּסִיל would again accord with אֲשֶׁר לֹא יָדַע in the following clause to which it serves as antecedent. We would thus translate עמל הכסילים תיגענו as "the work of the fool wearies him".

10₁₇ בֶּן־חוֹרִים. "A son of freemen". חוֹרִים derives from a root חָרַר (cf. Arabic حرر "to free")[35] denoting "free". The noun appears only in the plural (e.g. IReg 21₈. ₁₁ Neh 2₁₆ 5₇) and has the meaning "nobles". The expression בֶּן־חוֹרִים is found here only in biblical Hebrew, but בן חורין appears in the Mishna (Git 4₆). We may compare too בר חרן (free men, nobles) in *Aḥiqar* (217) and the term חרן(ו)ת "freedom" on the Jewish coins of the First Roman war (60–70 A.D.) and of the Bar-Kokhba revolt (132–135 A.D.)[36]. Dahood, however, equates our term with the personal name *bn ḥrm* found in Ugaritic (UT 400 I, 9)[37].

---

[30] Van Dijk loc. cit. 441.

[31] Reading *Qere* in agreement with פָּקוֹחַ in the next stich.

[32] Cf. Job 7₁₀ and Ps 103₁₆ וְלֹא יַכִּירֶנּוּ עוֹד מְקוֹמוֹ (and his place will not know him again). See Sarna, JBL 82 (1963), 318, and cf. also Van Dijk loc. cit. 442ff., for other possible instances of this **Taqtul* form. So Watson, Bibl 53 (1972), 199, suggests that תקעו in I Chr 10₁₀ is to be interpreted as a Hiphil ("they exposed") and so the initial letter is to be explained as a 3rd masc. pl. with a preformative ת.

[33] Cf. GK 90 kl (252f.).

[34] See Hummel, JBL 76 (1957), 94.

[35] Lane I ii 538 col. 1.

[36] See Kadman, IEJ 4 (1954), 150f., especially 165. Cf. too DISO 96, Ls. 8f.

[37] Bibl 39 (1958), 311.

10₁₇ᵦ בִּגְבוּרָה וְלֹא בַשָּׁתִי. "With strength and not in carousing". שָׁתִי,
from שָׁתָה "to drink", appears here only in the Old Testament, although
a feminine form שְׁתִיָּה is found in Est 1₈. Zimmermann maintains that
בגבורה is too strong a word here, and that some such term as "moderation" is required. He accordingly thinks that the original was the Eastern
Aramaic word בחוסנא (ܟܣܘܣܢܐ) meaning "with moderation". The translator failed to recognise this meaning in the word, taking it rather as
חוּסְנָא "strength", and so rendered it by בִּגְבוּרָה [38]. But בגבורה ולא בשתי
is in the nature of a comment on the preceding material, which emphasises
that effective rulership depends on "eating at the proper time", and as
such גְבוּרָה seems a suitable word.

10₁₈ בַּעֲצַלְתַּיִם יִמַּךְ הַמְּקָרֶה וּבְשִׁפְלוּת יָדַיִם יִדְלֹף הַבָּיִת. בעצלתים appears
to be dual (from עַצְלָה sloth), but for no obvious reason, although some
scholars regard it as a dual of intensity [39]. Dahood suggests that the form
may be explained by regarding the מ as "enclitic" in accordance with
Ugaritic and Phoenician usage [40]. However, the nominal form עַצְלוּת
occurs in Prov 31₂₇. It is thus possible that the original text was בְּעַצְלוּת
יְמַךְ, the ים of the present בעצלתים arising from a dittography of the ים־
of the following word [41]. עצלות would also provide a parallel to שִׂכְלוּת
in the next stich.

יִמַּךְ is the Niphal imperfect of מכך "to be low, sink". Elsewhere in
biblical Hebrew it is found only in Ps 106₄₃ and Job 24₂₄. We notice that
it is followed and paralleled here in Koheleth by יִדְלֹף "drip". This is
the only place in the Old Testament where these two verbs appear together, and Dahood sees in the verse a connection with the Ugaritic *l
ymk l tngṣn pnth l ydlp tmnh* [42]. But, apart from a lexical, there is no close
affinity between these two texts. For while דלף in Koheleth means "drip"
or "drop" (cf. Job 16₂₀ Ps 119₂₈) Ugaritic *dlp* has not this meaning. In
the two passages it is attested (*loc. cit.* and line 26) *dlp* parallels *ngṣ* "shake",
and therefore seems to connote "quake" [43]: "he did not sink down, his
face did not shake, his countenance did not quake".

הַמְּקָרֶה "the roof-structure". We recognise the underlying root קָרָה
"to meet, encounter": hence the word denotes something that "meets"

[38] Loc. cit. 26.
[39] E.g. BDB 782a; Gordis op.cit. 317; Hertzberg op.cit. 194; Galling op.cit. 118.
[40] Bibl 33 (1952), 194–195, and see also Hummel loc.cit. 94.
[41] Cf. Zimmerli op.cit. 237 n.1.
[42] Dahood, Bibl 33 (1952), 212, and Ugaritic-Hebrew Philology, 55; JQR 62 (1971),
84–87, Text (Baal III A, 17f.) as CML 82.
[43] See Speiser, JCS 5 (1951), 66.

or "fits into place" as a rafter of a roof. The nominal form מקרה appears only here, although we find the form קוֹרָה elsewhere in the Old Testament (e.g. Gen 19₈ Cant 1₁₇), and the form תְּקְרָה in the Talmud (e.g. Baba Metz 117a). It is to be observed that the participle with the article (Ps 104₃) is pointed הַמְקָרֶה (Pataḥ with Methegh) probably to distinguish it from the noun with the article הַמְקָרֶה (Pataḥ with Daghes Forte). שִׁפְלוּת, "a sinking down". The term appears here only in the Old Testament, but we find it in the Targum (שִׁפְלוּתָא) on Jer 49₂₄, and again in the Talmud (e.g. Sot 48a).

10₁₉ עֹשִׂים לֶחֶם. Compare Dan 5₁ where עֲבַד לְחֶם is used of preparing a feast.

10₁₉ᵦ הַכֶּסֶף יַעֲנֶה אֶת־הַכֹּל. The Septuagint ἐπακούσεται[44] and the Vulgate "obediunt" seem to take ענה as "obey, submit", while in its duplicate rendering ܡܣܟܢ ܣܟܐܠܐ the Peshitta associates the root with the meaning "to afflict, humble" (e.g. Isa 25₅ 31₄). But ענה has here rather the force of "provide for" (e.g. Gen 41₁₆ Hos 2₂₃₋₂₄)[45] or "pay"[46]: "Money pays for all".

10₂₀ בְּמַדָּעֲךָ. We find the noun מַדָּע (knowledge) in late biblical passages (IIChr 1₁₀₋₁₂ Dan 1₄. ₁₇). The Septuagint (συνειδήσει) and some exegetes likewise see this word in our text, although interpreting it as "thought" rather than "knowledge"[47]. It is, however, doubtful if this meaning for the term suits the parallel expression וּבְחַדְרֵי מִשְׁכָּבְךָ (in thy bedchamber) in the same line. The emendation בְּמַצָּעֲךָ (in thy couch) has been countenanced by more than one scholar[48], but attempts have also been made to discern a suitable meaning in the Massoretic text. Thus, connecting the word with the sexual connotation of the root ידע, Koehler and Baumgartner propose "bed-room"[49]. But this is synonymous, rather than parallel with ובחדרי משכבך. It is to be noted that ידע has also the meaning "to be quiet, to be at rest", and on this basis D. W. Thomas suggestively argues that מדעך (vocalised מִדְעֲךָ?) means "repose, rest"[50]. Dahood thinks that the word should be interpreted in the light of Ugaritic

---

[44] For text variation see Rahlfs, Septuaginta II, 257. Cf. also Gordis op. cit. 318.

[45] Gordis ibid. On the various meanings of ענה see our comments under 1₁₃ above.

[46] C.H. Gordon (UT 99 n. 1) notes that Akkadian apâlu has likewise the meaning "to pay" as well as "to answer".

[47] E.g. McNeile op. cit. 83; Barton op. cit. 179; Gordis op. cit. 319; Hertzberg op. cit. 197–198.

[48] See Kroeber op. cit. 108.

[49] KBL 497b.

[50] JTS 50 (1949), 177.

mnd^c which has the meaning "messenger". He would thus regard מדעך
as plural, and render "Even among your own messengers do not belittle
the king . . ."[51]. But while this proposal may be philologically possible,
it would not provide an adequate parallel to ובחדרי משכבך.

10 20 בַּעַל הַכְּנָפַיִם "Owner of wings". Compare the singular בַּעַל כָּנָף
in Prov 1 17; but the plural may be used here to balance עוֹף הַשָּׁמַיִם in
the previous clause.

---

[51] Bibl 39 (1958), 311 f.

11₁ שַׁלַּח לַחְמְךָ עַל־פְּנֵי הַמָּיִם כִּי־בְרֹב הַיָּמִים תִּמְצָאֶנּוּ "Cast thy bread upon
the face of the waters, for in many days you will find it". So we may
literally translate the passage, but as it seems to have a proverbial impli-
cation some uncertainty attaches to its meaning. The Targum, Talmud
and medieval Jewish scholars regarded it as an exhortation to charitable
works[1], and some later exegetes adopted a similar view[2]. Other commentators explain the verse as offering advice to those engaged in maritime
merchandise[3]. Again, Hertzberg and Galling suggestively argue that we
are to see the passage in the context of Koheleth's views on the uncertainty of the future (e.g. 3₁₁ 8₁₇ 9₁₁), and therefore as expressive of the
notion that the most unpromising venture may have an unexpectedly
successful outcome[4].

Zimmermann accepts the view that the verse is to be interpreted in
terms of maritime commerce, but claims that the meaning becomes clari-
fied if we see it in its original Aramaic form. Regarding the use of שַׁלַּח
with "bread" as unusual, he thinks that it arose from a misunderstanding
of the Aramaic verb פְּרַס. This could mean "spread out" as the sails of
a vessel, or it could mean "break", from which nominal forms occur with
the meaning "bread". The translator took the second meaning here, and
so offers לחמך in our text. He should, however, argues Zimmermann,

---

[1] See Ginsburg, Qoheleth, 447.
[2] E.g. Ginsburg ibid.; Wright, The Book of Koheleth, 226.
[3] E.g. McNeile, An Introduction to Ecclesiastes, 84; Gordis, Koheleth: The Man and His World, 320; Dahood, Bibl 39 (1958), 315f.
[4] Hertzberg, Der Prediger, 200f.; Galling, Der Prediger, 119. Humbert, Recherches sur les sources égyptiennes de la littérature sapientale d'Israël, 122, would ex- plain "upon the waters" after the Egyptian expression "on the waters of . . . (ḥr mw n)", meaning "devoted, obedient to" the deity, and thinks that in Koheleth it would have the force of obedience to Yahweh. He accordingly renders: "Cast thy bread out of obedience, for thou shalt find it after many days". But the theme of obedience to Yahweh is hardly a characteristic theme of Koheleth. On the other hand, Gemser, VTS 7, 1960, 102–108, notes that the recently edited Egyptian *Instructions of 'Onchsheshonqy* contains a saying "Do a good deed and throw it into the river; when this dries up you shall find it" which may be compared with our passage in Koheleth.

have rendered: "Set your sail upon the waters . . ."[5]. But if we are to
suppose that "bread" was originally "sail" or "ship" there would be
little point in the proverbial saying. A ship setting out to sea would
normally be expected to make a successful voyage, and there would be
nothing remarkable in its safe return to port. On the other hand, "bread"
thrown upon the water would be expected to disintegrate and disappear;
but our text states that, contrary to expectation, it will be found again.
We again notice that Zimmermann represents תֶּן־חֵלֶק (v. 2) by a sea
"venture". But this would be an unusual meaning of even the Aramaic
חֵלָק (cf. Ezr 4₁₆ where it means "possession" of land, and Dan 4₁₂. ₂₀
where it means "one's appointed lot").

11₃ שָׁם יְהוּא. Four MSS read הוא, and compare Job 3₁₉ קטן וגדול
שם הוא (the small and the great are there)[6]. However, the point of the
aphorism is that a tree will remain where it falls. Hence it is probable
that we have here the Qal imperfect of the Aramaic verb הֲוָא (הוה) "to
be" (cf. LXX ἐκεῖ ἔσται). The participle of הָוָה occurs in Koheleth 2₂₂,
and the form יהוא is known to us from Aramaic inscriptions[7]. On the
analogy of תֶּהֱוֵא (Dan 2₄₀) and לֶהֱוֵא (Dan 2₂₀) we may point יְהֱוֵא[8].

11₅ הַמְּלֵאָה. From the root מָלֵא "to fill"; hence "pregnant". The
term appears here only in biblical Hebrew, but we meet it in the Mishna;
for example יצאה מְלֵאָה (she went away pregnant, Yeba 16₁).

11₆ בַּבֹּקֶר . . . וְלָעֶרֶב. Compare Job 4₂₀ מִבֹּקֶר לָעֶרב "from morning
till evening". So the ב prefixed to בקר here seems to have the force of
"from". "From the morning sow thy seed, and till the evening do not
rest thy hand"[9].

11₉ בְּחוּרוֹתֶךָ "In thy youth". בחורות is an abstract noun in the form
of a feminine plural. Here and 12₁ are the only instances in which the
word is found in the Old Testament.

11₁₀ וְהַשַּׁחֲרוּת. The noun שַׁחֲרוּת appears here only in biblical Hebrew,
although the form שָׁחוֹר occurs in Lam 4₈. The term is connected with

[5] JQR 36 (1945/46), 31–32.
[6] Cf. Zimmerli, Das Buch des Predigers Salomo, 299 n. 2, who would adopt the
reading הוא.
[7] See, e.g. CIS ii (vol. 1) No. 200,3; No. 212,4ff.; see also DISO 62, Ls. 30f.
[8] The form יהוה appears often in extra-biblical Aramaic (cf. Cowley, Aramaic
Papyri of the Fifth Century B. C., 283), but, of course, neither יהוה nor יהוא
appears in biblical Aramaic, להוא being used instead. It may be noted that Dahood
(Bibl 47, 1966, 271) would read שָׁמִי הוא (that is its proper place) for the Massoretic
שם הוא. But it is doubtful if a tree always falls in "a proper place".
[9] Cf. Dahood ibid 281, and also under 5₁₄ above where we drew attention to the
interchange of ב and מ.

the root שָׁחַר which primarily means "to be black" [10], but it also signifies the time when the hair is black, that is, the period of youth and vigour; compare the Arabic شَخَر, early youth [11]. That שַׁחֲרוּת has such a meaning is corroborated by its proximity to יַלְדוּת "youth". In rendering ἡ ἄνοια (folly, so Peshitta), the Septuagint obviously misunderstood the meaning of the term. The Targum more discerningly interprets as יוֹמֵי אוּכָּמוּת שְׂעַר "the days of the blackness of hair".

---

[10] Hence it also denotes "the dawn"; e.g. שַׁחַר, I Sam 9 26 and Mesha Inscription, l. 15, מבקע השחרת (from the break of dawn).
[11] Freytag ii 401a; Lane iv 1515, col. 3.

12₁ בּוֹרְאֶיךָ בִּימֵי־בְּחוּרֹתֶיךָ. וּזְכֹר אֶת־בּוֹרְאֶיךָ can only be rendered "thy Creator", although it is plural in form. However the Versions and some MSS presuppose the singular בּוֹרַאֲךָ [1], and we find בֹּרַאֲךָ in Isa 43₁ where it parallels יֹצֶרְךָ. Gordis would regard בוראיך as a singular, on the assumption that it is an example of a ל״א verb being vocalised as a ל״ה (e.g. עֹשֶׂיךָ "thy maker", Isa 54₅) [2]. But, as Zimmermann rightly observed, "Creator" is strange in a context which has nothing to do with religion, and which is rather concerned with the theme of advancing old age. Zimmermann therefore thinks that the original Aramaic text made some reference to "health", and suggests that the translator misread בָּרְיָךְ "your health" (cf. Targum Ex 21₁₉) as בָּרְיָךְ "your Creator" [3]. However, even "health" is not suitable to the context, for one may enjoy good health in old age. The burden of the whole passage is that youth irrevocably passes to old age. From 11₉ onwards the author emphasises that one should enjoy life in youth. 11₉c, which mentions God judging one's acts appears to be a gloss. So it is highly probable that 12₁a is a gloss. 12₁b then follows naturally from 11₁₀a: "Remove sorrow from your heart and put away evil from your flesh ... before the evil days come". A religious editor would be tempted to insert 12₁a as a counterbalance to 11₉a which proclaims that one's heart should be glad "in the days of ... youth". As a word in an editorial clause, then, בּוֹרְאֶיךָ may be explained,

---

[1] This was adopted by Baer in his edition of the text, Quinqua Volumina, 1886, 68f., and so GK § 124 k (399). The MT is taken as "a plural of majesty" by some scholars (e.g. Franz Delitzsch, Commentary on the Song of Songs and Ecclesiastes, 402; Wright, The Book of Koheleth, 238; Zimmerli, Das Buch des Predigers Salomo, 242 n. 4). According to Midrash Koheleth the Mishnaic injunction concerning the origin, destiny and Judge of man (Aboth 3₁) is based on Koh 12₁, being derived from one word, namely, בורך "thy pit", בארך "thy well" and בוראך "thy Creator" (Midrash Rabbah VII (Ruth and) Ecclesiastes, Eng. ed. Cohen 299). But while this is an interesting piece of Midrashic word-play, it offers no evidence for the form and meaning of בוראיך in our text. The reading borᵉka (grave) is however preferred by Scott, Ecclesiastes, AB18, 1965, 253. 255, and Wright, CBQ 30 (1968), 333, on grounds of context.

[2] Koheleth: The Man and His World 330.

[3] JQR 36 (1945/46), 32. So Ginsberg, VTS 3 (1955), 145, would explain the original word, but renders by "vigour".

not in terms of an Aramaic original, but rather as a subsequent scribal error for the singular בּוֹרַאֲךָ[4].

12₁ь עַד אֲשֶׁר לֹא "before". Compare the Mishnaic עַד שֶׁלֹּא; for example, עַד שֶׁלֹּא נבחרוּ (before they are chosen, Mak 2₄).

12₃ שֶׁיָּזֻעוּ. From זוּעַ "to shake, tremble". Apart from here, the root occurs in biblical Hebrew only in Est 5₉ and Hab 2₇. We find it, however, in biblical Aramaic (Dan 5₁₉ 6₂₇) and also in the Targum (e.g. Judg 8₁₂) and Mishna (e.g. Aboth 5₂₂).

12₃ь וּבָטְלוּ. This is the sole instance of the root בטל occurring in biblical Hebrew. But it occurs in biblical Aramaic (Ezr 4₂₁. ₂₃. ₂₄ 5₅) and also in the Mishna (e.g. Aboth 1₅ 2₄). We again find a participial form (מבטל) in an Aramaic Palmyrene inscription of the second century A.D.[5]

12₄ שׁוּק "street". Besides here and verse 5 we find the word in the Old Testament only in Prov 7₈ and Cant 3₂. We meet it too in a few passages in Egyptian Aramaic[6], and again in Palmyrene and Nabatean inscriptions[7]. The word has thus a wide incidence in Aramaic sources, but we also find the Arabic سوق[8] and the Assyrian *sûqu*[9]. Dahood observes that in Phoenician settlements in North Africa a forum is calles *Sûq*, and that many modern villages in Algeria and Tunisia are similarly named. He therefore concludes that, whatever its origin, the word must have reached Koheleth through Phoenician mediation[10].

12₄ בִּשְׁפַל קוֹל הַטַּחֲנָה. שְׁפַל is here the infinitive construct of the verb שָׁפֵל "to be lowly" rather than the construct of the adjective שָׁפָל[11]: "at the sinking of the sound of the mill"; compare also Prov 16₁₉ שְׁפַל־רוּחַ (a humbling of spirit). הַטַּחֲנָה, from טָחַן "to grind". This form of the noun appears here only, but we find טְחוֹן in Lam 5₁₃. The older term was רֵחַיִם (e.g. Num 11₈ Isa 47₂) and we note the Ugaritic *rḥm* (dual, mill-

---

[4] Cf. also Sperber (A Historical Grammar of Biblical Hebrew 575) who notes inconsistencies in the use of *yodh* in nominal forms before the personal suffix; e.g. מַחֲנֶךָ ... וְהָיָה מַחֲנֶיךָ קָדוֹשׁ (thy camp ... and thy camp will be holy, Deut 23₁₅) where, as the verb and adjective show, מחניך is singular as in the first instance.

[5] CIS ii (vol. 3), 3913 i, 10 (p. 46), and 55 for date. Cf. too Wagner, Die lexikalischen und grammatikalischen Aramaismen im alttestamentlichen Hebräisch, No. 39 (p. 34).

[6] Cowley, Aramaic Papyri of the Fifth Century B. C., Nos. 5₁₂. ₁₄ (11); 13₁₄ (37).

[7] DISO 317–318.

[8] Freytag ii, 378a.

[9] Bezold, Babylonisch-Assyrisches Glossar, 1926, 208b.

[10] Bibl 33 (1952), 215. It may however be observed that the "Street-market" in modern Jerusalem is also called "Suq".

[11] Cf. GK § 45c (123).

stones) [12]. We may compare too the Vulgar Arabic نطحنة and طاحون which
are used for the earlier رَحَا [13].

124ᵇ .וְיָקוּם לְקוֹל הַצִּפּוֹר. Many scholars accept the Massoretic text:
"and he rises at the voice of the bird" [14]. ויקום is not, however, a parallel
to וְיִשַּׁחוּ (and are depressed) in the following stich. The reading וְיִקְמַל
has been proposed [15], which, though graphically close to the Massoretic
text, denotes "to decay" or "to be mouldy" (Isa 19₆ 33₉), and is therefore
scarcely applicable to "voice". Ginsberg argues that the Ugaritic *ql*,
perhaps from the root *qwl* or *qll*, "to fall, drop" underlies our text, and
accordingly suggests the reading *wyql qwl hṣpwr* "and the voice of the bird
becomes faint" [16].

124ᵇ בְּנוֹת־הַשִּׁיר "the daughters of song"; hence "song birds". The
construction is common; compare, for example, בְּנוֹת יַעֲנָה "young of the
ostrich", Job 30₂₉ Isa 43₂₀ Mic 1₈. We may note too Ugaritic *bnt hll*,
"the daughters of praise", applied to the *kṭrt*, the female singers [17].

125ᵃ יִרְאוּ וְחַתְחַתִּים. Many MSS, G Sʰ KΣ read יִרְאוּ "they see".
However, "they fear" with the Vulgate *timebunt* (cf. Syriac ܢܕܚܠܘܢ) seems
preferable. It is thus possible to regard the Massoretic consonantal text
 יראו as *defective* for יִירְאוּ "they fear". Compare I Sam 17₁₁ where יְרָאוּ
occurs for יִירְאוּ "they fear" (as v. ₂₄) [18]. It will further be observed that
as in I Sam 17₁₁ יראו is immediately preceded by ויחתו (√חתת, and they
were terrified), so here in Koheleth it is immediately followed by the
noun חתחתים "terrors". The noun appears here only [19], but such forms
of duplication appear elsewhere; for example, תלתלים (√תלל) "palm-
branches" (Cant 5₁₁), גלגל (√גלל) "wheel" (Ez 10₂ Koh 12₆). Such formations are, however, more frequent in the Mishna [20].

125ᵇ .וְיָנֵאץ הַשָּׁקֵד וְיִסְתַּבֵּל הֶחָגָב וְתָפֵר הָאֲבִיּוֹנָה. Obscure allegory and
textual uncertainty combine to make this line one of the most difficult

---

[12] UT No. 3216 (483).

[13] Wright op. cit. 493. For the vulgar Arabic see Wehr, Arabisches Wörterbuch,
1956 edn., 502b; for the older form see Freytag ii, 134a.

[14] Cf. Barton, The Book of Ecclesiastes 195; Gordis op. cit. 334; Hertzberg, Der
Prediger, 205 and 207; Kroeber, Der Prediger, 111.

[15] E. g. BH³; Strobel, Das Buch Prediger (Kohelet), 161 n. 8; cf. also McNeile,
An Introduction to Ecclesiastes, 88.

[16] Syria 33 (1956), 99–101. Cf. too UT No. 2227 (478a). Galling (Der Prediger 120)
follows Podechard in reading וידום (√דמם) "be silent"; cf. Sym παύσεται.

[17] Gordon, UT No. 769 (390).

[18] For further examples of the defective *yodh* see Sperber op. cit. 568.

[19] Hence Strobel (op. cit. 161 n. 10) thinks there may be confusion with תחתים
(below); but this is unlikely since חתחתים serves as a parallel to "they fear".

[20] Segal, Mishnaic Hebrew Grammar, 112.

in Koheleth[21]. The *Qere* and many Versions (G Sʰ K S V) render יָנֵאץ
by "blossom", as if the root is נצץ; and modern commentators generally
accept this, thus equating the MT with יָנֵץ (imperf. Hiph.), the א being
regarded as a vowel in a *plene* orthography[22]. But citing Ibn Ezra, among
others, C. D. Ginsburg argues that the root is rather "to despise"[23], and
McNeile[24], Podechard[25] and Strobel[26] are likewise of this opinion. This
view of the verb carries the interpretation that delicacies formerly enjoyed
become "despised" in old age. Yet, although the precise meaning of the
phrase וינאץ השקד remains obscure[27], the reading of the Versions cannot
lightly be discarded, and it is possible that, since the almond tree blossoms
in January, its white blossom is a symbol of winter and the white hair
of old age.

וְיִסְתַּבֵּל הֶחָגָב. The root סבל means "to bear a load" (e. g. Gen 49₁₅
Isa 53₄), and the Pual participle has the meaning of "laden" (Ps 144₁₄).
The Hithpael, which appears here only in biblical Hebrew, should accordingly have some such force as "burden oneself". Many MSS read
ויסתכל[28] signifying "to be confused, foolish"[29], and if we accept the view
that an old man is the subject of the allegory, this is not an impossible
reading. However, in rendering "grows fat" the Septuagint (παχυνθῇ),
the Vulgate *impinguabitur* and Arabic (تسمن) seem to reflect the notion of
the corporal infirmities of old age indicated by the Hebrew. The Targum
(יתנפחו) "swells" and the Peshitta (ܣܡܢ) "grows" seem to represent
similar interpretations of יסתבל. The noun חָגָב is normally regarded as
"locust" or "grasshopper" elsewhere in the Old Testament (e. g. Lev 11₂₂
Num 13₃₃ Isa 40₂₂), and the Septuagint, Vulgate and Peshitta so take it
here. But Jewish exegesis identified the term with parts of the body:
thus the Targum translated by "ankles" (אסתורי), the Midrash by "joints"
(קרסוליו), while the Talmud (Shab 152a) rendered by העגבות "the but-

---

[21] Cf. Moore, JBL 10 (1891), 55–64.
[22] E. g. Barton, The Book of Ecclesiastes, 180 and 196; Gordis op. cit. 335; Hertzberg op. cit. 207; Kroeber op. cit. 120; Zimmerli op. cit. 243; Barucq, Ecclésiaste, 182.
[23] Coheleth, 462.
[24] An Introduction to Ecclesiastes, 89 and 111.
[25] L'Ecclésiaste, 463.
[26] Op. cit. 161. So the MS. Bodl 2333 reads ינאץ, imperf. Qal of נאץ (Textus 5,
1966, 107).
[27] Cf. Franz Delitzsch op. cit. 412f. and Wright op. cit. 257f. for a survey of the
various views that have been proposed.
[28] K-de R.
[29] See Jastrow II, 991 for Targumic and Talmudic usage.

tocks"[30]. This Talmudic rendering may however offer a clue to the connotation of the term here; for it suggests that we might connect חגב with the Arabic حجب which denotes the region of the hips[31]. Accordingly יסתבל החגב may represent the figure of an old man with stiff-joints dragging himself along with difficulty[32].

תָּפֵר in the text is the Hiphil imperfect of פרר "to break". But G S[h] K Σ read Hophal תָּפַּר "is broken". תפרה "to bear fruit" is presupposed by Aquila, and, on grounds of dittography arising from the ה at the beginning of the following word, a few scholars have entertained this reading[33]. But our reading of תפר depends largely on our interpretation of the noun אביונה.

הָאֲבִיּוֹנָה. The term appears here only in biblical Hebrew, but we find it in the Mishna (Mass 4₆) where it means "caperberry", and it is translated as such by both the Septuagint (κάππαρις), Vulgate (capparis) and Peshitta (ܟܦܪ). The berry had the effect of stimulating the appetite[34], and for this reason it seems to be so called in Hebrew. The Peshitta, as we observed, translated by ܟܦܪ, but immediately commented ܟܐܒܘܬܐ ܘܢܬܒܛܠ (and want shall cease), as if connecting אביונה with אֶבְיוֹן "want"[35]. Nevertheless there is a persistent Jewish tradition which explains האביונה as sexual passion. According to the Midrash it is the התאוה (the desire) "which brings peace between man and wife"[36]. The Targum interpreted the word as ותתמנע מן מַשְׁכְּבָא "and you will cease from sexual intercourse", while the Talmud (Shab 152a) explained it as זוּ חֶמְדָּא "that is, sexual desire". There is thus a strong exegetical link between האביונה and the capacity for sexual enjoyment. And, if this is what Koheleth meant by the word, the verb תפר should accordingly be interpreted

[30] Jastrow II, 1040.
[31] Lane Bk I ii, 516 (col. 1). Moore, however, (loc.cit. 64), points to the incongruity of "almond", "caper" and "locust", and therefore suggests that חגב should be connected with the Arabic كَبَّك indicating "a kind of melon" (dialect of Yemen). See also his comments on 62.
[32] Cf. Delitzsch op. cit. 415 and Gordis op. cit. 335.
[33] E.g. Moore loc.cit. 64 and Hertzberg op.cit. 207.
[34] Cf. Plutarch (Symposia VI, ii, 4) where in common with the salted olive it restores the strength and the appetite. So Pliny (Historiae Naturalis XX, lix) mentions that its daily use reduces the risk of paralysis and disorders of the spleen.
[35] Some such interpretation seems to underlie Symmachus' καὶ διαλυθῇ ἡ ἐπίπονος "and want (sorrow) shall be dispersed". See Wright op.cit. 264f. and F. Field, Origenis Hexapla II, 403f.
[36] Cohen op.cit. 301.

as signifying "be broken, made impotent": "and the sexual instinct will become impotent" [37].

12₅ₑ בֵּית עוֹלָמוֹ. This is the sole instance of the expression in biblical Hebrew. But בבית עָלְמֵיהּ is the Targum on בביתו (in his tomb) in Isa 14₁₈, while we find בית עלמין (the cemetery) in the Talmud (Sanhed 19a). The expression is also common in Palmyrene inscriptions where it means "house of eternity" [38]. Thus in one such inscription from the end of the second century A.D. we read, בת עלמא קברא דנה די בנה זבדעתה "the house of eternity, that grave which Zabdeateh built" [39]. The Greek historian Diodorus Siculus (c. 60 B.C.) relates that the Egyptians too referred to their graves as αἴδους οἴκους (eternal houses) [40]. In discussing בֵּית עוֹלָמוֹ Dahood mentions a Punic inscription from the fourth-second century B.C. which contains the words הדר בת עלם "the chamber of the tomb" [41]. He thus argues that while the sepulchral terminology of the inscriptions was probably of Egyptian origin, Koheleth was directly indebted to the Phoenicians for his use of the phrase in our text [42]. עוֹלָם with the pronominal suffix וֹ is again unique in biblical Hebrew, and Dahood would likewise connect this with Ugaritic ʿlmh "his eternity" (UT 52₄₆) and ʿlmk "thy eternity" (UT 68₁₀) [43]. However, we meet עולמו in the Talmud; for example, Ab Zar 10b, where it is used of eternal life: יש קונה עולמו בשעה אחת ויש קונה עולמו בכמה שנים (one man may acquire eternity in a single hour, another may acquire it after many years).

12₆ יֵרָחֵק: from רָחַק "to be far". This does not give a satisfactory meaning here, unless it was a technical term in connection with חֶבֶל הכסף (the silver chord), the significance of which now eludes us. Most Versions (G S Σ V) read יִנָּתֵק "is torn" (cf. 4₁₂) which seems suitable. The *Qere* and some MSS strangely read יֵרָתֵק "joined".

12₆ וְתָרֻץ appears to be the imperfect Qal of רָצַץ "to break", after the analogy of ע״ו verbs; compare יָרֹן from רָנַן "to sing" (Prov 29₆). But many scholars [44] would point תֵּרֹץ in accordance with the Niphal form נָרֹץ of the same verb in the following line. However, G Sʰ S T accept

---

[37] Hertzberg (op.cit. 213) doubts if האביונה is to be explained in this way. But Kroeber (op.cit. 150) remarks that as תענוגת בני האדם is mentioned in 2⁸ at the end of a catalogue of joys, so it may be referred to here at the end of a catalogue of losses.

[38] See Jouon, Syria 19 (1938), 99–100.

[39] CIS ii (vol.3), No. 4192 (298).

[40] Book 1, Ch. 51₂.   [41] Text, CIS i (vol. 3) No. 124 (157).

[42] Bibl 33 (1952), 216.   [43] Bibl 39 (1958), 316.

[44] E.g. BH³; McNeile op.cit. 90f.; Hertzberg op.cit. 207; Kroeber op.cit. 110; Galling op.cit. 120.

תָרָק and consistently read יָרָק in 6b (the golden bowl *breaks* ... and the wheel *breaks*). In reading *recurrat* the Vulgate identifies תָרָק with the root רוּץ "to run", but *confringatur* in the next line takes נָרֹץ as from רצץ.

12₆ גֻלַּת הַזָּהָב. The noun גלה "bowl" is found elsewhere in the Old Testament (e.g. Jos 15₁₉ I Reg 7₄₁ f. pl.). In Zach 4₂-₃ it surmounts a golden candle-stick and holds within it seven lamps. There is again mention of "a golden bowl", *gl ḫrṣ*, in Ugaritic[45], and Dahood thinks that our phrase in Koheleth is but a rendition of this[46].

12₆b כַּד "jar"; compare Arabic كد, a vessel of hard material in which ingredients are compounded[47]. Dahood notes the attestation of the word in Ugaritic (*kd*, UT No. 1195, p. 417), and draws attention to the Greek transcriptions of the Phoenician כד (κάδος, κάδδος)[48]. But we find the word too in Egyptian Aramaic[49], while it also appears frequently in early Old Testaments books (e.g. Gen 24₁₄. ₁₇. ₄₃ Judg 7₁₆ I Reg 17₁₂).

12₆b הַגַּלְגָּל. In other Old Testament passages it has the meaning "wheel" (e.g. Isa 5₂₈ Jer 47₃ Ez 10₂), and it is generally so interpreted here by commentators. Dahood argues that "wheel" does not provide an adequate parallel to "jar", and suggests that we should rather render "water-pitcher"[50]. In support of this he mentions a vase on which גלגל is inscribed in Punic characters, and also states that the Akkadian "gul-gullu" means "a water-pitcher". "Gulgullu", however, primarily means "skull", although it has also the meaning of "cooking-pot"[51].

12₇ וְיָשֹׁב. The form is that of the jussive of שׁוּב. We would expect the imperfect, as תָשׁוּב in the second stich, and therefore some scholars point וְיָשֻׁב[52]. But according to GK (§ 109K, p. 323) the jussive may be used for the imperfect, especially when it stands at the beginning of a sentence where it may serve a rhythmical purpose. So Franz Delitzsch thought that it is used as a subjunctive here, and pointed to Job 13₂₇ as an example of the interchange of the full and abbreviated forms[53].

---

[45] Keret 72 (UT 250a) and 165 (UT 251b).

[46] Bibl 33 (1952), 216.

[47] Freytag iv, 16a.

[48] Bibl 33 (1952), 216. Cf. also Autran. Phéniciens (Essai de contribution à l'histoire antique de la Méditerranée), 1920, 5. 46, who mentions κάδος as one of the Greek words derived from Phoenician.

[49] DISO, 115, Ls. 21f.

[50] Bibl 33 (1952), 216f.

[51] CAD 5, 128 sec. 2.

[52] E.g. BH3; Galling op.cit. 120; Kroeber op.cit. 110; so 15 MSS (Kennicott, Vetus Testamentum Hebraicum; Cum Variis Lectionibus II, 561).

[53] Op.cit. 425.

12₉ᵦ וְאָזֵן וְחִקֵּר תִּקֵּן מְשָׁלִים הַרְבֵּה. אזן is here usually understood as meaning "weigh, ponder" and is connected with the Arabic وزن "to weigh" and מאזנים "scales" (e. g. Isa 40₁₅ Dan 5₂₇)⁵⁴. If this is to be accepted, it is the only instance in biblical Hebrew in which אזן has such a meaning. All the Versions interpret it otherwise. The Septuagint took it as οὖς "ear" (καὶ οὖς ἐξιχνιάσεται κόσμιον παραβολῶν, and the ear will trace out the ordering of the parables). Both the Syro-Hexaplar and Coptic Versions follow the Septuagint. Yet the noun "ear" is strange here; and Aquila (ἠνωτίσατο), Peshitta (ܨ) and Targum (וַאֲצִית) read "heard", while the Vulgate freely renders *et enarravit quae fecerat* (and he declared what he had done). It will moreover be observed that in reading κόσμιον (ordering) the Septuagint presupposes the noun תֹּקֶן or תְּקוּן (compare Mishnaic תִּקּוּן, order, arrangement, Git 4₆) rather than the verb תִּקֵּן⁵⁵. It is therefore probable that we should render: "and he listened and considered the arrangement of many proverbs".

12₁₀ וְכָתוּב יֹשֶׁר. כָּתוּב is here vocalised as a passive participle, and was apparently so understood by the Septuagint which represents the phrase by καὶ γεγραμμένον εὐθύτητος (and that which is written is of uprightness). We notice that it parallels בִקֵּשׁ at the beginning of the line, and 5 Hebrew MSS (de R.) and some Versions (A Σ S V) took it as the perfect וְכָתַב. It is, however, possible to regard it as an infinitive absolute consecutive and point as וְכָתוֹב⁵⁶. Dahood would explain the Massoretic vocalisation on the basis of Phoenician orthography. He points out that the Proto-Semitic *ā* which developed as *ô* in Hebrew became *û* in Phoenician, and thus thinks that כָּתוּב may be accepted as an infinitive absolute⁵⁷.

12₁₁ כַּדָּרְבֹנוֹת וּכְמַשְׂמְרוֹת. The first term דרבנות is apparently the plural of a singular דָּרְבֹנָה. We meet the word דָּרְבָן in I Sam 13₂₁ where it is a sharp instrument like an axe, and was probably used as a goad for driving cattle; compare Arabic ذرب, to sharpen an iron instrument⁵⁸. So in Judg 3₃₁ we find the phrase בְּמַלְמַד הַבָּקָר denoting an instrument to drive or direct (cf. למד "to teach") cattle.

---

⁵⁴ Cf. Barton op. cit. 199; BDB 24b; Gordis op. cit. 342; Hertzberg op. cit. 218; Kroeber op. cit. 113.

⁵⁵ Cf. Wright op. cit. 441; Driver loc. cit. 234.

⁵⁶ E. g. BH³ and Gordis op. cit. 343.

⁵⁷ Bibl 47 (1966), 281.

⁵⁸ Lane I iii, 959 col. 1,2. We may compare too the Ugaritic *drb* which, although uncertain in itself (Gordon UT No. 699, 387a), is in a context (UT No. 2050: 5ff.) which mentions such terms as "two knives", "two javelins". See, Dahood, Bibl 47 (1966), 282.

The root of the second term, מַשְׂמְרוֹת, is dubious, but it is probably to be connected with סָמַר "to bristle" (cf. Job 4₁₅ Ps 119₁₂₀). So in the Mishna we find בְּסַנְדָל הַמְסוּמָר, "with a nail-studded shoe". (Shab 6₂). Again מַסְמְרוֹת appears in Jer 10₄ and מִסְמְרוֹת in IIChr 3₉, both terms signifying "nails" or "fasteners". And as מַשְׂמְרוֹת here in Koheleth is a synonym for דָּרְבֹנוֹת "goads" it is likely that it denotes objects such as "nails".

12₁₁ בַּעֲלֵי אֲסֻפּוֹת. This expression occurs nowhere else in the Old Testament, and its meaning is uncertain. The Versions offer little help, their authors clearly experiencing difficulty with the passage as a whole. The Septuagint οἱ παρὰ τῶν συνθεμάτων (which by those in agreement) is vague, and the Vulgate renders as *magistrorum consilium* (counsel of masters). The Peshitta represents בעלי אספות as ܡܪ̈ܝ ܐ̈ܣܟܦܬܐ (masters of the threshold), while the Targum interprets as רבני־סנהדרין (masters of the Sanhedrin). The phrase בַּעֲלֵי אֲסֻפּוֹת does appear in the Talmud (Sanhed 12a) where it means "masters of assemblies"; but this meaning is hardly applicable here in Koheleth, since בעלי אספות seems to be parallel to דִּבְרֵי־חֲכָמִים (words of the wise) at the beginning of the line. In a Phoenician inscription from Piraeus dated in the year 96 B.C. we find the expression בנאספת, normally translated "in assembly"[59]. Dahood would divide these letters as בן אספת "the members of the assembly", and so thinks that this is equivalent in meaning to בעלי אספות in our text[60]. But this, again, would not offer a suitable parallel to דברי־חכמים. Strobel has made the interesting suggestion that instead of בַּעֲלֵי we should read בְּעֹל (in the yoke of). He thus sees "yoke" as a figure of Wisdom and cites Ben Sira 6₂₉ and 51₂₆ where Wisdom is so described. He accordingly translates, "The words of the wise are as goads and nails implanted in the yoke of the Wisdom Literature"[61]. And while some obscurity remains in the interpretation of the line as a whole, the notion of "the yoke or wisdom of collected sayings" has the merit of offering a parallel to "the words of the wise"[62]. The singular of אֲסֻפּוֹת is not found in biblical

---

[59] Cooke, A Text-Book of North Semitic Inscriptions, 1903, 94. See too DISO 173, ls. 14f.

[60] Bibl 33 (1952), 217f.

[61] Op. cit. 170.

[62] So in Lam 3₂₇ we read that "it is good for a man to bear the yoke in his youth", since it leads to an understanding of the nature and compassion of God (v. ₃₁f.). We may compare too the saying of Jesus (Matt 11₂₉), "Take my yoke upon you and learn from me" in which "yoke" seems to have the force of "Wisdom" or "ideology", as the sequel "and you shall find rest for your souls" suggests.

Hebrew, but on the analogy of אֲגֻדַּת־ (knot, Ex 12₂₂, pl. אֲגֻדּוֹת Isa 58₆) it would be אֲסֻפָּה "collection": compare Talmudic אֲסִיפָה (Hag 18a).

12₁₂ᵇ וְלַהַג הַרְבֵּה. להג occurs here only. It is usually rendered "study" (noun) and connected with the Arabic لَهِج "to be devoted, attached"[63]. Noting that the Versions represent the term by "study" or "meditation" (e.g. LXX μελέτη, Vul *meditatio*), Dahood observes that such a rendering is semantically different from لَهِج. He accordingly suggests that the Versions understood the consonants להג as the preposition ל prefixed to a noun from the root הגה. This term would have the force of "a dative of reference", and the noun in its original Phoenician form would be הג instead of the Hebrew הגה. He further notes that in a Ugaritic text *hg* is found in parallelism with *spr* (Krt, 90–91, UT p. 250b), just as הג occurs with סְפָרִים here in Koheleth[64].

Insofar as Dahood's argument implies that להג is to be understood as the preposition ל prefixed to a noun הגה, it is, at least, suggestive. Apart from Koheleth 12₁₂ᵇ, להג is found neither in the Hebrew bible nor in Rabbinical literature[65]. The verb הגה, on the other hand, often occurs in the Old Testament (e.g. Jos 1₈ Ps 1₂ 143₅) with the meaning "study, reflect". The noun הֶגֶה appears too in the primary sense of "moaning, uttering" (Job 37₂ Ps 90₉; cf. Isa 8₁₉), while in Ps 49₄ הָגוּת has the meaning "meditation". Again in Rabbinical Hebrew הֶגֶה has the force of "study"; thus אֵין הֶגֶה אֶלָּא תּוֹרָה "*Hegeh* is nothing except study of the Torah" (Midrash Rabbah on Gen 49₂). We need not, however, assume an original Phoenician orthography to explain the Massoretic text. It could easily arise from haplography; that is, an original להגה הרבה could become the present להג הרבה.

12₁₃ᵃ סוֹף דָּבָר הַכֹּל נִשְׁמָע, The Greek and Coptic Versions represent נשמע by the imperative singular, and so does the Syriac, which however adds ܟܡܣܬ "in its entirety". The Vulgate takes הכל as a subjective collective plural *omnes*, and renders נשמע by *audiamus*, "let us all hear". So Hertzberg[66] and other commentators[67], although taking הכל objectively, regard נִשְׁמָע as a Qal cohortative plural, with pausal pointing, and render "last uns hören" (let us hear). But הַכֹּל נִשְׁמָע is similar in construction to הַכֹּל נִשְׁכָּח in 2₁₆ where נִשְׁכָּח appears to be the third person singular

[63] Freytag iv, 129.　　　　　　　　[64] id. 219.

[65] This verse from Koheleth is quoted in the Talmud (Erub 21b), but it is explained in terms of הֶגֶה. Cf. also Midrash Rabbah on Ecclesiastes 12₁₂b where להג is similarly explained (להגות to talk about).

[66] Op.cit. 217.

[67] Galling op.cit. 123; Kroeber op.cit. 113 and 121; Strobel op.cit. 170.

Niphal, with pausal pointing. Compare נִשְׁכַּח זכרם (3rd per. sing. Niph.) in 9₅ where the context and meaning are similar. Accordingly נִשְׁמָע here seems to be the pausal form of the third person singular Niphal: "all has been heard". This interpretation of the phrase would moreover appear to be a more suitable comment than "Let us hear all" on סוף דבר. Zimmermann contends that the phrase as a whole should be understood in terms of an Aramaic original which read, "The end of the matter-everything will be understood, כלא משתמע"[68]. But this, again, is hardly an improvement on the Hebrew "The end of the matter, all has been heard".

12₁₃c כִּי־זֶה כָּל־הָאָדָם. This is an obscure phrase, and the Versions provide little illumination[69]. Zimmermann asserts that זה is a mistranslation of an Aramaic דין which the translator took as דֵּין "this" instead of דָּיֵן or דִּין "judge"[70]. But while this yields an intelligible clause, it is of doubtful relevance to the context, especially in view of the reference to "judgement" in the next line. Gordis considers זה כל־האדם "as a pregnant idiom, characteristically Hebrew", and renders "this is the whole duty of man". In support of this, he cites such passages as Ps 110₃ עמך נדבת "thy people are freely offering themselves" and Ps 120₇ אני שלום "I am seeking peace"[71]. But these passages hardly bear directly on the force of זה כל־האדם. That the Talmudic teachers themselves thought the expression difficult may be seen from Bera 6b where it is asked, "What does זה כל האדם mean?" Rabbi Eleazar there answered that the whole world would not have been created "except for this", אֶלָּא בִשְׁבִיל זֶה. To him the phrase meant that due recognition of God was the purpose of life. It is thus possible that instead of כָּל־ we should read the Mishnaic כְּלָל "general rule, principle"[72]; this would be an example of haplography easily incurred by a scribe accustomed to writing כל־האדם elsewhere in Koheleth (3₁₃ 5₁₈ 7₂). The reading "for this is the rule of man" would be a meaningful comment on the previous line. However, the possibility remains that the Massoretic זה כל־האדם represents an idiom whose force now escapes us.

---

[68] Loc. cit. 40.

[69] Some scholars (e.g. BH³; Galling op. cit. 123; Kroeber op. cit. 112) would remove דבר from the beginning of the verse and insert it immediately after כי זה. But, דבר is already a meaningful word in its present position, while the authenticity of its connection with סוף seems to be attested by סופא די־מלתא, Dan 7₂₈.

[70] Loc. cit. 26.

[71] Op. cit. 345.

[72] E.g. זה הכלל "this is the general rule" (Hul 3₁). There are a number of Mishnaisms in Koheleth (cf. below 137 f.), and it 'would not be surprising to find כלל here.

XIII. AN ASSESSMENT OF ZIMMERMANN'S VIEW

Our examination of the language of Koheleth suggests that there is little to indicate that the book is a translation from an Aramaic original. Equally improbable is the view that the work was originally composed in Phoenician orthography and shows the influence of Phoenician syntax and morphology. As we shall see from the following considerations, both of these positions seem to be based on questionable presuppositions and doubtful methodology. We will first consider the approach of Frank Zimmermann.

Fundamental to Zimmermann's explanation of the language of Koheleth is the assumption that the person who translated it into Hebrew frequently failed to understand the Aramaic before him. Indeed Zimmermann lists over thirty instances in which this is supposed to have occurred. But it is strange that a translator should undertake such a task if his knowledge of the original was so imperfect. Nor are the reasons for translating the book obvious, since Koheleth is essentially secular rather than religious in nature. If it were a predominantly religious document we could understand that a reader, recognising its value, would undertake to translate it even at the risk of inadequately performing his task. But no such claim could be made for Koheleth, and a reader would only be tempted to embark on a project of translation if he understood and appreciated the subtleties and sophistications with which the book abounds. There would be little point in translating into Hebrew a document in which the translator did not recognise that the original meant "No man succeeds on earth in doing good without doing evil" instead of "There is no man righteous on earth, who does good and does not sin"[1]; or again, that he should have rendered "sail" and not "bread", and "health" instead of "Creator"[2]. On the translation theory the real significance of such passages is missed, and the purpose of translating the book defeated.

Zimmermann indeed argues that this misunderstanding of an original occurs quite frequently in the ancient Versions of the Bible, such as the Septuagint, Peshitta and Targum[3]. But while lapses in translation are

---

[1] See under 7 20.
[2] See under 11 1 and 12 1.   [3] JQR 40 (1949/50), 80.

recognised in the Versions, they are confined mostly to a confusion of similar letters in the original and a misinterpretation of a metaphor or idiom. The mistakes in translation assumed by Zimmermann's theory of Koheleth are of a different nature; for there we have mistakes ranging from the misunderstanding of a single particle to a misconception of the grammatical structure and language of whole passages.

Torrey observed that the unorthodox religious philosophy of Koheleth was more likely to be composed in Aramaic for popular consumption than in Hebrew, but that later, when it was desired to preserve the work as a specimen of Solomonic wisdom, it was decided to translate it into Hebrew[4]. But if this were a popular Aramaic work we should expect that the translator would have been familiar with all aspects of its thought and meaning. It is thus surprising that, according to the translation theory, he should have so frequently misunderstood the original. Moreover, if the present text is to be regarded as a translation from Aramaic, it is strange that the Aramaisms are not translated.

It is, again, questionable if the Aramaic original which Zimmermann claims to discover offers a more acceptable text than the Hebrew. Thus, as we noted under 3₁₄, he maintains that יַעֲשֶׂה in the line כל אשר יַעֲשֶׂה האלהים הוא יהיה לעולם should be the perfect עָשָׂה. The misunderstanding arose, he says, from the ambiguity of the Aramaic participle עָבֵד. It is, however, as logical to say "Whatever God does, it will be for ever" as "Whatever God did, it will be for ever". Indeed the imperfect would seem preferable in a sentence which expresses the principle of the continuous activity of God; compare, Isa 43₁₃ אפעל ומי ישיבנה (I will work and who will hinder it). Again, it will be recalled that in 5₅ he suggests that instead of the present Hebrew text לַחֲטִיא אֶת־בְּשָׂרְךָ we should read לְחַיֵּב אֶת בשרך as a more correct rendering of an Aramaic לְחַיָּבָא לבשרך (to condemn thy body) However, not only have we biblical precedence for the causative use of חָטָא (e.g. Deut 24₄ Isa 29₂₁), but לחטיא is as intelligible as לחיב here. The contention that the phrase ואין משלחת במלחמה in 8₈ conceals an Aramaic "one cannot lay aside armour in battle" is likewise scarcely obvious on logical grounds; for, as we previously remarked, it is no more suitable to the context than the Hebrew "and there is no discharge in battle". Zimmermann regards וְאַחֲרָיו אל הַמֵּתִים in 9₃ as a misrepresentation of an original וַאֲחוֹרוֹהִי לְמֵיתַיָא (and his back is turned to the events to come). But, however we interpret the Hebrew ואחריו, המתים (the dead) is more acceptable than למיתא (to

---

the events to come), since it provides a parallel, by way of contrast, to
בחייהם (in their lives) in the previous clause. Finally, there is no reason
to regard Zimmermann's Aramaic וכלא משתמע (and everything will be
understood) in 12₃ as preferable to the Hebrew הכל נשׁמָע (everything
has been heard).

Many passages which Zimmermann attempts to solve on the translation theory seem also to find a more natural explanation on grounds
of editorial insertions, glosses and scribal errors. Thus he regarded the
phrase ואל מקומו שׁואף זורח הוא שׁם (and unto its place it pants, it shines
there) in 1₅ as a translator's misinterpretation of an Aramaic ודנח שמשא
ועל שׁמשׁא ולאתריה תאב דנח הוא תמן (The sun shines and the sun sets; and
he returns to his place where he rests). But this is hardly suitable to the
context. Our consideration of the passage led us, on the other hand, to
regard it as an intrusion in the text. Its removal would enable us to see
in the context as a whole a meaningful reference to the cardinal points.
He would likewise explain למטה לארץ (downwards to the earth) in 3₂₁
as deriving from an Aramaic לְאָרַע. The translator, he thinks, did not
know how to take the term and so expressed it by a doublet[5]. Yet לארץ
in the Hebrew text may be due to a glossator who, while not attempting
to identify the place indicated by the previous למעלה (upwards), knew
that למטה could only denote "to the earth". Similarly, it will be remembered that Zimmermann thinks that the awkward ויתרון דעת החכמה in
7₁₂ is a misreading of an Aramaic ויותרן מנדע דחוכמתא (but an advantage
is knowledge, for wisdom . . .). We, however, are of the opinion that
the phrase ויתרון דעת is misplaced and should replace ויתר in the previous
verse. The parallelism and logic of both verses would then be considerably improved[6].

Zimmermann further draws attention to the irregular use of the
article in Koheleth, and considers it another proof that the work is a
translation from an Aramaic original[7]. He argues that such usage is due
to a translator failing to observe the distinction between the Absolute
(e.g. גבר man) and Emphatic (e.g. גברא the man) States in Aramaic. It
is true indeed that we have many examples of the irregular use of the
article in Koheleth. Thus in the phrase כל הַדְּברים יגעים (all things are
wearisome, 1₈) we would expect that דברים should not have the article.
So in גם כל הָאָדם אשר נתן־לו האלהים (even every man to whom God has
given, 5₁₈) it is strange that אדם has the article. Again in the phrase

---

[5] JQR 36 (1945/46), 42f. So Ginsberg, Studies in Koheleth, 20.
[6] See under 7₁₂.   [7] JQR 36 (1945/46), 20ff.

וסגלת מלכים וְהַמְּדִינוֹת (and treasures of kings and [governors?, or] provinces, 2₈) we observe that מדינות has the article while מלכים has not. Similarly in לשׂחוק עשׂים לחם ויין ישׂמח חיים וְהַכֶּסֶף יענה את־הכל (for laughter they make bread, and wine cheers the living, but (the) money pays for all, 10₁₉) we notice that כסף is alone determinate. Again in 10₂₀ קול has the article, while the parallel דבר has not: כי עוֹף השׁמים יולִיך את־הַקּוֹל ובעל הכנפים ⁸יַגִּיד דָּבָר (for a bird of the air carries the voice and a feathered creature declares a word).

But, while with Zimmermann we could cite other such instances of the irregular use of the article in Koheleth, this is not a feature peculiar to the book. There is no regularity in the use of the article in Phoenician, and indeed Dahood cites this as another indication of Phoenician influence on Koheleth⁹. More significant, however, is the fact that the irregularity is found in various parts of the Old Testament. Thus in I Chr 8₂₈ we find אלה ראשׁי־אבות (these are the heads of the fathers), but in I Chr 9₃₄ אלה ראשׁי־הָאבות. In I Chr 10₁ we have ופלשׁתים נלחמו בישׂראל (and the Philistines fought against Israel), but we find the article with פלשׁתים in a similar passage in 11₁₃, וְהַפלשׁתים נאספו שׁם. So in I Chr 12₁₄ we have ראשׁי־הַצבא (captains of the army), but in 12₃₃ צבא appears without the article: מזבלין יוצאי־צבא (From Zebulun those of the host who went out). Similarly in II Reg 15₂₅ we find בית־מלך, but in II Reg 16₈ we have בית־הַמלך. Again in Isa 48₁₃ we find ימינ₁ טפחה שׁמים (my right hand spreads out the heavens), but in 45₁₈ בורא הַשׁמים (creator of the heavens). So in Jos 1₃ we read כל־מקום אשׁר תדרך כַּף, but כל־הַמקום אשׁר תדרך כף רגלכם בו, רגלכם בו in Deut 11₂₄.

We likewise find variations in the use of the article by different writers. Thus in II Sam 7₂ we have בבית ארזים (in the house of cedars), but in the corresponding phrase in I Chr 17₁ בבית־הָארזים. In II Sam 5₂₄ we read את־קוֹל צעדה (the sound of the marchers), but in the corresponding clause in I Chr 14₁₅ את־קוֹל הַצעדה. In the foregoing examples we noticed that while the later text of the Chronicler has the article, it is omitted in the earlier material of Samuel. Conversely, in the following examples we find the article in the text of Kings, but its absence in the later version of the Chronicler. For example, in I Reg 9₂₂ we have כי הם אנשׁי־הַמלחמה while in II Chr 8₉ כי המה אנשׁי־מלחמה; in I Reg 10₁₅ we find וכל־מלכי הָערב, but in II Chr 9₁₄ וכל־מלכי־ערב.

---

⁸ So Massoretic pointing. BH³ reads יַגֵּיד, but cf. Sperber, A Historical Grammar of Biblical Hebrew, 437, for inconsistency in the use of the vowels *Hireq* and *Sere* in the Imperfect; cf. also 434f.

⁹ Bibl 33 (1962), 200f.

Such examples show, then, that inconsistency in the use of the article is not confined to the book of Ecclesiastes, and therefore, that the inconsistencies found there are not necessarily a sign of translation from an Aramaic original. Zimmermann, as we have noted, attributes this indiscriminate use of the article to a translator's confusion of the determinate and indeterminate States of Aramaic. While this is highly improbable, it is nevertheless possible that Koheleth's use of the article is to some extent influenced by Aramaic usage. For, as Zimmermann obseıves[10], we find inconsistency of usage in this respect in the book of Daniel. Thus in 5ı and ⁊ we find the Emphatic forms חמרא (חמרא שתה, he drank wine) and המנוכא[11] (המנוכא די־דהבא, a chain of gold) when we should expect the Absolute. So in 2₄₄ we have מלכו די לעלמין לא תתחבל והיא תקום לעלמיא . . . (a kingdom which shall never be destroyed . . . and it will stand for ever) in which לעלמין is Absolute, although it has the same force as לעלמיא which is Emphatic.

That however there are Aramaic elements in the book of Koheleth is undeniable. Apart from Aramaic words, we can detect certain Aramaic idioms underlying the Hebrew text, especially in proverbial material. But this is not surprising, for, as we shall show on a later page (147 f.), when Koheleth was composing his work Aramaic was a significant and formative factor in the linguistic environment. The Aramaisms of the book as a whole may therefore be more naturally regarded as indications of Aramaic influence than as evidence of translation from an Aramaic original.

---

[10] JQR 36 (1945/46), 23 n. 2.
[11] For variants on the spelling of the initial part of the word, see BH3.

XIV. AN ASSESSMENT OF DAHOOD'S VIEW

Basic to Mitchell J. Dahood's approach to the language of Koheleth is the supposition that the original composition was written in Phoenician orthography. Believing that the *matres lectionis* first appeared in Hebrew literature in about the sixth century B.C., he thinks that they gradually became more frequent until the period of the Dead Sea Scrolls when vowel letters were used to represent even short vowels. A work therefore which, like Koheleth, was composed in the normal Hebrew orthography of the fourth century B.C. would have been sufficiently supplied with *matres lectionis* to avoid confusing, for instance, the singular and plural forms of the verb, or the singular and plural forms of nouns in the construct[1]. Thus, as we noted under 1 10, Dahood thinks that the final הָיָה of the phrase היה אשר לעלמים היה should, with some readings (5 MSS K–de R), be the plural היו, and that accordingly the Massoretic Text is due to a scribe misunderstanding the consonantal הי of the text before him[2]. But, as we there pointed out, the notion "age" may be expressed by the singular עולם or the plural עולמים. In denoting emphasis rather than plurality לעלמים does not therefore logically demand a plural form of the verb. Dahood similarly argues that היה in the phrase כל־אשר־היה in 1 16 should, with some authorities (1 Ms De–R, GSV), read the plural היו. He attributes this "grammatical blunder" to the copyist who wrote היה as the simplest form of the consonants הי[3]. The rendering "any" is, however, as likely here as "all"; for כל־ with the force of "any" occurs more than once in biblical Hebrew. Thus, in Num 30 5 we read . . . וְקָמוּ כל־נדריה (and all her vows will stand), but in the next verse we find the verb in the singular כל־נדריה . . . לא יקום (any of her vows . . . will not stand). It is to be noted that the Septuagint and Peshitta read the plural of the verb in both passages. In Gen 5 23 we have another example of כל־, with a plural meaning, having a singular verb: וַיְהִי כל־ימי־חנוך (and all the days of Enoch were). The Septuagint and Peshitta naturally represent the verb by the plural. There are, moreover, many instances in the Old Testament in which the Massoretic Text has a singular form of the verb, but which in the idioms of

---

[1] Bibl 33 (1952), 36.   [2] Ibid.

[3] Bibl 33 (1952), 37. Cf. also his remarks on נעשה in 1 13 (36).

the various Versions are more naturally rendered in the plural[4]. For example, in a passage in Gen 35₂₆, אלה בני־יעקב אשר ילד לו (these are the sons of Jacob which were born to him), the verb יָלַד is in the singular, but it is rendered by ἐγένοντο in the Septuagint and by ܐܠܕ in the Peshitta. Again while the Hebrew verb in Ex 29₁₀, וְסָמַךְ אהרן ובניו את־ידיהם (and Aaron and his sons will place their hands) is singular, the Septuagint translates as the plural ἐπιθήσουσιν. Nor indeed is the Hebrew text always consistent in its use of the verb. For while here in v. 10 of Ex 29 it uses the singular, in v. 15 it has the plural וְסָמְכוּ אהרן ובניו את־ידיהם. Another such example is found in I Sam 14₄₅. At the beginning of the verse we read וַיֹּאמֶר הָעָם, where הָעָם is regarded as collective and singular, but at the end of the verse we find וַיִּפְדּוּ הָעָם where הָעָם is conceived as plural. Dahood again notes that the verb in Koh 2₇ וּבְנֵי־בַיִת הָיָה לִי (and sons of the house I had) is represented by some authorities (3 MSS K–de R, GS) as the plural הָיוּ, and accordingly doubts if we can defend the Massoretic הָיָה[5]. But such a usage is not peculiar to Koheleth. For example, in I Chr 24₂₈ we find וְלֹא־הָיָה לוֹ בנים, which the Septuagint renders καὶ οὐκ ἦσαν αὐτῷ υἱοί.

Nor can we assume with Dahood that in the period of the fourth and third centuries B.C., when he thinks Koheleth was composed, Hebrew orthography was amply supplied with vowel letters. J. W. Wevers argues that when the Old Testament was translated into Greek "the Hebrew text preferred the *scriptio defectiva*". In a consideration of the variants of the Books of Kings he notes, for example, that in I Reg 15₂ the Hebrew אֲבִישָׁלוֹם is represented in the Septuagint by Ἀβεσσαλώμ, which suggests that the form before the translator was אַבְשָׁלוֹם, as in II Chr 11 20[6]. So in II Reg 3₄ the Septuagint has Μωσὰ for the Hebrew מֵישַׁע (Mesha), indicating that the translator's text read מֵשַׁע. Again in II Reg 23₁₁ the Massoretic text has מַרְכְּבוֹת, while the Septuagint reads τὸ ἅρμα, presupposing an underlying *defective* Hebrew form מרכבת (chariots)[7].

It is, moreover, uncertain when the system of *matres lectionis* was introduced into Hebrew writing[8], nor have we any evidence that it was

---

[4] Cf. Rabin, Textus 2 (1962), 74f.   [5] Loc. cit. 37.

[6] An interesting parallel to אבשלום and אבישלום is provided by two recently discovered texts: one, dating from the 8–7th centuries B.C., contains the name אבגד; the other, an Aramaic inscription from about the 1st. century A.D., has the *plene* form אבגיד. See Avigad, IEJ 18 (1968), 52–53.

[7] Wevers, ZAW 61 (1945–48), especially 70.

[8] According to Cross and Freedman it was borrowed by the Israelites from the Arameans in the 9th century B.C., Early Hebrew Orthography: A Study of the Epigraphic Evidence, 1952, 57.

consistently used. Certainly the Massoretic text shows both the *defective* and the *plene* writing existing side by side throughout the Old Testament. For example, in Gen 21₁₁ we find אוֹדֹת (concerning), but אֹדוֹת in v. 25. So we have דוֹרוֹתֵינוּ (our generations) in Jos 22₂₇, but דֹרֹתֵינוּ in v. 28. In Judg 14₁₂ we find חֲלִפֹת (festal garments), but חֲלִיפוֹת in v. 13. The forms הוֹלִיד and הֹלִיד appear in I Chr 5₃₀, while similarly in Joel 1 v. 10 and 12 we find הוֹבִישׁ and הֹבִישׁ. So in Koh 11₉ we have בְּחוּרוֹתֶיךָ, but בְּחוּרֹתֶיךָ in 12₁. Again we find the plural form of the verb with attached suffixes written both *defective* and *plene*. Thus in Gen 24₅₄ we have שַׁלְּחֻנִי (they sent me), but שַׁלְּחוּנִי in v. 56. Likewise in Jer 37₈ we meet the form שְׂרָפָהּ (they burnt it), but שְׂרָפוּהָ in 38₁₈. Similarly we find examples of *defective* and *plene* writing in the case of plural nouns with suffixes. Hence, in Num 15₂₀ we have עֲרִסֹתֵכֶם (your grains of corn), but עֲרִסֹתֵיכֶם in the following verse. So in Deut 23₁₅ we find מַחֲנֶךָ (your camp) and מַחֲנֶיךָ [9].

There is, further, no standardisation of orthography in the extra-biblical Hebrew literature of the second and first centuries B.C. In a bill of sale dating from the second century we observe a scribe writing a woman's name in the *defective* שלמ, but in a few lines later she herself writes it in the *plene* שלום [10]. In the oldest surviving manuscript of Ben Sira, the Masada Scroll, dating from about 75 B.C.[11], we similarly notice a number of orthographical inconsistencies. Thus in 42₂₁ we have the *defective* גברת (strength, fem. pl.), but we have the *plene* עתות (seasons) in 43₆. In 43₉ and 43₁₈ we find תור (beauty) which seems to be a phonetic spelling for תאר (B. Marg. תואר), the form appearing in 42₁₂ and 43₁. Likewise we have the phonetic מזנים (scales, root אזן) in 42₄, but we find the full etymological מאזנים earlier in Isa 40₁₂. ₁₅, and later in the B Marginal text of Ben Sira. So we find the *defective* עלם in 41₉ᵦ, but the *plene* עולם in 42₁₈ and 44₁₃.

Again, in the Dead Sea Scrolls, in which we have an extravagant use of the *plene* script, there is little orthographic uniformity. Thus in a few fragments of Koheleth discovered at Qumran we have כיא (MT כי) in the text of 5₁₄, כי in 6₄, and כ (כמה for MT כי מה) in 6₈. So although א is superfluously inserted in כיא, it is, as a radical consonant, curiously

---

[9] It will be observed from the Old Testament examples quoted above that even the Massoretes did not attempt to impose orthographic uniformity on the text. It was rather their concern to preserve the Textus Receptus. Cf. Gordis, JBL 74 (1955), 106.

[10] See Milik, RB 61 (1954), 182f., especially 183 for text.

[11] Yadin, The Ben Sira Scroll from Masada, 1965, l. 4–5.

absent from a word in 7₈ where we find מרשיתו for the Massoretic
מֵרֵאשִׁיתוֹ (from its beginning)[12].

We cannot therefore assume that *plene* writing was the norm in any
period of Hebrew literature. Consequently we may question the validity
of Dahood's supposition that errors in Koheleth which he ascribes to a
copyist misunderstanding the *defective* spelling of his text is an indication
that that text was written in Phoenician orthography. If such errors were
made, they could equally arise from instances of *defective* spellings in the
Hebrew orthography which Koheleth himself, irrespective of his date,
employed.

Dahood, again, has a tendency to explain words and phrases in
Koheleth in terms of Phoenician and Ugaritic syntax, morphology and
lexicography. But, considering adequate parallels may be cited from the
Old Testament, this is doubtful methodology. Thus he notes that the
construction of an independent pronoun in a relative clause introduced
by אשר is attested three times in Phoenician[13]. But, as we noted under
4₂ᵦ, this construction is common in biblical Hebrew (e.g. Deut 1₃₉
Neh 2₁₃ Ez 43₁₉) while it is also found in Aramaic (e.g. Dan 6₂₇ 7₁₇)
and again in the Mishna (e.g. Mik 10₄). It is likewise doubtful procedure
to refer to one example of a nominal clause in Phoenician, כי מלך צדק
הא (for he is a just king), and imply that instances of the structure occurring in Koheleth (e.g. 3₁₃ 4₈ 6₂) are modelled on it[14]. This is all the
more surprising when we remember that this particular usage occurs not
only in biblical Hebrew, but also in Aramaic and the Mishna. Thus in
Deut 1₁₇ we read כי המשפט לאלהים הוא (for the judgement is God's)
and in Num 3₂₇ אלה הם משפחת הקהתי (these are the family of the Kohathi-
tes). So in Dan 6₂₇ די־הוא אלהא חיא (who is the living God) and in Ezr 5₁₁
אנחנא המו עבדוהי (we are his servants) we have a similar construction.
Likewise in the Mishna we read אלו הן הממונים (these are the overseers,
Shek 5₁) and אני הוא הטמא (I am the unclean, Naz 8₁). So commenting
on אשר להיות in 3₁₅, which is an example of the periphrastic future,
Dahood cites three Punic examples[15]. But there is little need to assume
Punic influence here, since the usage is known in various periods of
Hebrew literature. For example: Gen 15₁₂, וַיְהִי הַשֶּׁמֶשׁ לָבוֹא (and as the
sun was about to set); II Chr 11₂₂, וַיַּעֲמֵד לָרֹאשׁ רְחַבְעָם (and Rehoboam
appointed to be chief); Dan 10₁₂ נתת את־לבך להבין (thou hast set thine
heart to understand).

---

[12] See Muilenburg, BASOR 135 (1954), especially 22 for a facsimile of the text.
[13] Bibl 33 (1952), 197.
[14] Ibid. 197.   [15] Bibl 33 (1952), 51.

Dahood again contends that forms like מַתַּת in 3₁₃, נָחַת in 4₆, מִשְׁלַחַת in 8₈ and כָּל־עֻמַּת in 5₁₅ are evidence of the influence of Phoenician morphology[16]. The ending *at* as the absolute state is found, however, in other Old Testament passages. For example: מָחֳרָת (the morrow, Gen 19₃₄); פֹּרָת (a beautiful tree, Gen 49₂₂); שִׁפְעַת (company, II Reg 9₁₇); יִתְרָת (abundance, Jer 48₃₆; cf. יִתְרָה Isa 15₇); בָּרְקַת (emerald, Ez 28₁₃)[17]. It may also be observed that in the Mesha Inscription we find במת (high place, l. 3) and מסלת (highway, l. 26).

Nor is it clear that Koheleth is largely indebted to both Phoenician and Ugaritic lexicography. Thus in our consideration of 10₆ we noticed that רַבִּים is probably to be taken as "the aged". Dahood would accept this interpretation, but thinks that it reflects Phoenician lexicography. However, as we there noted, רבים has that meaning in other biblical passages (e.g. Job 4₃ 32₉) and also in passages in the Manual of Discipline. Similarly he thinks that סֹפְדִים (mourners) in 12₅ is to be associated with Ugaritic *mšspdt* (mourning women) in I Aqht 1, 172 and 183[18]. But we find סֹפְדִים, the same term as in Koh 12₅, in Isa 32₁₂, while the verb occurs in a number of instances (e.g. I Sam 25₁ 28₃ I Reg 14₁₃. ₁₈). לַחַשׁ (charmer) in 10₁₁ is another word which Dahood thinks Koheleth used under Phoenician influence. Noting that the feminine form occurs once in Phoenician and that *lḫšt* (whisper) appears three times in Ugaritic, he declares that לחשׁ, with the meaning of charm or incantation, is, apart from this instance in Koheleth, found only twice elsewhere in biblical Hebrew (Isa 3₃ Jer 8₁₇)[19]. But in Isa 3₂₀ we find the plural form of the noun, לחשים, denoting "charmers or amulets", while in Ps 58₆ we have the Piel Participle plural מלחשים with the meaning "charmers".

Much of the Phoenician and Ugaritic material cited by Dahood provides interesting parallels to certain passages in Koheleth rather than indicate that Koheleth himself was dependent on such material. Thus in 11₂ we have mention of an act which should be performed לשבעה וגם לשמונה, "to the extent of seven and even eight times". As Dahood observes, this is a literary device to denote repetition and multiplicity, and was common in the ancient Orient. He further notes that this particular "seven-eight" gradation occurs six times in Ugaritic and once in Phoenician, and from this he concludes that our reference in Koheleth reflects Canaanite influence[20]. But this "seven-eight" enumeration occurs in

---

[16] Bibl 33 (1952), 46f.
[17] See GK § 80, 223–224.
[18] Bibl 39 (1958), 314. Text as UT 246b.
[19] Bibl 33 (1952), 212.
[20] Bibl 33 (1952), 212f. Cf., however, Loewenstamm, IEJ 15 (1965), 121–135, who notes Akkadian infuence in the Seven Day numerical scheme in Ugaritic.

Mic 5₄, while the "three-four" sequence is common throughout Am chapters 1–2, Prov chapter 30 (vv. 15. 18. 21. 29) and Ben Sira 26₅. The "six-seven" series is similarly found in Job 5₁₉ and Prov 6₁₆. The category "two-three" again occurs in Ben Sira 23₁₆, while that of "nine-ten" appears in 25₇[21]. Dahood similarly remarks that כד (jar) in 12₆ is richly attested in Ugaritic. But in biblical Hebrew the word occurs in Genesis (e.g. 24₁₄. 18. 43), Judges (e.g. 7₁₆. 19) and Kings (e.g. I Reg 17₁₂ 18₃₄).

Referring to שֶׁמֶן רוֹקֵחַ in 10₁, Dahood further cites Ugaritic *lg šmn rbḫ* (a log of perfumer's oil)[22]. But interesting as the appearance of this phrase in Ugaritic is, it does not prove that Koheleth is indebted to it for the proverb he quotes here. We read of the oil (שמן) which is the product of the perfumer (מעשי־רקח) in Ex 30₂₅, and also of the fragrance of oil (ריח שמן) in Cant 1₃ and 4₁₀. With regard to 10₉, "He who moves stones (אבנים) is hurt by them, he who splits trees (עצים) is endangered by them", Dahood likewise points out that the frequent biblical pair *ᵓªbanim-ʿeṣîm* is found in Ugaritic (*labnm wl ʿṣm*) and also that the nuance "logs" for *ʿeṣîm* is apparently found in the phrase *iky aškn ʿṣm* (how can I deliver logs?)[23]. This, however, is no more than a case of cognate languages using common terms for such ordinary nouns as "stones" and "trees". So, even if we accept Dahood's explanation of חגה in 12₁₂, the Ugaritic *spr* (number) and *hg* (reckoning), which he cites as parallels to ספרים ... להג[24], would be no more than lexical equivalents, although the contents and nature of the two passages in question are very different. Dahood again compares שפחות ובני־בית (handmaids and domestics) in Koh 2₇ with Ugaritic *(k)rt bnm il wšph lṭpm wqdš* (Keret is the son of El, and the offspring of Lutpan and Qudsu)[25]. But while both phrases contain the roots *šph* and *bn*, they have little else in common.

Of little more significance is the parallelism between Koh 10₁₈, ידלף ... ימך (sink ... drip) and Ugaritic *ymk ... ydlp*[26]. עוֹלָמוֹ in Koh 12₅ is indeed the only instance in the Old Testament in which עוֹלם occurs with a suffix. It is accordingly of some interest that we find such a structure in more than one passage in Ugaritic. Thus in text 68₁₀ we read *tqḫ mlk ʿalmk* (you shall take your eternal kingship) and again in I Aqht 1, 154

---

[21] Cf. Roth, VT 12 (1962), 300–301, who points out that the second of two numbers in which the second is one unit higher than the first occurs some 38 times in the Old Testament and Ecclesiastes (especially 301 f.).

[22] Bibl 47 (1966), 278.

[23] Loc. cit. 279.

[24] Bibl 33 (1952), 219.

[25] Bibl 47 (1966), 267.

[26] Dahood, Bibl 33 (1952), 212. See above under 10₁₈.

ᶜnt brḥ pᶜlmh (now a fugitive and for ever)[27]. Yet it is doubtful if we are to regard the structure of עולמו as exhibiting Ugaritic influence. Its force is that of an adjective, and a noun with a suffix does serve such a function in biblical Hebrew. For example: זרוע כחו (the arm of his might, *his mighty* arm, Isa 44 12); זרוע עזו (the arm of his strength, *his strong* arm, Isa 62 8); נוה קדשך (the habitation of thy holiness, *thy holy* habitation, Ex 15 13); שם קדשך (name of thy holiness, *thy holy* name, I Chr 16 35). Moreover, as we noted earlier, עולמו is used in Rabbinic literature (e.g. Ab Zar 10 b) in the same sense as it is used in Koh 12 5.

We welcome, of course, any light which Ugaritic and Phoenician may shed on the language of Koheleth. Our interpretation of עלם in 3 11 as "ignorance" finds a basis in Job 28 21 and 42 3, but it is reassuring to discover that the Ugaritic ᶜglm has a similar meaning. רבים with the meaning "aged" occurs in 10 6 and is again attested in Job 4 3 and 32 9, but this meaning finds confirmation in the Ugaritic rb. It is likewise revealing that mrr has the force of "strength" in Ugaritic, and we may in this wise interpret מַר of Koh 7 26, and indeed Ez 3 14. The fact that ᶜm has the force of "like" in Ugaritic again supports our attribution of such a meaning to עם in Koh 2 16 4 15 and 7 11.

It is similarly instructive to find that בית עלם has the meaning of "grave or cemetery" in Phoenician (cf. Koh 12 5) and that על may have the sense of "from" (cf. Koh 1 5). So it confirms Hebrew usage to observe that the Phoenician infinitive absolute may be followed by a personal pronoun (cf. Koh 4 2), that a personal pronoun may serve in an emphatic capacity (cf. Koh 2 15) and that *y* is a form of the third person masculine singular suffix (cf. Koh 2 25).

But while such instances confirm otherwise doubtful or isolated usages in Koheleth, they do not necessarily indicate that the author of that work was directly indebted to Ugaritic or Phoenician influence[28].

---

[27] Texts as UT 180a and 246b.

[28] Nor is there any evidence that the work originated in Phoenicia. Thus Albright, who declared himself as being in substantial agreement with Dahood's approach to Ecclesiastes, thought that Koheleth lived in the Coastal Plain, probably in southern Phoenicia, and that his orally transmitted aphorisms were collected after his death and put into writing in Phoenicia, "Some Canaanite-Phoenician Sources of Hebrew Wisdom", in: Wisdom in Israel and in the Ancient Near East, VTS 3 1955, 14–15. Accordingly he would explain "*MLK* in Jerusalem" (1 12) as meaning "counsellor in Jerusalem", pointing *MLK* either as *môlēk*, like the Amarna *mâlik*, or as *mallak*, after the Phoenician **mallok*, (loc. cit. 15 n. 2). But for the Palestinian location of the work, see H. W. Hertzberg, "Palästinische Bezüge im Buche Kohelet", in: Baumgärtel-Festschrift, 1959, 63–73, and K. Galling, Der Prediger, 76.

At most they show that such terms had a common, though perhaps restricted, currency in the North-West Semitic Languages[29].

---

[29] As recognised above, Ugaritic makes a valuable contribution to the understanding of Hebrew usage and philology. Cf. Stanley Gevirtz, JNES 20 (1961), 41–46; Moshe Held, JBL 84 (1965), 272–283; F. C. Fensham, The Bible Translator, 18 (1967), 71–74. On the other hand, Herbert Donner makes a plea for a judicious use of Ugaritic in our interpretation of the Psalms, ZAW 79 (1967), 322–359; and more recently Fensham reminds us, VT 22, (1972), 296–303, that we must be concerned with concepts as well as etymology in our comparison of Hebrew and Ugaritic words and phrases.

C. Reconstruction

I. LINGUISTIC CHARACTERISTICS OF KOHELETH

(1)

Having considered the inadequacies of the theories of Zimmermann and Dahood, we now proceed to our own view of the language of Koheleth. In our analysis of the text we have seen that it consists of various elements of linguistic material. Certain phrases indicate that the author was familiar with the literature and language of the Old Testament. Thus 5₁₄ כאשר יצא מבטן אמו ערום ישוב ללכת כשבא (as he came forth from the womb of his mother, naked will he return as he came) is clearly based on Job 1₂₁ ערם יָצָתִי מבטן אמי וְערם אשוּב שמה. So 8₄ וּמי יאמר לו מה־תעשׂה (and who says to him, What doest thou?) is reminiscent of Job 9₁₂ מי־יאמר אליו מה־תעשׂה. Some unusual constructions in Koheleth find their explanation, again, in earlier biblical usage. In the phrase וְקָרוֹב לשמע of 4₁₇b, קרוֹב is the Infinitive Absolute. As we noted earlier (ad. loc.), we would expect קרוב to have the pointing of the Infinitive Construct קָרֹב which would agree with the following and parallel מִתֵּת (than the giving). However, parallels for this use of the Infinitive Absolute are found in Job 25₂, הַמְשֵׁל ("dominion", for הַמְשִׁיל Inf. con.), and Jer 10₅, הֵיטֵיב ("doing good", for הֵיטִיב Inf. con., e.g., Lev 5₄). Again in Koh 5₁₀. ₁₂ we have the noun בעל with a plural form of the pronominal suffix, although the meaning of בעל is clearly singular. But, as we observed in discussing these passages (ad. loc.), this is in agreement with classical usage. For example, Ex 21₂₉ הועד בבעליו (and it had been testified to its owner) and Ex 22₁₁ וְלקח בעליו (and its owner shall accept it). So נפש in 6₇ must be interpreted in the sense of "appetite" as in Isa 5₁₄, לכן הרחיבה שאול נפשה (therefore Sheol enlarged her *appetite*) and Prov 16₂₆ נפש עמל עמלה לו (the *appetite* of a labourer laboureth for him). שאלת על־זה in 7₁₀ is similarly to be interpreted as וָאשאלם על (and I asked them concerning) in Neh 1₂. The Infinitive Absolute continuing the force of a finite verb in 8₉ ראיתי וְנָתוֹן (I saw and gave), and 9₁₁ שבתי וְרָאֹה (I turned and saw), is, again, to be explained in the light of the usage in such passages as Gen 41₄₃,

וְנָתוֹן ... וַיִּקְרְאוּ, and Neh 9₈, וְכָרוֹת ... וּמצאת. The construction of an
imperfect followed by an infinitive to express a hypothesis or intention,
which find in 8₁₇c וְגַם אִם־יֹאמַר הֶחָכָם לָדַעַת (and even if the wise man
claims to know), finds, likewise, a precedent in II Sam 21₁₆ וַיֹּאמֶר לְהַכּוֹת
אֶת־דָּוִד (and he thought to kill David) and in II Chr 32₁ וַיֹּאמֶר לְבִקְעָם
אֵלָיו (and he thought to capture them for himself). Similarly the phrase
מלא כף נחת (the fill of the hand of rest) in 4₆ is to be compared with
I Reg 17₁₂ מלא כף־קמח (a handful of meal). Lastly we may note that the
line כי אם יפלו האחד יקים את־חברו (if they fall, the one will raise his
friend) in 4₁₀ is to be explained by such earlier idioms as Judg 6₂₉ וַיֹּאמְרוּ
אִישׁ אֶל־רֵעֵהוּ (and they said, a man unto his neighbour) and Isa 47₁₅ אִישׁ
לְעֶבְרוֹ תָּעוּ (each according to his way they err).

(2)

But as well as consisting of much that is of the nature of classical
Hebrew, Koheleth also contains a number of Aramaisms. As examples
of these we may cite תְּקַף in 6₁₀, עַל־דִּבְרַת שׁ in 7₁₄, פֶּשֶׁר in 8₁, עֲבָדֵיהֶם
in 9₁, גוּמץ (pit, Syriac ܓܘܡܨܐ) in 10₈, and שִׁפְלוּת in 10₁₈.
Now this tendency of Koheleth to use occasional Aramaic words
and expressions finds an instructive parallel in the Masada Scroll of Ben
Sira and in the Marginal readings of the B Text. Thus in 41₁₄ the Scroll
and B Marginal have the Aramaic שִׂימָה (store) for אוֹצָר of the B text.
In 41₁₈c they both read the Aramaic מְשׁוּתָּף (from a partner) for the
Hebrew חוֹבֵר of the B text, while again in 42₃ they read שׁוּתָּף for the B
text חוֹבֵר[1].
It may further be observed that there are some words and verbal
usages in Koheleth which, apart from instances in the Mishna, occur
elsewhere only in Ben Sira. Thus שִׁלְטוֹן (governor) appearing in Koh
8₄. ₈, appears again only in Ben Sira 4₇. So מִסְכֵּן (poor) in Koh 4₁₃ and
9₁₅. ₁₆ is found again in Ben Sira 4₃. חֶשְׁבּוֹן (reckoning), occurring in three
passages in Koheleth (7₂₅. ₂₇ 9₁₀), likewise occurs in Ben Sira 42₃ and
42₄b (B. Marg.)[2]. ענה is followed by ב (to be occupied with) in Koh 1₁₃

---

[1] See Yadin, The Ben Sira Scroll from Masada, 9a.
[2] As noted above under 7₂₉ חשבנות (sing. חשבון) occurs there, where however, its
meaning is doubtful. It is also found in II Chr 26₁₅ where it seems to connote
"contrivances". But while there is probably an etymological connexion between
חשבון and חשבנות the term חשבנות as used in II Chr 26₁₅ has a different connotation from חשבון in Koh 7₂₅. ₂₇ 9₁₀.

and 3₁₀, and it is likewise construed with the preposition in Ben Sira 42₈ עֻנֶּה בזנות (occupied with harlotry)³. Again נָהַג, although found in classical Hebrew (e. g. Deut 4₂₇ II Reg 4₂₄), has the meaning "behave" only in Koh 2₃ and Ben Sira 40₂₃. So לָוָה means "to accompany" in Koh 8₁₅, and it has this meaning elsewhere only in Ben Sira 41₁₂.

---

³ Marginal, cf. Yadin op.cit. 23.

II. KOHELETH AND BEN SIRA

(1)

These linguistic affinities between Koheleth and Ben Sira prompt us to inquire whether there are further points of contact between the two works. For, since we can date the composition of Ben Sira with reasonable accuracy[4], it would help us to understand the complex nature of the language of Ecclesiastes if we could relate it chronologically to Ben Sira. There is in fact much in Koheleth which bears a likeness to certain passages in Ben Sira. This is particularly true of the proverbial material which is an element of each book.

Now, in attempting to explain this similarity, commentators commonly assume that Ben Sira is dependent on Koheleth. Thus Gordis claims to be able to demonstrate the priority of Koheleth from the following passages[5]:

Koh 4₈	Ben Sira 14₄
ולמי אני עמל ומחסר את־נפשי מטובה	מונע נפשו יקבע לאחר ובטובתו יתבעבע זר
(and for whom do I work and deprive myself of enjoyment)	(He that deprives himself gathereth for another, and in his possessions a stranger exulteth)

There is nothing, however, to suggest that Ben Sira is here dependent on Koheleth. At the beginning of the verse Koheleth refers to the futility of a childless man working hard and amassing wealth. Then, adapting a current proverb to his own situation, he remarks, "For whom do I work and deprive myself of enjoyment?". The passage in Ben Sira, on the other hand, naturally continues the thought of v. 3 concerning a miserly and covetous man. So, v. 5 continues with the unattractive characteristics of the mean man. Thus while the line in Ben Sira is integral to a unified context, that in Koheleth is rather a secondary personal reflection on the common theme of the miser. Moreover, only two words, נֶפֶשׁ and טוֹבָה,

---

[4] See below p. 132.
[5] Koheleth—The Man and His World, 46 ff.

are common to each passage, and even these are in different forms. Gordis further cites Koh 6₂, כי איש נכרי יאכלנו, as a phrase underlying Ben Sira 14₄. But this has only a vague association with the thought of Ben Sira here, and it might equally be suggested that Koheleth had in mind Job 31₈, ואחר יאכל (and another eateth).

Koh 7₁₄

ביום טובה היה בטוב וביום רעה
ראה גם את־זה לעמת־זה
עשה האלהים על־דברת שלא
ימצא האדם אחריו מאומה

(In a prosperous day be in prosperity, but in an evil day be circumspect: even this as well as this God did, so that man will not find anything after him)

Ben Sira 33₁₅

ἀπέναντι τοῦ κακοῦ τὸ ἀγαθόν, καὶ ἀπέναντι τοῦ θανάτου ἡ ζωή. οὕτως ἀπέναντι εὐσεβοῦς ἁμαρτωλός. καὶ οὕτως ἔμβλεψον εἰς πάντα τὰ ἔργα τοῦ ὑψίστου, δύο δύο, ἓν κατέναντι τοῦ ἑνός

(Good is the opposite of evil, and life the opposite of death. So the sinner is the opposite of the godly. Look upon all the works of the Most High; they likewise are in pairs, one the opposite of the other)

Koheleth is concerned to make the point that since God has unalterably decreed our circumstances we must accept life as it is. We should, however, enjoy life in good times, but be circumspect in evil times. Unfortunately the Hebrew of Ben Sira is not extant here, so we cannot compare the passages linguistically. Nevertheless, it is clear from the Greek that we have an allusion to the principle of opposite pairs: good and evil, life and death, sin and saintliness. So the works of God are similarly designed, and Ben Sira is satisfied that there is no unresolved conflict in nature. But there is nothing in this to indicate that he is influenced by Koh 7₁₄. If we were to look for biblical influence we might mention Isaiah 45₇ "I form light and create darkness, I make weal and create woe, I Yahweh do all these things". However, it is more likely that, although no dualist himself, Ben Sira is here using the language of Persian Dualism and of the Greek principle of Opposites[6].

---

[6] For Persian Dualism cf. Yasna 30₃f., "In the beginning . . . the twins revealed themselves in thought, word and deed as the Better and the Bad . . . they generate life and the absence of life . . ." (trans. by Bode and Nanavutty, Songs of Zarathustra 1952, 49f.). For the Greek principle of the Opposites see, for example,

Koh 3₁₁   Ben Sira 39₁₆

את־הכל עשה יפה בעתו   מעשי אל כלם טובים
                                    וכל צורך בעתו יספיק

(Everything he made beautiful in   (The works of God are all good,
his time)   and every need he supplies in his
                                     time)

We notice that the passage in Ben Sira is in a context which is in the
nature of a doxology. On the other hand, the passage in Koheleth is, as
we noted above (ad. loc.), clearly an intrusion. But even so, it bears little
similarity to Ben Sira either in language or thought. Indeed it could be
more cogently argued that if we are to recognise any biblical reminiscence
in Ben Sira it is the phrase ככל־צרכך (according to all thy need) in
II Chr 2₁₅.

Gordis and others[7] further claim that Ben Sira is directly quoting
from Koheleth in the following passages:

Koh 3₁₅ᵦ   Ben Sira 5₃

והאלהים יבקש את־נרדף   כי ייי מבקש נרדפים
                                    (for Yahweh seeks the persecuted)

It is to be observed at the outset that the term נִרְדָּף in Koheleth is difficult
of interpretation. The Septuagint (διωκόμενον), Peshitta (ܟ݁ܝ݂ܶܡ݂ܰ) and
Targum (דְרִדֵף), take it as "persecuted", the meaning it necessarily has
in Ben Sira (Do not say, Who has power over me?, for Yahweh seeks
the persecuted). But such a meaning is not suitable to Koheleth, where
the context refers to the unchangeable and perpetual state of nature:
מה־שהיה כבר הוא וְאשר להיות כבר היה (3₁₅ₐ). It will be remembered that

---

Aristotle, The Physics I, v. In an article entitled "Kohelet's Concept of Opposites", Numen 19 (1972), 1–21, Horton Jr. agrees with Gordis's view (op, cit. 51)
that the "golden mean" referred to in Koh 7₁₄₋₁₈ is different from Aristotle's
ethical interpretation of the term. Horton then comments that "Koheleth's mean
is more implicit than explicit and represents a dislike of extremes" (3), and on a
later page (20) he observes that Koheleth's view of the processes of nature is not
that of opposites generating each other as in Plato, or transforming each other
into different substances as in Heraclitus. With this we would agree, and it is
accordingly questionable if, despite Horton's title, Koheleth had a "view of opposites" at all.
[7] Gordis op. cit. 47; Barton The Book of Ecclesiastes, 107; Hertzberg, Der
Prediger, 47 f.; Kroeber, Der Prediger, 66.

a passage similar to this occurs earlier in chapter 1₉ₐᵦ, מה שהיה הוא
שיהיה ומה שנעשה הוא שיעשה. Immediately following we have the comment
וְאֵין כָּל־חָדָשׁ תַּחַת הַשָּׁמֶשׁ (1₉ᶜ, and there is nothing new under the sun).
Likewise it is probable that Koheleth, or an editor, wishing to make a
similar remark on the substance of 3₁₅ₐ, inserted וְהָאֱלֹהִים יְבַקֵּשׁ אֶת־נִרְדָּף.
On the analogy of 1₉ᶜ, נִרְדָּף (Ni. pt.) must convey some such meaning
as "repetition, the same": compare the Vulgate, *Deus instaurat quod abiit*
(God restores that which passes away). The semantic development underlying נרדף in Koh 3₁₅, then, seems to have been, "pursues—passes
again—the same". We may compare too the Arabic مترادف "synonymous"⁸. But this connotation of the term is not appropriate to Ben Sira
where נרדפים is clearly used in its primary sense of "pursue or persecute".

Koh 8₁

חכמת אדם תאיר פניו
וְעֹז פניו ישנא

(the wisdom of a man illuminates
his countenance and the boldness
of his face is changed)

Ben Sira 13₂₄

לב אנוש ישנא פניו

(the understanding of a man
changes his face)

There is, of course, a general similarity of thought here. We have, however, little reason to postulate Ben Sira's dependence on Koheleth. The
two terms which they have in common—the verb שנא and the noun
פניו—are in different sequence. In Ben Sira the verb comes first, and
recalls משנה פניו of Job 14₂₀. In Koheleth the noun comes first, and so
פניו ישנא reminds us of (Q) אנפוהי אשתני in Dan 3₁₉. It may indeed further
be argued that in language and meaning Ben Sira 13₂₄ is closer to Prov
15₁₃ לב שמח ייטב פנים (a glad heart enlivens the countenance) than it is
to Koh 8₁.

Koh 7₁₆

וְאַל־תִּתְחַכַּם יוֹתֵר

Ben Sira 32₄ (35₄)

ובל עת מה תתחכם

(and not a time when you should
be wise)

Koheleth declares here that it benefits one little to be too wise, and
reminds us of *Aḥiqar*, 147. אל תסתכל כביר (be not overcrafty). As the
context shows, Ben Sira rather implies that there is a right and a wrong

---
⁸ Lane I iii, 1068 col. 3.

time to display one's wisdom. There is accordingly little to suggest that Ben Sira is here indebted to Koheleth.

It is likewise assumed[9] that Koh 7₂₈ ᵇ, אדם אחד מאלף מצאתי, under-lies Ben Sira 6₅, ובעל סודך אחד מאלף (But the confidant (lord) of thy private counsel be one in a thousand). The passage in Koheleth is, how-ever, quite unconnected in its context, and its significance is doubtful. The passage in Ben Sira is, on the contrary, a meaningful stich, and natu-rally completes part of a larger proverbial saying (אנשי שלומך יהיו רבים) "Let thy friends be many, but . . .". It is true that the phrase אחד מאלף is common to both passages, but both alike could have been influenced by Job 33₂₃ מליץ אחד מני־אלף (an interpreter one in a thousand).

Ben Sira 43₂₇, וקץ דבר הוא הכל (and it is the end of the matter, He is the all) is similarly thought to depend on Koh 12₁₃ סוף דבר הכל נשמע . . . כי זה כל־האדם[10]. קץ דבר and סוף דבר have indeed the same meaning, although סוף דבר equally invites comparison with סופא די מלתא of Dan 7₂₈[11]. But הוא הכל of Ben Sira has even less connection with any term in Koh 12₁₃. As the context shows, הכל in Ben Sira refers to God and his works. On the other hand, הכל נשמע in Koheleth applies to "all" which has been heard, while כל before האדם, whatever its precise mean-ing[12], clearly relates to "man".

The assumption is also made that the words of Ben Sira 4₂₀, בני עת וזמן שמר, are based on Koh 3₁, לכל זמן ועת[13]. It should first be noted that the Hebrew MS of Ben Sira (B Marg.) reads בני עת המון שמר, and that וזמן is Shechter's emendation[14]. וזמן may be the right reading, since המון yields no intelligible meaning. But, if it is correct, there is no valid reason for thinking that it depends on Koh 3₁. Indeed it may be more confidently argued that the contrary is the case. For זמן is used here only in Koheleth, and in a phrase (לכל זמן) which is unnecessary to the context. The following words, וְעֵת לכל־חפץ תחת השמים (and a time for everything under the heavens) would appear to be a more apt introduction to a section (3₂₋₈) which is an elaboration of the theme "everything in its season", and in which עת is used no less than 28 times. לכל זמן might therefore be a gloss at the beginning of the line, or, if used by the author himself, might appear to show an awareness of Ben Sira 4₂₀.

---

[9] E.g. McNeile, An Introduction to Ecclesiastes, 35; Hertzberg op.cit. 48.

[10] E.g. McNeile op.cit. 35; Barton op.cit. 54; Hertzberg op.cit. 48; Kroeber op.cit. 66.

[11] It will be noted that the phrase in Daniel completes the account of Daniel's visions.

[12] See above under 12₁₃.

[13] E.g. McNeile op.cit. 34.   [14] The Wisdom of Ben Sira, 41.

Finally it is commonly accepted that Ben Sira 13₂₄, אם לטוב ואם לרע, rests on Koh 12₁₄, אם טוב וְאם רע. Yet, despite the similarity of language, the relationship between the passages is in reality superficial. These words in Koheleth constitute the final phrase in the book, and seem to be a comment on the preceding material. The phrase in Ben Sira, on the other hand, suitably completes the proverb לב אנוש ישנא פניו אם לטוב ואם לרע (the heart of a man changes his face, whether for good or evil). Moreover, both טוב and רע are, as the context indicates, adjectives in Koheleth, while they are nouns in Ben Sira. Both terms are, again, prefixed by the preposition ל in Ben Sira, a usage common in the Old Testament: for example, אם לרע IIChr 18₁₇ and לרע Ps 56₆; לטוב Deut 6₂₄ and Jer 15₁₁.

(2)

These and other passages in Koheleth and Ben Sira are, then, commonly adduced as evidence for the belief that Ben Sira draws on Koheleth[15]. Rarely, however, have they more than one or two words in common. Again, while in many cases such passages are difficult and seem secondary in Koheleth, they are essential to their contexts in Ben Sira. In none of these passages is there anything either in thought or language to indicate the priority of Koheleth. Indeed so uncritical and inadequate is the evidence offered in support of the claim that the question might be legitimately raised whether, on the contrary, Ben Sira was the earlier writer.

We could, of course, speak with greater confidence of the character of Ben Sira's Hebrew if we had the entire Masada Scroll which dates from about a century after the composition of the work[16]. For, although the Manuscripts A and B and other fragments from the Cairo Genizah may be regarded as representing substantially genuine texts, it is likely that some passages reflecting Mishnaic and Talmudic usage are secondary[17]. However, apart from such material, we find passages which on linguistic

---

[15] See the lists proposed by, for example, Barton op. cit. 54; McNeile op. cit. 34; Gordis op. cit. 46–47; Hertzberg op. cit. 47–48; Kroeber op. cit. 65–66.

[16] See Yadin, The Ben Sira Scroll from Masada, 1965, 4 n. 11.

[17] See e.g. Di Lella, The Hebrew Text of Sirach, 1966, 106f., who thinks that such passages are examples of later retroversions from the Syriac Version. On the other hand, Rüger, (Text und Textform im hebräischen Sirach, 1970, e.g. 8f. 112f.) argues that such material is in the nature of direct glosses and insertions by Palestinian Jewish commentators, and is therefore not to be regarded as deriving from Syriac or Greek sources.

grounds might be claimed to be earlier than the corresponding passages in Koheleth. Thus in Ben Sira 40₁₁ we read כל מארץ אל ארץ ישוב ואשר ממרום אל מרום (everything from the earth returns unto the earth, and that which is from on high (returns) on high). Now it is assumed that this verse depends on the lengthy passage in Koh 3₂₀₋₂₁ הכל היה מן העפר והכל שב אל־העפר ... היא למטא לארץ. It is, however, likely that the contrary is the case, or, if one is not dependent on the other, at any rate that Ben Sira is the earlier. It will be observed that Koheleth has a tendency to use the preposition ל instead of אל. Thus in 8₄ we find ומי יאמר־לו מה תעשה. This, as we noted earlier, is clearly a quotation from Job 9₁₂, where, however, we have אליו instead of לו. The phrase is again quoted in Dan 4₃₂, ויאמר לה מה עבדת, where, of course, we have לה, the preposition אל (to, unto) not being used in biblical Aramaic[18]. Koheleth is thus nearer in usage to the Aramaic of Daniel than to Job. So here in 3₂₁ Koheleth characteristically uses the preposition ל (לארץ) while in the corresponding passage Ben Sira uses אל (אל ארץ). Similarly in discussing the relationship between Koh 8₁ and Ben Sira 13₂₄ we noticed that in reading וְעֹז פניו ישנא Koheleth's order of words is that of Dan 3₁₉, אנפוהי אשתני, while, in reading ישנא פניו, Ben Sira follows the order of Job 14₂₀, משנה פני. We observed too that commentators assume that Ben Sira 43₂₇ depends on Koh 12₁₃. Inasmuch, however, as Ben Sira has קץ and Koheleth the later סוף it is likely that Ben Sira is the earlier passage. So we recall that Koh 12₁₄ has אם־טוב ואם־רע, but in a parallel phrase Ben Sira has אם לטוב ואם לרע. The use of the preposition ל before טוב and רע is in accord with earlier classical usage (e.g. Deut 6₂₄ Ps 56₆).

It may again be noted that the Waw Consecutive, so characteristic of classical Hebrew, appears in a number of places in Ben Sira. As examples of the construction with the imperfect we may cite: ויכהו עד כלה (10₁₃, and he smote him utterly); וישב — for וַיּוֹשֶׁב — (וישב ענים תחתם 10₁₄, and he set up the poor instead of them); וישבתו כאשר שבתו (44₉, and they ceased when they came to their end); ויאמצהו (45₂, and he made him mighty); ויחזקהו (45₃, and he strengthened him); וישמיעהו (45₅, and he made him hear); וישימהו (45₇, and he established him); וילבישהו (45₈, and he clothed him). In contrast to this usage of Ben Sira, the Waw Consecutive with the Imperfect appears only three times in Koheleth: וָאראה in 4₁ and 4₇, and וָאתנה in 1₁₇, where, however, it may be secondary.

---

[18] אל is, again, only rarely used in the Mishna (Segal, A Grammar of Mishnaic Hebrew, 142).

So, while the perfect with Waw Consecutive occurs in Ben Sira 42₈,
והיית (and thou shalt be) and 42₁₁, והבישתך ¹⁹ (and she will shame thee),
it is not found at all in Koheleth. On the other hand, while the perfect
with simple (conjunctive) Waw occurs but a few times in Ben Sira (e. g.
והתבוננתי and I considered 39₃₂; ובא and he came 44₂₀ ᵦ; ומת and died 48₁₁),
it appears very frequently in Koheleth. For example: ופניתי אני (2₁₁),
וסבותי אני (2₁₇), ושנאתי את־החיים (2₁₅), ואמרתי אני בלבי (2₁₃), וראיתי אני
(2₂₀), וראיתי את־כל־ (8₁₅), ושבחתי אני (5₁₃), ואבד העשר ההוא ... והוליד בן
(8₁₇), ומלט־הוא (9₁₅ ᵦ), וסגרו ... וחשכו ... ובטלו הטחנות (12₃₋₄). In this
decided preference for the simple Waw rather than the Consecutive tense,
Koheleth is nearer than Ben Sira to the usage of the Mishna. For, apart
from citations from biblical Hebrew, the Waw Consecutive has virtually
disappeared from Mishnaic Hebrew ²⁰.

We further notice that the relative ש does not occur in Ben Sira.
It is used, however, almost as often as אשר in Koheleth ²¹. As we observed
earlier, ש is employed increasingly in late Hebrew literature, and it is
significant that it is normal usage in the Mishna.

(3)

The linguistic evidence indicating the priority of Ben Sira to Koheleth is confirmed from a comparison of some of their views. This is
particularly noticeable in their outlook on life. Ben Sira's views are
largely based on traditional Judaism and in the concept of Wisdom found
in Prov chapters 1–9. All things are created and sustained by God (e. g.
33₁₀₋₁₃ 43₂₇₋₃₃), and, provided man accepts the dictates of Wisdom, he
encounters but few difficulties in life (4₁₁₋₁₈ 6₂₃₋₃₁). Koheleth, on the
other hand, approaches the problems of life with no such presuppositions ²². Applying his mind to the conditions of human experience, he
finds, on the contrary, that man's lot is one of misery and toil (1₁₂₋₁₄).
Unable to accept the assumptions of traditional religion, he regards life
as vain and purposeless (2₁₆₋₁₇ 4₄ 6₂). But even less could he accept the
religious optimism of Ben Sira. Ben Sira thinks of God as a merciful
being in close association with man (15₁₉ 17₁₉. ₂₉ 18₁₃): Koheleth conceives of him as remote in the heavens, detached from the affairs of men

---

¹⁹ Text והושבתך for והבישתך. See Lévi, The Hebrew Text of the Book of Ecclesiasticus, 1951, reprint, 54.
²⁰ Segal op. cit. 72.
²¹ See above p. 7 f.
²² Cf. Müller, VT 18 (1968), 507–521, especially 520f.

(5₁, Heb.). Ben Sira accepts that God's will prevails on earth (39₁₆):
Koheleth declares that man lives in utter uncertainty of the outcome of
events (8₇). Ben Sira believes in a due reward for the righteous (44₁₆f.
15₁₇. ₁₉): Koheleth is convinced that the same fate awaits the righteous
and wicked alike (9₂).

It is thus not improbable that, though Koheleth shows a dependence
on Ben Sira[23], his views are to some extent a reaction against the orthodox
but uncritical views of that book[24]. On the other hand, aware of the
sceptical nature of his own work, and of the likelihood that it would not
gain unanimous acceptance, Koheleth, or his editor, astutely ascribed
it to the unassailable authority of Solomon. It is doubtless mainly on this
ground that the book was finally accepted in the canon[25].

That the earlier and more orthodox Ben Sira did not find a place
in the canon may be explained by the contents and history of the book.
In eulogising the great figures of Israel's past, Ben Sira gives noticeable
prominence to Aaron and his priestly line. God, he declares, "made an
everlasting covenant with him, and gave him the priesthood of the people.
He blessed him with splendid vestments . . . No outsider ever put them
on, but only his sons and his descendants perpetually" (45₇. ₁₃, RSV).
But a passage of this nature could only prove embarrassing to the Jewish
leaders who in 140 B.C. declared that Simon of the usurping Hasmonean
house "should be their leader and high priest for ever" (IMac 14₄₁)[26].
Thus it is likely that at this time the book of Ben Sira was withdrawn
from circulation by the religious authorities. Two fragments of the text
of Ben Sira were, however, recovered from Cave II in Qumran in 1952[27],
which suggests that a copy of the work was deposited there by supporters
of the Zadokite priesthood. But already in about 800 A.D. other copies
were discovered in a cave and brought to Jerusalem, where they seem
to have been eagerly studied by the Karites. The text then seems to have
been circulated for a few centuries, during which further copies were
made. But, apparently, the Rabbis suppressed the text again, and finally
consigned the surviving copies to the Genizah. It was, accordingly, from

---

[23] See further below p.163.
[24] It has been suggested by Braun (Kohelet und die frühhellenistische Popularphilosophie 1973, 174) that we can recognise a reaction in Ben Sira against the
Hellenising tendencies in Koheleth. But the thought, like the language, of Ben
Sira is quite intelligible for the period round 180 B.C., while the language of
Koheleth, being demonstrably later, is naturally the vehicle of equally later thought.
[25] On the canonisation of the book, see R. Kroeber, Der Prediger, 69–73.
[26] See further below p. 145.
[27] See Baillet, RB 63 (1956), 54f. See also ibid. 49.

the Genizah in Old Cairo that the Hebrew text of Ben Sira emerged again in the year 1896[28].

Thus it was that, suppressed by the Rabbis from the second century B.C. onwards, Ben Sira was precluded even from consideration for admission to the canon. Koheleth, on the other hand, contained nothing that was offensive to their ecclesiastical views. Indeed inasmuch as it was sceptical of traditional doctrine, it might be regarded as lending support to the changes the Rabbis themselves contemplated[29]. Even so, it is likely that Koheleth's speculations were the source of no little embarrassment to his editors, who more than once introduced an element of orthodoxy into his book (e.g. 5 7a. 20 11 9c 12 1a). They further represented him as one who studied and composed proverbs (12 9). Apparently they already knew from Ben Sira (18 29 44 4-6) that this was an honourable and pious occupation.

---

[28] See Kahle, The Cairo Geniza, 1959, 9–27. Cf., however, Rabin who thinks the banning of Ben Sira by the Rabbis was part of an anti-Sectarian movement. Ben Sira, he argues, was similar to the literature produced by the Sectarians who would in turn "pass off the whole Sectarian books as respectable old literature". Hence, the entire literature produced by the mother community of the Rabbis and Sectarians had to be banned. The Historical Background of Qumran Hebrew, in: Scripta Hierosolymitana IV, Aspects of the Dead Sea Scrolls, 1965^2, 160.

[29] E.g. the introduction of the principle of "Oral" as well as "Written" Law. Cf. Kahle op. cit. 22–23.

III. HISTORICAL AND LINGUISTIC EVIDENCE
FOR THE DATE OF KOHELETH

(1)

We know from external evidence that Ben Sira was writing at the beginning of the second century B.C. His grandson translated his work into Greek in the year 132 B.C., and therefore Ben Sira could scarcely have written it later than 180 B.C.[1] The privileges which the Jews enjoyed during the early years of Seleucid government are clearly reflected in the buoyant mood of the work[2]. On the other hand, the pessimism and uncertainty which pervades the writings of Koheleth suggest the darker days of Maccabean times.

But Koheleth is, of course, placed earlier than this. Middendorp thinks that he was active at somewhat the same time as Ben Sira, and therefore prior to the Maccabean revolt[3]. Gordis again believes that the work shows no trace of the Maccabean persecutions, and assigns it to about 250 B.C.[4] Dahood, as we have seen, places the work on grounds of orthography in the fourth-third centuries B.C.[5], and on Zimmermann's view the Aramaic original is to be dated at about 300 B.C.[6] So Scott connects the book with the end of the fourth or early third century B.C.[7]. Muilenburg, again, accepts a date in the third or late fourth century B.C. for the composition of the book, while Zimmerli and Kroeber place it roughly in the middle of the third century B.C.[8] In the absence of con-

---

[1] See e.g. Pfeiffer, History of New Testament Times, 1949, 364–367.

[2] The Seleucids gained control of Palestine from the Ptolemies in 198 B.C., and from then until the reign of Antiochus IV (Epiphanes, c. 175–164 B.C.) the Jews lived in peaceful circumstances.

[3] Middendorp, Die Stellung Jesu ben Siras zwischen Judentum und Hellenismus, 1973, 85–90.

[4] Koheleth: The Man and His World 67.

[5] Bibl 33 (1952), 36.

[6] JQR 36 (1945–46), 39 n. 3.

[7] Proverbs, Ecclesiastes, AB, 1965, 198.

[8] Muilenburg, A Qoheleth Scroll from Qumran, BASOR 135 (1954), 24; Zimmerli, Das Buch des Predigers Salomo, 128; Kroeber, Der Prediger, 7–8. So Hengel, Judentum und Hellenismus, 1973², 212f., would place the work between 270–220 B.C.

crete evidence, Galling would only suggest that the book derives from the beginning of the third century B.C.[9], while in an equally cautious approach Loretz refers to that century as the generally accepted date for the work, but adds that an earlier date is not to be excluded[10]. Finally, Braun would accept the view of those scholars who assign the work to the second half of the third century B.C.[11].

On the other hand, in considering the date of Koheleth, some scholars claim to detect references to historical figures in his work. Thus in 4₁₃₋₁₆ Schunck sees a reference to three Seleucid rulers: the "foolish king" is Antiochus II, the man "from prison" Seleucus II, and "the second lad" Antiochus the Great (III). He accordingly thinks that Koheleth lived throughout the years 246–200 B.C., and wrote his book at the end of that period[12]. So Barton thought that the old and foolish king in 4₁₃₋₁₄ is Ptolemy IV (Philopater) who died in 205 B.C., while the poor and wise youth in the same passage is Ptolemy V (Epiphanes) who was only five years old when he succeeded to the throne[13]. The text and meaning of this passage are, however, too uncertain to allow us to base a historical occasion on it[14]. But if we are to see in it a child who succeeded to the office of a king, it is equally possible to identify him with Antiochus V (Eupator) who was only eight years of age when he suceeded his father Antiochus IV (Epiphanes) in the year 163 B.C.[15]. But, as in the case of the child Ptolemy V, we have no evidence that Antiochus V was "poor". Nor again could a child of eight years, scarely more than one of five, be regarded as "wise". Barton further argues that the phrase "woe to you, O land, when your king is a child, and your princes feast in the morning" (10₁₆) refers to the Seleucid Antiochus III (223–187 B.C.)[16]. But we may equally see the eight-year old son of Antiochus IV (Epiphanes) as the "child" here. Barton again thinks that חורים in 10₁₇ is to be taken

---

[9] Der Prediger 74f.

[10] Loretz, Qoheleth und der Alte Orient, (1964), 22–29.

[11] Braun, Kohelet und die frühhellenistische Popularphilosophie, 1973, 14. 177. So, it may be noted, Odeberg (Qohaelaeth, 1929, 94) regarded "250 as a probable *terminus post quem*".

[12] VT 9 (1959), 192–201.

[13] The Book of Ecclesiastes 61.

[14] Cf. above under 4₁₄.

[15] Haupt thought that the foolish king was Antiochus IV, but that the poor youth was Alexander Balas: The Book of Ecclesiastes, 1905, 2. However, as Balas did not immediately succeed Antiochus IV, and did not rule till some 14 years later, his identity with the "poor youth" is scarcely possible.

[16] Op. cit. 62.

as "well-born"[17]. On that interpretation, the term could apply to any
ruler of honourable family, and be no more than a generalisation. It is,
however, probable that בן־חורים means "free-people"[18], and so may
conceivably refer to the period following 163 B.C., when the Jews under
Judas Maccabeus gained temporary freedom from the Seleucids[19]. In
claiming to see references to such figures as Ptolemy V and Antiochus III,
Barton confesses that he is influenced by the assumption that Koheleth
is earlier than Ben Sira and cannot therefore be much later than the beginning of the second century B.C.[20]. Hertzberg, again, would associate such
passages as 5 7f. 8 22ff. 10 5. 7. 16 with events in Palestine at the end of the
third century B.C., and so maintains that Koheleth wrote his book then,
or possibly in the early years of the following century[21]. But, like Barton
and other commentators, Hertzberg too starts from the assumption that
"Ben Sira knew and used Qoheleth" (p. 49). Yet this is an assumption
which cannot be defended on either historical or linguistic grounds, and
seems to rest on nothing more than the belief that Ben Sira, being Apo-
cryphal, must necessarily be later than Koheleth which happens to be
"canonical". Apart from this supposition it is possible to associate the
passages in question with more than one ruler in the second century
B.C., and indeed Graetz argued that 4 13-14 is a reference to Herod the
Great who ruled from 37–4 B.C.[22].

The tenor of such passages is thus too general to enable us to identify
particular persons in them. The most that can be claimed for 4 13-14 is
that it belongs to that type of Hebrew proverbial literature which regards
wisdom essential to the successful rule of a king (cf. Koh 9 13-16 Ben Sira
10 3 Prov 8 14-16). The disastrous consequences of a child-king in 10 16 is
again an obvious generalisation, and is reminiscent of Isa 3 4 where a

---

[17] Op. cit. ibid.   [18] See above under 10 17.
[19] We recall that the Jews struck a coin with חרות on it in their revolt against the
Romans.
[20] Op. cit. 62.   [21] Der Prediger 51 f.
[22] Graetz, Kohélet oder salomonische Prediger, 78 f. The Targum, on the other
hand, regards the "poor youth" as Abraham, and the "foolish king" as Nimrod.
So Malamat, BA 28 (1965), 55, identified the "child" with Jeroboam and the
"second child" with Rehoboam. Again Dornseiff, ZDMG 89 (1935), 248–249,
thought that there is here a reference to Joseph and Pharaoh, while verses 15-16
contain a reference to Absalom and David. Also in 9 14-15 and 7 19 he saw an allusion
to Miltiades, one of the ten Athenian Generals. Miltiades advised an attack on
the Medes at Marathon, but though successful in that venture, later suffered a
reverse at Paros for which, a wounded and dejected figure, he was reprimanded by
the Athenians (Herodotus 6 109-186).

child-prince or ruler betokens woe and oppression. The injunction in
10₁₇ that a king should avoid drunkenness is similarly in harmony with
the teaching of Prov 31₄₋₅.

But while we cannot claim to find an allusion to an historical figure
or event in the book of Koheleth, it contains some material which points
to a definite period in Jewish history. A unique feature of the work is
that, while it has some forty references to God, it never refers to him
as *Yahweh* but always as *Elohim*. This can hardly be due to Aramaic
influence, since the Aramaic אֱלָהּ would more naturally be represented
by אֱלֹהַּ which appears in late Hebrew literature (Deut 32₁₇ Dan 11₃₈
Hab 1₁₁). Koheleth's use of *Elohim* seems rather to find its explanation in
the religious environment of the early Maccabean period. Antiochus Epiphanes installed the cult of the Syrian deity Baal Shamim[23] in the temple
at Jerusalem, and in calling it the temple of Olympian Zeus (II Mac 6₂,
cf. I Mac 1₅₄) doubtless also wished to identify Yahweh with Zeus. We
likewise read that the Samaritan temple in Gerizim was now called *Zeus
Xenion* (II Mac 6₂), and, according to Josephus (Antiq xii v. ₅), this was
in response to a request made by the Samaritans themselves. More significant, however, is the record that there were many in Jerusalem who
were now attracted to "the Greek way of life" (II Mac 4₁₀), and further
that "many even from Israel gladly adopted" the "religion" of Antiochus
Epiphanes (I Mac 1₄₃)[24]. The Books of Maccabees were indeed written
later than the time of Antiochus[25], and probably exaggerate the extent
to which "lawless men came forth from Israel and mislead many" (I Mac
1₁₁). Nevertheless, we may accept that there were some in Judah who
were attracted to the novelty of Greek religion; and it is likely that Koheleth, who took a discriminating attitude towards traditional Judaism,
would contemplate it with interest. The concept of a transcendant and
impersonal deity appears to have made a particular appeal to him, and
it is thus probable that Greek notions underlie his view of God as remote
in the heavens, having little converse with man on earth (5₁ Heb.)[26].

---

[23] So Dan 11₃₁ (cf. 12₁₁) where השקוץ משמם (the abomination that makes desolate)
has since Nestlé (ZAW 4, 1884, 248) been regarded as an intentional change for
"Baal Shamim". See Tcherikover, Hellenistic Civilisation and the Jews (Eng.
trans. 1961), 195 and the literature cited in 475 n. 30, and also: Eissfeldt, Ba'l-
šamēm und Jahwe, in: Kleine Schriften II, 1963, 171—198, especially 195f.

[24] See further below p. 165.

[25] Cf. Pfeiffer, History of New Testament Times, who places I Maccabees round 100
B. C. (490). II Maccabees is, of course, but an epitome of a five-volumed work by
Jason of Cyrene (II Mac 2₃₅) who wrote about the same time (Pfeiffer 514f.).

[26] See further p. 166.

Hence inasmuch as *Elohim* is a general term for deity, it would be more acceptable to his theological outlook than *Yahweh*, with its limiting connotation as the national God of Israel.

In expressing his doubt about the destiny of the human spirit, Koheleth again seems to presuppose the teaching on the subject which we find in Daniel and the second book of Maccabees. We read in Dan 12₂ that "many who sleep in the dust of the earth shall awake, some to everlasting life, and some to shame and everlasting contempt". It is natural, and probable, that speculations regarding the ultimate fate of man should, for the Jews, first emerge in the severe religious persecutions of the reign of Antiochus Epiphanes. Thus we read in Maccabees of a Jew who, on being painfully put to death for his faith, exclaimed, "The king of the universe will raise us up to an everlasting renewal of life" (II Mac 7₉). So the last words of another victim to his torturers were, "One cannot but choose to die at the hands of men and to cherish the hope that God gives of being raised again by him. But for you there will be no resurrection to life" (II Mac 7₁₄).

But, while such utterances contain a doctrine of resurrection to eternal life, Koheleth thinks that man is but little different from the beast. Both die and alike return to the dust whence they came. It appears indeed that Koheleth would make a distinction between the body and the spirit; but if so, he is scarcely more hopeful of the destiny of the spirit (3₂₁). For he believed that the same spirit (רוח) animates both man and animal (3₁₉); and therefore no one knows whether the spirit of man goes upwards, or whether, like that of the beast, it goes downwards to the earth. In casting doubt on a tenet of contemporary Jewish belief, Koheleth appears again, as we shall see later²⁷, to be influenced by a Greek view of the ultimate destiny of man and beast.

(2)

The probability that Koheleth was aware of the teaching of the book of Daniel is strengthened by the consideration that his language seems to be later than that book which is a product of the years 167–164 B.C.²⁸ Unfortunately the material on which we may attempt a linguistic comparison of the books of Koheleth and Daniel is limited; and where we recognise points of contact it may be possible to argue that Koheleth

²⁷ p. 167.
²⁸ Cf. e.g. Fohrer, Introduction to the Old Testament (Eng. edn. 1970), 477f.

was influenced by usages anterior to Daniel, or that both writers drew from a common source[29]. Nevertheless, it is noteworthy that there are Aramaisms in Koheleth which appear elsewhere in the Old Testament only in the Aramaic of the book of Daniel. Thus פֶּשֶׁר in Koh 8₁ is found frequently in Daniel (e.g. 2₄₅ 4₃ 5₁₅)[30]. The phrase עֹשִׂים לֶחֶם is used in Koh 10₁₉ of "making a feast", and עֲבַד לְחֶם is used in the same sense in Dan 5₁. The expression עַל־דִּבְרַת שֶׁ in Koh 7₁₄ is likewise to be compared with the expression עַל־דִּבְרַת דִּי in Dan 2₃₀ and 4₁₄. Again, it will be recalled that Job 9₁₂, מִי־יֹאמַר אֵלָיו מַה־תַּעֲשֶׂה, is the basis of Dan 4₃₂, וְיֹאמַר לֵהּ מָה עֲבַדְתְּ. But in writing וּמִי יֹאמַר־לוֹ מַה־תַּעֲשֶׂה Koheleth's (8₄) use of לוֹ instead of אֵלָיו seems to be influenced by the Aramaic לֵהּ in Daniel. Moreover, a phrase which originally had a religious application may in the course of time be used in a secular sense. Hence, in applying the phrase in question in proverbial fashion to a ruler, it is likely that Koheleth is writing after the composition of the book of Daniel. The fact that the Hebrew of the book of Daniel frequently employs the Waw Consecutive[31] is a further indication that it is earlier than the Hebrew of Koheleth.

Another characteristic of Koheleth, and no less significant for the dating of its language, is the number of words and phrases which are found elsewhere only in the Mishna and Talmud[32]. Thus עִנְיָן which occurs often in Koheleth (e.g. 1₁₃ 2₂₃ 3₁₀) appears frequently in the Talmud; for example, Kid 6a עֲסוּקִין בְּאוֹת עִנְיָן (employed with this matter), Baba Bat 114b מֵעִנְיָנָא לְעִנְיָנָא (from one matter to another). The

---

[29] For the use of Aramaic in determining the date of a biblical text, compare the caution epxressed by Hurvitz, IEJ 18 (1968), 234ff. He would, however, admit that Aramaisms may be utilised as a criterion for lateness "when evaluated in the light of other linguistic phenomena associated with the text in which these Aramaisms occur" (240). It is our belief that such phenomena are to be found in the text of Koheleth.

[30] For the occurrence of the word in extra-biblical Aramaic, see Wagner, Die lexikalischen und grammatikalischen Aramaismen im alttestamentlichen Hebräisch, No. 239 (96).

[31] For example, in chapter 8 alone we find, among others: וַיָּבֹא (and he came, v.₆); וַיִּךְ (and he smote, v.₇); וַתִּגְדַל (and it became great, v. 10); וָאֶשְׁמְעָה (and I heard, v. 13). The fact that these are in prose constructions is immaterial. For, as we have seen earlier (p. 129), Koheleth uses the Perfect with Simple Waw in passages which are decidedly prosaic.

[32] The Mishnaic period probably extended from the beginning of the second century B.C. to the end of the third century A.D. The Talmudic period began shortly afterwards, and the Talmud was probably committed to writing by 500 A.D. Cf. Segal op.cit. 1–5.

expression חוּץ מִן (except) in Koh 2₂₅ is found again only in post-biblical Hebrew: we may mention Bera 6₁ חוץ מן היין (except wine), and Shab 2₅ חוץ מן הפתילה (except the wick). Outside Koh 11₅ the word מְלֵאָה (pregnant) appears only in the Mishna; for example, Jeb 16₁ יצאה מלאה (she went away pregnant). The only place in the Old Testament where אִי (woe) occurs is Koh 10₁₆, but it is found more than once in the Mishna; thus in Yeb 13₇ we read אי לו על אשתו ואי לו על אשת אחין (woe to him on the loss of his wife, and woe to him on the loss of his brother's wife). Koh 12₅ is similarly the only instance in the Old Testament where we find אֲבִיּוֹנָה (caperberry). It, however, occurs in the Mishna; for example, Maas 4₆ אין מתעשר אלה אביונות (only the caperberries are tithed). Likewise בֵּית־עוֹלָם is found in biblical Hebrew only in Koh 12₅, but we find, for example, בית עולמים in Tos Bera 3, and בית עלמין in San 19a. So בבית עלמיה is the Targumic rendering of בביתו (in his tomb) in Isa 14₁₈. Again, whatever our view of בעלי אֲסֻפּוֹת in Koh 12₁₁, it is significant that the phrase occurs nowhere else except in the Talmud (e. g. San 12a). Finally, although חורים appears more than once in the Old Testament (e. g. I Reg 21₈. ₁₁) the expression בֶּן־חוֹרִים in Koh 10₁₇ is paralleled elsewhere only in Rabbinical literature (e. g. Git 4₄. ₆).

We observe, moreover, that words are used with the same secondary meaning in Koheleth as in the Mishna and Talmud. Thus the basic meaning of חֵפֶץ is "pleasure" (e. g. Isa 54₁₂) or "desire" (e. g. Job 31₁₆), but in Koh 3₁. ₁₇ 5₇ and 8₆ it has the force of "matter" or "thing". In the Mishna חפץ has a similar meaning: for example, Bab Metz 4₁₀ בכמה חמץ זה (how much is this thing?). Similarly in the Talmud (Bera 5a) we read אדם מוכר חפץ לחרבו (a man sells a thing to his fellow). Again in Koheleth 6₉ מַרְאֵה עֵינַיִם has the meaning of "pleasure or enjoyment". So in the Talmud (Yoma 74b) we find the phrase מראה עינים באשה (the pleasure of looking at one's wife). A similar meaning attaches to מראי־עיניך in Koh 11₉. In 3₁₁ and 5₁₇ יָפֶה (adj.) is used in the sense of "good, appropriate". The term has a similar meaning in the Talmud; thus, יפה דנתי (have I argued rightly?, Bera 4a), and ומעוטן יפה (but a little is good, Bera 34a).

We again notice some similarity of syntactical usage between Koheleth and the Mishna. In Koheleth the pronoun אֲנִי is frequently used pleonastically with the first person of the verb. Thus we find אמרתי אני in 2₁ and 2₁₅, and ראיתי אני in 2₁₃ and 2₂₄. So in Kethu 13₅ we have אלו אף אני לא אמרתי (If I had assigned myself) and in Taan 1₁ אני פסקתי לעצמי (I did not indeed say). Koheleth also uses the pronoun with a participial construction. For example: כי (7₂₆); שם הֵם שָׁבִים לָלֶכֶת (1₇); וּמוֹצֵא אֲנִי

גַם יוֹדֵעַ אָנִי (8₁₂). In the Mishna we likewise read יודע אני שיש נדרים
(I know that there are vows, Nedar 11₇) and again . . . הוא רצה (he is
willing . . ., Bab Bath 6₆). As in the Mishna too, such participial constructions are often used with אין: thus כִּי אֵינָם יוֹדְעִים לַעֲשׂוֹת רַע (4₁₇);
כַּאֲשֶׁר אֵינְךָ יוֹדֵעַ (9₂); וְלַאֲשֶׁר אֵינֶנּוּ זֹבֵחַ (11₅). Mishnaic examples are: Nedar
11₇ איני יודע שיש מפירין (I did not know that they could be revoked);
Nedar 2₁ שבועה שאיני ישן שאיני מדבר (an oath that I will not sleep, that
I will not speak).

We recognise a further correspondence between Koheleth and the
Mishna in the use and omission of the definite article. As we noted
earlier (p. 109) Koheleth exhibits some inconsistency in this respect.
Thus in the line כִּי עֵת לְכָל־חֵפֶץ וְעַל כָּל־הַמַּעֲשֶׂה שָׁם (3₁₇) חפץ has not the
article while מעשה has, although both terms have the same logical force.
On the other hand, the article is missing when we would expect it.
For example, in the phrase עַד אֲשֶׁר לֹא יָבֹאוּ יְמֵי־הָרָעָה וְהִגִּיעוּ שָׁנִים (12₁)
we should expect שׁנים to be determinate. Similarly in the Mishna the
article is omitted in such expressions as תלמוד תורה (the study of the
Torah, Peah 1₁), כהן גדול (the High Priest, Yoma 1₁); but we find it
in such instances as בעל הבית (the master of the house, Shab 1₁) and
בית המדרש (the house of study, Shab 16₁). We again find ככר זו (this
loaf) in Sheb 3₇, but הַמָּעוֹת הָאֵלּוּ (this money) in Maas Shen 3₃.

We may note here too that in the Dead Sea Scrolls there is some
inconsistency in the use of the article. Thus in the Manual of Discipline
(IQS) we find the article used in iii 19, רוחות האמת והעול (the spirits of
truth and evil), but in a few lines later (iii 25) it is absent in the phrase
והוא ברא רוחות אור וחשך (and he created the spirits of light and darkness).
Again the article is used with שחת in the phrase עם אנשי השחת (with the
men of corruption) in ix 16, but it is absent in verse 22 where עם אנשי
שחת has the same meaning [33].

(3)

The affinities which Koheleth exhibits with post-biblical usage
suggest that, when he was writing, the Mishnaic idiom constituted a
considerable element in the linguistic environment. In attempting to

---

[33] Cf. Leahy, Bibl 41 (1960), 151f. On the other hand, we observe certain classical
features in this Scroll, including the frequent use of the Waw Consecutive (cf.
Gordis, Bibl 41, 1960, 406). But these may be conscious imitations of biblical
Hebrew rather than representative of the language of the day. However, until we
can determine more precisely the date of the Scrolls we cannot make a profitable
comparison of their language with that of Koheleth.

define further the period of Koheleth's literary activity it will be instructive to consider the main characteristics of the language of the Shema and The Eighteen Benedictions. For these are the earliest representatives of Jewish liturgical language and are thought to date from pre-Maccabean times[34]. The Shema is the earlier, and is mentioned in the Mishna (Bera 2₂) as having been recited daily, morning and evening. Central to the Shema are the three Pentateuchal passages, Deut 6₄₋₉ 11₁₃₋₂₁, and Num 15₃₇₋₄₁. These passages are preceded by two Benedictions and followed by two Thanksgiving Prayers[35]. In these Benedictions and Prayers there are, moreover, many devotional passages from the Psalms and other biblical books. Hence, under the influence of such Old Testament material, the Shema as a whole is cast in language approximating to that of biblical Hebrew. Nevertheless, we recognise in it some Mishnaic elements. Thus we find the use of שֶׁ for אשר: שמו שֶׁל־מלך (the name of the king)[36]; שֶׁהוא ראשון (who is the first)[37]; שֶׁעשית (which thou hast done)[38]. We find instances too in which the pronoun of the third person is used as a copula: עזרת אבותינו אתה הוא מעולם (thou hast been the help of our fathers from of old)[39]; אמת אתה הוא ראשון ואתה אחרון (it is true that thou art the first and thou art the last)[40]. Compare the Mishnaic אם אני הוא הטמא . . . אם אני הוא הטהור (If I am the unclean . . . if I am the clean, Naz 8₁)[41]. Again we observe the use of אֶת as a demonstrative: אֶת־שֵׁם האל המלך . . . קדוש הוא (the name of the divine king . . . holy is he)[42]. Compare the Mishnaic אֶת שיבלת בעינו (the one which has a wart in his eye, Bera 6₁₀)[43].

The Eighteen Benedictions consists of a collection of eighteen prayers which were said three times daily in the synagogue[44]. Like the Shema, they were composed largely in the devotional language of the Psalms and prophetical books. Yet we detect too some Mishnaic modes of expression. As in the Shema, we find the frequent use of שֶׁ for אשר: שאתה הוא יי אלהינו (for thou art Yahweh our God)[45]; ועל נסיך שֶׁבכל־יום

---

[34] See Elbogen, Der jüdische Gottesdienst in seiner geschichtlichen Entwicklung, 1962⁴, 14–60. Cf. too Hertz, The Authorised Daily Prayer Book, 1946, xviii.
[35] The Shema is found in Hertz op.cit. 108ff.
[36] Hertz 108.   [37] Hertz ibid.
[38] Hertz 110.   [39] Hertz 126.
[40] Hertz 128.   [41] See Segal op.cit. 198f.
[42] Hertz 112.   [43] See Segal op.cit. 202.
[44] See Mishna, Bera 4₁. They were also known as Tefillah, the Prayer *par excellence*. Cf. too Taan (Mishna) 2₂. The Benedictions may be found in Hertz op.cit. 131f.
[45] Hertz 150.

שֶׁבְּכָל־עֵת . . . עמנו ועל נפלאותיך (and for thy miracles which are daily with
us, and for thy wonders which are (wrought) at all times)[46]. We also
observe the use of the pronoun with the participle: מוֹדִים אֲנַחְנוּ לָךְ (we
give thanks to thee)[47]. Compare Ps 75₁ הודינו לך אלהים הודינו and Ps 79₁₃
נספרו . . . . נודה לך לעולם . . . where we have the first person plural of the
verb. Again, the pronoun הוא serves as a copula between subject and
predicate: שאתה הוא אלהינו (for thou art our God)[48]; ישענו אתה הוא
לדור וָדור (thou art our salvation to generation and generation)[49]. Finally
we notice the absence of the article: מכלכל חיים בחסד מחיה מתים ברחמים
רבים (who sustains the living with loving-kindness, revivest the dead
with great mercy)[50].

Our purpose in thus considering the Shema and The Eighteen
Benedictions is to ascertain whether their language is earlier or later
than that of Koheleth. On reading the Jewish Prayers we are aware of
their clarity of thought and expression. Their authors show such a
familiarity with the forms of the biblical language that the few Mishnaisms
they use are relatively unobtrusive. The style of Koheleth, on the other
hand, is often laboured and inelegant. He frequently appears to be
writing in an idiom which, although doubtless an element of the vernacular, had as yet attained little literary grace. It is, of course, true that
our respective authors deal with different themes. The Jewish Liturgies
are devotional and lend themselves to facile expression in the traditional
style. Koheleth, while familiar with Job and Proverbs, was, nevertheless,
in his own peculiar way reflective, sceptical and unorthodox. To some
extent, therefore, we might expect a break with the thought and language
of tradition. But, making due allowance for differences of subject matter
and approach, the Shema and the Eighteen Benedictions are written
with perceptibly greater ease and seem nearer than Koheleth to the age
of classical Hebrew. There are, again, more Mishnaisms in Koheleth
which in itself suggests that it was composed in a period when the
Mishnaic tongue was beginning to be widely used.

(4)

It is, moreover, significant that the Shema and the Eighteen Benedictions were known to the Qumran Sectarians in an order similar to

---

[46] Hertz ibid.
[47] Hertz ibid.   [48] Hertz ibid.
[49] Hertz ibid.   ˙[50] Hertz 134.

that in which they appear in the Jewish Liturgy[51]. The Prayers are, therefore, common to both the Sectarians and Pharisaic Judaism, and must
accordingly date from a time when they formed a single religious
community. Now it is likely that this mother community is to be identified with the Hasidim of Maccabean times[52]. We read in I Mac of "a
company of the Hasideans" (2₄₂) joining the ranks of Mattathias and
opposing the forces of Antiochus Epiphanes. We also read that "all
who became fugitives to escape their troubles joined them and reinforced
them" (v. ₄₃). The movement against Hellenism and the Seleucid power
had thus a popular as well as a religious basis. This would lead to the
social changes by which the lower and peasant classes acquired an influence in national affairs. The persecutions and conflicts of the Maccabean period would, again, lead to a disruption of cultural continuity.
One effect of this would be the decline of the classical forms of the
language and the emergence into prominence of the colloquial speech.
And when it is remembered that dialectical Hebrew was the vernacular
of the Jews since the time of Ben Sira, if not earlier[53], this development
would be all the more natural[54].

But while the social changes connected with the Maccabean crisis
brought the Mishnaic idiom into prominence, it must have been some
time before it was generally accepted as a literary medium. Through
lack of early literary documents we cannot claim to trace the phases of
this literary development. The Mishna indeed contains material dating
from the early second century B.C.[55], but as such material was orally

---

[51] See Rabin, The Historical Background of Qumran Hebrew, Scripta Hierosoly-
mitana IV, Aspects of the Dead Sea Scrolls, 1965², 153 ff.; and also Talmon, The
Calendar Reckoning of the Sect from the Judean Desert, ibid. 187 ff. See also
Talmon, RdQ 8 (1960), 475–500.

[52] Cf. Rabin loc. cit. 156 f.; cf. too Morgenstern, HUCA 38 (1967), 59–73, who
would, however, trace their origin to the early post-exilic age.

[53] Birkeland ("The Language of Jesus", in: II Hist.-Filos. Kl, 1954, No. 1, 6 ff.)
and Chomsky (JQR 42, 1951/52, 195 ff.) in particular argue that dialectical Hebrew
was always the speech of the Palestinian populace. See too Grintz, JBL 79 (1960),
32 ff., especially 46–47.

[54] According to Birkeland the Mishnaic language "started with" the "oral teaching"
of the Jewish Schoolmen, the Soferim and the Tannaim. It was they who "made
the revolutionary step of leaving BH and creating new standard Hebrew" (loc. cit.
20). But in view of the fact that Mishnaic Hebrew was in origin the spoken language of the populace, it is likely that now after the Maccabean revolt there was
also a considerable secular impetus in its development.

[55] See Rabin loc. cit. 155.

transmitted till as late as the second or third century A.D.[56] we have
no intermediate Mishnaic documents which might offer a chronological
view of the development of the language.

The general opposition of the Jews to Hellenism in Maccabean
times would doubtless be a powerful motive for the use of Hebrew in
either its classical or colloquial form[57]. It is likely, moreover, that the
popular nationalism which attended the victories of their military
leaders was decisive in fostering the more widespread adoption of the
Mishnaic idiom. The appointment of Jonathan to the office of High
Priest in 152 (I Mac 10 15ff.) would provide considerable support for
this movement. Jonathan was a member of the Hasmonean house[58], and
the elevation of one who was not of Zadokite lineage to this office was
contrary to tradition[59]. But while such an appointment would be resented
by the old Zadokite families[60], it would, on the other hand, be welcomed
by the peasant and artisan elements of the population. Nor did Jonathan
fail to sustain their admiration of his achievements. By the year 145 B.C.
he even controlled part of southern Samaria (I Mac 11 19-37), and when
in 142–141 he was succeeded by his brother Simon we read that "the
yoke of the Gentiles was removed from Israel" (I Mac 13 41). Indeed such
was the degree of independence now enjoyed by the Jews that the first
year of Simon was regarded as the beginning of a new era (I Mac 13 42).

---

[56] See Liebermann, Hellenism in Jewish Palestine, 1950, 83–89, for a statement on the
orally transmitted form of the Mishna.

[57] Cf. e.g. II Mac 7 21 where those persecuted by Antiochus speak "in the language
of their fathers" and also verse 27 where a mother comforts her son "in their native
tongue". So it is significant that while Ginsberg would place the composition
of the Aramaic "original" in the third cent. B.C., its translation into Hebrew could,
he says, be only in the Maccabean age (Studies in Koheleth 44).

[58] So-called from "Asamoneus" who according to Josephus (Antiq XII 61) was the
great-grandfather of Mattathias, father of Jonathan.

[59] Cf. Ez 40 46 43 19 44 15 I Chr 29 22. Cf. also I Mac 7 5. 12ff., where there is mention
of Alcimus of the house of Aaron. Aaron was a descendant of Levi (Ex 6 16-20),
and in Ez 43 19 Zadok is represented as of the tribe of Levi. According to Hauer,
JBL 82 (1963), 89ff., Zadok was a Jebusite priest who seceded to David prior
to the capture of Jebus by the Hebrews.

[60] Some scholars regard the Zadokite Documents discovered in Cairo, and first
published by Schechter in 1910, as the composition of a Priestly group who were
opposed to the elevation of an Hasmonean to the High Priesthood. A passage
thought to be particularly relevant is VI 12: "All those that have been brought
into the covenant ... have come into the sancturay so as to kindle his altar in
vain ..." (text as Rabin, The Zadokite Documents 1954, 22–23). See e.g. Kahle,
The Cairo Geniza, 1959, 19f. Whatever the date of these documents the Zadokite
priesthood is eulogised in more than one place: e.g. IV 1ff. V 5 XII 21.

These circumstances would together be conducive to the development and promotion of the Mishnaic idiom as the national tongue.
Almost a generation had passed since the beginning of the Maccabean
persecutions. The rising generation as a whole would become more
accustomed to the use of Mishnaic Hebrew, and by the year 140 or so
it must have been used extensively as a literary medium.

(5)

It is likely, however, that Koheleth was written before this date.
For while it has some Mishnaic elements, it still retains too many of the
characteristics of biblical Hebrew to suggest that it was composed in a
period which was likely to be predominantly Mishnaic. Corroborative
evidence for this view may perhaps be found in the Zadokite Documents and similar material discovered at Qumran[61]. For when the Sectarians departed there, they apparently took with them a copy of the
Book of Koheleth[62]. If therefore we could determine the date of their
departure we could establish a *terminus ante quem* for the composition
of the work. We have noticed earlier (p. 143 n. 60) that the Sectarians
appear to have been opposed to the promotion of a non-Zadokite to
the Jerusalem High Priesthood. But the immediate circumstances of
their flight seem also to be connected with a risk of incurring persecution for their views. Jonathan, as we have seen, became High Priest in
152, but for the remainder of his career he seems to have been too occupied with military and political problems to concern himself with the
relatively minor issues of religious controversy (I Mac 10₆₇–12₄₆). Even

---

[61] This is, of course, on the assumption that the historical background of the found-
ing of the Sect at Qumran is the Maccabean-Hasmonean period. See e.g. Rowley,
The Zadokite Fragments and the Dead Sea Scrolls, 1952, 64 ff.; Kahle, The Cairo
Geniza, 1959, 19 f.; Rabinowitz, VT 3 (1953), 175–185; Cross, Jr., The Ancient
Library of Qumran, 1958, 80 ff. Other scholars place the Scrolls considerably
later. Cf. e.g. Roth, The Historical Background of the Dead Sea Scrolls, 1958,
who argues that, while the Sect traced its history back to the early second century
B.C., it was not till the second half of the first century B.C. that its activities began
(especially pp. 63 ff.); Driver, The Judean Scrolls, 1965, who regards the Scrolls
as contemporary with the writings of the New Testament (589 f.). Archaeological
evidence indicates however, that the site of Qumran was occupied at least as early
as the reign of Alexander Janneus (103–76 B.C.). Cf. Cross op.cit. 43; de Vaux,
L'archéologie et les manuscrits de la Mer Morte, 1961, 53; Mansoor, The Dead
Sea Scrolls, in: The Book and The Spade, 1975³, 19–26.
[62] See Muilenburg, BASOR, 135 (1954), 20–28, who thinks that the Scroll dates
from about 150 B.C.

at the time of his death in 142, Syrian soldiers still occupied the garrison of Acra in Jerusalem. But shortly after his accession, Simon succeeded in overwhelming the final remnants of Syrian rule. This naturally endeared Simon to his people, and in the year 140 B.C. they posted in the precincts of the Temple a decree outlining the terms of his rulership. This decree contained the following significant clauses: "And the Jews and their priests decided that Simon should be their leader and high priest for ever . . . and that he should take charge of the sanctuary . . . and that he should be obeyed by all . . . And none of the people or priests shall be permitted to nullify any of these decisions or to oppose what he says, or to convene an assembly in the country without his permission . . . whoever acts contrary to these decisions or nullifies any of them shall be liable to punishment" (I Mac 14 41-45). It was the object of this document that Simon should henceforth be acknowledged as the supreme authority in ecclesiastical and civil affairs. However, in referring to him as "high priest for ever" it deliberately contravenes the statement earlier expressed in Ben Sira that the house of Zadok should hold the office of "high priesthood for ever", כהונה גדולה עד עולם (45 24).

That Simon, a Hasmonean, was accorded this title could only be regarded with dismay by the supporters of the Zadokite claim to the High Priesthood; and they might well have been tempted to continue their opposition to the appointment. But such a course would clearly be in defiance of the published decree and incur the displeasure of Simon. To avoid persecution they accordingly seem to have migrated to a retreat in the desert[63], taking with them copies of the scriptures, one of which was the book of Koheleth. It is then probable that the migration took place soon after the publication of Simon's decree in the year 140 B.C.[64] But Koheleth must have been composed earlier than this;

---

[63] Cf. e.g. Zadokite Documents VI 5. 19 VIII 14r.

[64] Cf. Cross, The Ancient Library of Qumran, 103 ff. Some scholars would place the migration earlier than this. See e.g. Kahle op.cit. 19, who would place it in the reign of Antiochus Epiphanes (c. 175–164 B.C.); Rabinowitz loc.cit. 183, who places the composition of the Damascus Fragments as early as 167–165. Of course, Menelaus was High Priest from 172–163, and according to II Mac (3 4 4 23 ff.) he was of the tribe of Benjamin, and therefore of non-Zadokite descent; but Old Latin sources represent him as of the family of Bilgah, which is mentioned in Neh 12 5 in connection with "the priests and the Levites" (12 1). Again, according to Josephus (Antiq XII v 1) "Menelaus" was but another name for "Onias". Cf. Rowley, Menelaus and the Abomination of Desolation, in: Studia Orientalia Ioanni Pedersen, 1953, 303 ff. It is also possible that "Benjamin" may be a corruption of *Miniamin*, an order of priests. See Pfeiffer, History of New Testament Times, 11 and n. 7. However, it was not till the decree in 140 that there

for, apart from the consideration mentioned above (p. 144) that it
must have been written before the Mishnaic language became predo-
minant, we must allow a certain lapse of time for its circulation and
recognition. These observations, together with our earlier contention
(p. 136f.) that the language and thought of Koheleth are later than the
book of Daniel, suggest that Koheleth was written sometime between
Daniel and Simon's decree.

It is, of course, maintained that we can hardly conceive of such a
work being composed and accepted as scripture in the environment of
the awakened national and religious consciousness of the Maccabean
age [65]. It is true that we could scarcely place the work in the early days
of the Maccabean struggles, when, under the leadership of Judah
(c. 165–160 B.C.) passions were inflamed against Seleucid rule. But in
152 when Jonathan was appointed ruler and High Priest by Alexander
Ballas the situation changed. Appointment to a priestly office on the
authority of the secular power was in accordance with Greek custom,
and as this was previously a Zadokite hereditary office it had far-reach-
ing effects. For it denoted a departure from traditional Judaism and a
movement in the direction of Greek practice [66]. Koheleth who seems
to have been an interested observer for some time would be fully aware
of the significance of these developments, since their implications would
accord with his own negative attitude to Judaism and his susceptibili-
ties to Hellenic culture. He would thus now be encouraged to give
literary form to his views, and, novel as they were in an Israelite context,
they would not be disturbing to those Jews already attracted to Greek
thought. It would then appear that Jonathan's appointment as ruler and
High Priest in the year 152 was the background of Koheleth's literary
activity.

---

was any indication that a non-Zadokite would permanently hold the office. The
prime object of this decree was to establish Simon and his family in the office
"for ever". There was now, therefore, every reason why the supporters of the
Zadokite claim should emigrate and conduct their worship in accordance with their
own religious views. We are not, of course, concerned here with the date of the
composition of the Zadokite Documents which tell of the migration (VI 5,19
VII 14f.). If this took place in 140 B.C., then the composition of the Documents
would be later still.

[65] So e.g. Ginsberg, VTS 3 (1955), 148.

[66] Cf. Bickerman: "Judah's lifework had been to prevent the threatening Helleni-
sation of Judaism and the surrender of the Torah ... Jonathan and his successors,
his brother Simon and Simon's descendants, will now seek to accommodate
Hellenism to Judaism. Under them Judea becomes a Hellenistic principality"
(The Maccabees, Eng. trans. 1947, 64).

IV. CONCLUSIONS

In this period the various linguistic features of the work become explicable. The Aramaisms which led Zimmermann to think that the book is a translation from an Aramaic original composed about 300 B.C. find their explanations in the complex pattern of the linguistic environment during and after the Maccabean wars[67]. For while Aramaic had influenced the Hebrew language since the days of the Persian empire, it is likely that its influence was greater now than at any time. Hastened by the disruptions of the Antiochene persecutions (167–164), classical Hebrew had declined, and, in consequence, Aramaic assumed a more significant place even in the religious life of the Jewish community. Only thus can we explain the inclusion of an Aramaic portion in the book of Daniel. For however we account for the origin and purpose of this material, it would hardly be incorporated in the book unless Aramaic was intelligible to the people at large[68]. Nor need it surprise us that we can detect Aramaic as an element in the linguistic background of Koheleth. For Koheleth was no traditionalist, and readily accepted the linguistic materials to hand. Thus he did not hesitate to use such current idioms as אנפי מלך (8₂) and שלא ימצא האדם אחריו מאומה (7₁₄). אנפי מלך appears in Aḥiqar 101 and no doubt should be read instead of the meaningless אני פי מלך of the Massoretic text[69]. The phrase seems to have become popular through proverbial usage, and as our author is making use of such material here he chose to quote it in the language in which it was commonly known. So it is likely that we are to recognise the Syriac idiom ܐܫܟܚ ܒܐܬܪ (to find something after, to find fault with) in שלא ימצא האדם אחריו מאומה in 7₁₄. If Koheleth wished to express

---

[67] Cf. Kutscher (The Language and Linguistic Background of the Isaiah Scroll, 1 Q Isaᵃ, 1974, 11 f.) who refers to the "confusion of languages that must have reigned" in Palestine during the late Second Commonwealth.

[68] That Aramaic was generally understood in Palestine somewhat later may be seen from the Aramaic inscriptions which have been discovered. Thus we find on the tomb of Jason Aramaic inscriptions dating from the early first century B.C. See Avigad, IEJ 17 (1967), 101–111. Similarly we have an inscription in Aramaic on a coin of Alexander Janneus pertaining to the years 83 and 78 B.C. See Naveh, IEJ 18 (1968), 20–25.

[69] See above ad loc.

himself in Hebrew here, he might have used some such phrase as we find in Jer 12₆ קראו אחריך מלא (they call after you loudly), which the Targum renders אמרו עלך מלין בישין (they speak evil words concerning you)[70]. It seems that Koheleth used the idiom in our text because it had become part of the vernacular of his time. Again in 11₃ we find the proverbial saying, "In the place where the tree falls, *there it will be* שָׁם יְהוּא". It is thus likely that יהוא, the third person singular imperfect of the Aramaic הֲוָא, is original, and that the verb "to be" was commonly expressed in Aramaic at this period. It will further be recalled that in 10₈ the word for "pit" is גוּמָץ. This is the term employed in the Targum to translate שׁוּחָה (pit) in Prov 22₁₄ and 23₂₇, and again שַׁחַת (pit) in Prov 26₂₇. It was thus apparently used by Koheleth here because it was the common word for "pit" in his day.

But, as Koheleth himself exemplifies, there was also a movement in the direction of Mishnaic Hebrew at this time. Hence, while the irregular use of the definite article, which Zimmermann regards as a mark of translation from Aramaic, may to some extent be due to Aramaic influence, it is probable that it also reflects the influence of Mishnaic usage. Dahood's view that Koheleth was composed in Phoenician orthography in the fourth-third centuries B.C. is, as we have seen, open to some criticism. It may now be further observed that it is unlikely that a work composed in this period would exhibit such late linguistic traits as Aramaic and Mishnaic usages and the virtual abandonment of the Waw Consecutive.

Equally inadequate to account for the linguistic peculiarities of Ecclesiastes is the view generally accepted by commentators that it was composed in the fourth or third century B.C. The syntax, vocabulary and usage of much of the book indicate a time when the Hebrew language was in a state of transition from biblical to Mishnaic Hebrew, and contained, moreover, a considerable admixture of Aramaic. But at no time before the Maccabean-Hasmonean struggles was this true of Hebrew. A date therefore within the period 152–145 B.C. satisfies both the historical and linguistic considerations for the composition of the book.

---

[70] Cf. Driver, VT 4 (1954), 230 n. 2. Cf. also above ad.loc.

D. The Thought of Koheleth

I. GENERAL CHARACTERISTICS

The thought of Koheleth is no less unusual than his language. According to Barnes, "This strange book should be used cautiously (if at all) as an authority, for it gives the speculations of a recluse, and not any generally accepted doctrine". So in the opinion of Dillon, the book consists of "A tissue of loose disjointed aphorisms and contradictory theses, concerning the highest problems of ethics and metaphysics. The form of the work is characterised by an utter lack of plan; the matter by almost impenetrable obscurity"[1]. There appears to be some justification for this estimate of the work; and this seems to be more surprising when it is realised that we can hardly explain such inconsistencies on the grounds of diversity of authorship. For while in the past some scholars attributed the work to more than one hand[2], modern scholarship is inclined to regard it, apart from the initial (1_{1-2}) and final (12_{8-12}) verses, as essentially the composition of a single author[3]. It is thus on the assumption that the work derives substantially from Koheleth himself that we must consider its contents and thought.

Koheleth is primarily concerned to study and portray the conditions in which man lives, but he seems to approach his task with the conviction that all experience of life is "vain" (1_{14} $2_{1.11.15.17}$). Thus it is pointless for a man to engage in work, for although he may amass goods and possessions he never enjoys them. Indeed these possessions are the

---

[1] These quotations appear among the interesting opinions about the book collected in the Frontispiece of Ecclesiastes or The Preacher by A. D. Power, 1952.

[2] E.g. Siegfried who detected five different authors in addition to two editors and two epilogists, Prediger Salomonis und Hoheslied, 1898², 2–12; Jastrow, who recognised substantial additions by "pious" commentators, "maxim" commentators, as well as miscellaneous comments and glosses, A Gentle Cynic, 1919, 71 ff. 245 ff.; Haupt who not only argued that a great part of the work consists of glosses, but also proposed a radical rearrangement of the existing material (The Book of Ecclesiastes, 1905, 8–33).

[3] Cf. e.g. Hertzberg, Der Prediger, 35–42; Kroeber, Der Prediger, 30–40; Loretz, Qoheleth und der Alte Orient, 212–217; Braun, Kohelet und die frühhellenistische Popularphilosophie, 166.

source of his misery. A man may possess riches, but for some reason God does not allow him to enjoy them, and so they pass to another (6₁ff.) who may even be a fool (2₁₈ff.). Or, again, a man may hoard wealth only to lose it in an unlucky venture, with the consequent impoverishment of himself and his heir (5₁₃). Accordingly "all man's days are painful, his task is irksome, and even at night his mind cannot rest" (2₂₃). Such speculations prompt the notion that it is an unhappy lot which God has bestowed on man (1₁₃ 3₁₁).

This "vanity" of living seems to spring from man's inability to discern his place and function in life, and from his utter ignorance of the future. "Who knows", he asks, "what is good for man while he lives the few days of his vain life, which he passes like a shadow . . . who can tell what will be after him under the sun?" (6₁₂). Again he complains, "that which is, is far off, and deep very deep, who can find it out?" (7₂₄); but even more pessimistic still is his statement, "man cannot find out the work that is done under the sun. However much man may toil in seeking, he will not find it" (8₁₇). Our author tells us that he is resolved to acquaint himself with wisdom and folly, but, alas, discovers that wisdom is but vexation, and that knowledge only increases sorrow (1₁₇f.). One fate befalls the wise man and the fool alike, for no one remembers the wise man any more than the fool (2₁₅f.). Life is confused and chaotic. Even the roles of various levels of society are reversed; the fool sits in a place of honour, while the man of consequence sits in a low place; so slaves ride on horseback while princes go on foot (10₆₋₇). In a world where values are so confused, effort is futile; "the race is not to the swift or the battle to the strong", nor has the man of wisdom and skill any advantage over the fool (9₁₁). All man's toil is for his mouth, but even so he is not satisfied (6₇). Some pleasure may indeed be gained from food and wine (10₁₉) and from the comforts of a wife and home (9₉). But even the pleasures of wine have their limits, and although Koheleth deprived himself of nothing that his eyes desired, he failed to find satisfaction in life (2₃. 10f.).

Life, then, is a weary, futile, round of existence; and this may even be inferred from nature. The sun rises and sets, the wind blows and veers to the four points of the compass, streams continuously flow to the sea, yet it is no fuller (1₅₋₇). This repetitive process produces unutterable weariness (1₈), and compels the belief that there is nothing new, all has happened before. Past events are not remembered, nor will future events be noted; they will all be forgotten in the oblivion which has overwhelmed past ages (1₉₋₁₁): "That which is, already has been;

that which will be already is . . ." (3_{15}). This pointless cycle of existence, with all its cares and miseries, is even worse by reason of the manifest injustice in it. The righteous and the wicked, the good and the evil are alike rewarded (8_{14} 9_{2}); the righteous man perishes in his righteousness, and the wicked prolongs his life in his wickedness (7_{15}). The weak and oppressed are in tears and there is no one to comfort them, while the powerful oppressors are merciless (4_{1}). Accordingly Koheleth regards the dead as more fortunate than the living, but better than both are those yet unborn and so are oblivious of the evil that is done on earth (4_{2-3}). Nor has man, since he is no different from the animal, any hope for the future: "As one dies, so does the other. They all have the same breath, and man has no advantage over the beasts . . . all go to one place; all are from the dust, and all turn to dust again. Who knows whether the spirit of man goes upward and the spirit of the beast goes down to the earth?" (3_{19-20}). Their destiny thus appears to be the same, and in the judgement of Koheleth they are both destined for extinction.

Such aspects of Koheleth's thought have raised the question of their origin. Are they the product of Koheleth's own thinking, or can we recognise external influences in them? These are questions which have been variously answered.

II. THEORIES OF BABYLONIAN AND EGYPTIAN INFLUENCE

Babylonian literature which affords so many parallels with earlier Hebrew writings is naturally thought to have been a source for Koheleth's work. Thus Barton thought that 9 7-9 is to be associated with a passage from the *Epic of Gilgamesh*:

> When the gods created mankind
> Death for mankind they set aside,
> Life in their own hand retaining.
> Thou, Gilgamesh, let full be thy belly,
> Make thou merry by day and by night.
> Of each day make thou a feast of rejoicing,
> Day and night dance thou and play!
> Let thy garments be sparkling fresh,
> Thy head be washed; bathe thou in water.
> Pay heed to the little one that holds on to thy hand,
> Let thy spouse delight in thy bosom!
> For this is the task of (mankind)! [4]

Not only did Barton pronounce the passage in Koheleth as "strikingly similar" to this, but thought that in parts the Hebrew seems to be a translation of the Babylonian [5]. More recently Loretz has argued that Koheleth's view of *hbl* (Windhauch) is already discernible in Gilgamesh's remark to his companion Enkidu, "All what you do is merely Wind (*šāru*)!", and he thus regards the Babylonian work as "a partial forerunner of the book of Qoheleth". A comparison between Koh 9 7-9 and the speech of the ale-wife in the *Epic of Gilgamesh* further leads him to think that Koheleth was acquainted with the Epic in its entirety or in the form of an abstract [6].

---

[4] Translated by Speiser in ANET, 90a iii.

[5] The Book of Ecclesiastes 39.

[6] Op. cit. 126–128. Loretz, on the other hand, fails to see either Egyptian or Greek elements in the book, 89 and 56. The notion of Greek influence is equally unacceptable to Gordon who proposes an exclusively Babylonian milieu for the work, IEJ 5 (1955), 85–88. Cf. too Rainey who favours a similar milieu, CTM 35 (1964), 149 f. However, while maintaining that Koheleth must have known the Gilgamesh

Egyptian literature, with which so much Israelite proverbial material is associated, has again been proposed as the source of Koheleth's teaching. Humbert has been the principal advocate of this view, and has offered much evidence in support of his claim[7]. He contends that the assumption of royal authorship, the style and contents of the book, can only be explained in terms of Egyptian influence. Thus such didactic compositions as *The Instruction for King Merikare*, and *The Instruction of King Amememhet*, ascribed to Egyptian rulers, account for Koheleth's pretentions to royal status (107). Koheleth's sayings which are in the form of a dialogue (e. g. 2_1 1_{16} 2_{15}) again find literary precedence in the *Lamentations of Khekheperre-Sonbu* and in the *Dialogue of the Weary Man* in which the authors speak to their hearts and confide their sorrows in them (109). Koheleth's attempts to attain a distinctive style, together with his editor's corroboration of this (12_{9-10}), is similarly to be compared with *Khekheperre-Sonbu* in which a priest in Heliopolis expresses the hope "to find unknown words, original phrases, expressed in novel language never used before . . ." (109)[8]. So the expression "under the sun" which Koheleth uses so frequently represents an Egyptian notion symbolising the world, or "that which the sun traverses in its course" (110). Pessimism, which is so prominent a feature of Koheleth's thinking, is again characteristic of Egyptian literature (110). Its classic expression is the *Dialogue of the Weary Man* who claims, "Death stands before me today like the return of invalids to health or going out after an illness. Death stands before me today like the scent of myrrh . . .". It is this pessimism which gives rise to the attitude of *carpe diem*, the notion that man should enjoy life while he can; and so the *Song of the Harpist*, which was sung at funeral banquets and describes the vanity of existence, ends with a plea to enjoy the pleasures which life affords: "Follow your desires as long as you live. Put perfumes on your head; deck yourself with fine linen and anoint yourself with the most precious substances of those offered to the gods . . . Make each day a feast and do not tire of it. Look, no one can take his possessions with him, look, none of those who have left us return". Similarly the Weary Man himself

---

Epic in some form or another, Forman thinks that his teaching has also points of contact with the pessimism of Egypt and the *Aḥiqar* collection (JSS 3, 1958, 336–342).

[7] *Recherches sur les sources égyptiennes de la littérature sapientiale d'Israël*, 1929, 107–124.

[8] The text of the Egyptian quotations throughout our consideration of Humbert's views is an English rendering of the French translation offered by him.

says, "Follow the good day, forget care", while in an inscription on the
tomb of Petosiris (c. 333 B.C.) we read, "Drink, get drunk, feast continually. Follow (the inspiration of) your hearts while (you are) on the
earth . . . When a man leaves his goods are lost" (112). It is, therefore,
against a background of such thought that we should view such passages
in Koheleth as 2₂₄ 5₁₇ and 9₇-₉ (110–112).

Humbert now claims (113f.) that his general conclusions so far
drawn are strengthened by reference to detailed passages in our author.
Thus Koheleth 2₄f., which mentions the building of houses and the
construction of pleasure grounds, is to be linked with the maxim of *Ani*,
"You have ploughed lands with hedges, you have planted a ring of
sycamores. But one grows tired of all that" (*Maxims of Ani* § 23). So
the mention of women singers and such persons in verse ₈ could hardly
relate to a Jewish environment where such luxuries were rare, but would
be quite explicable in an Egyptian setting of the harem and of female
singers performing seductive dances (115). Again Koheleth's mention
of time and season in 3₁-₈ recalls a thought to be found in the Insinger
Papyrus 2₁-₂: "Food is good in its time and . . . sleep is good in time
of feebleness . . .". Koheleth's reference to social injustice in 3₁₆ and
acts of oppression in 4₁ are likewise to be compared with the social
diatribes common in Egyptian literature. For example, in the *Peasant's
Lament* we read, "See, in your land justice is badly administered, it is
banished from its rightful place. State officials commit crimes . . . Those
who should investigate steal. The man who should arrest a man guilty
of deception makes himself liable to the same accusation" (§ 26). When
again Koheleth speaks contemptuously of hierarchical officialdom (5₈),
he reminds us of the political anomalies and social scandals complained
of in the *Advice of an Egyptian Sage*, the *Lamentations of Khekheperre-Sonbu*
and the *Prophecies of Nefer-rehu* (116). Koheleth's warning against multi-
plying words in worship and his depreciation of sacrifice in comparison
with the silent homage of the heart (4₁₇-5₁) is likewise in harmony with
the sentiments of Egyptian Wisdom literature. Thus in *Ani* we read,
"God's sanctuary, what he abhors is noisy demonstrations. Pray humbly
with a loving heart, whose words are all expressed in secret. He will
protect you in your doings, he will listen to your word . . .". *Amenemope*
again recommends the same ideal of silence when he contrasts the silent
man who is discreet and modest with the man who is unrestrained and
noisy (117f.). In Koh 10₆-₇ there is mention of the fool and the slave
occupying the places of rich men and princes. This too, argues Humbert,
owes something to the Egyptian moralist who in the *Advice of a Sage*

wrote: "In truth the poor now own riches and he who could not afford sandals possesses treasures . . . He who had no servants is now master of (numerous) slaves and he who was important now looks after his own affairs" (121). Humbert again naturally compares Koh 10₈, referring to the fate of a man who digs a pit, with the Egyptian proverb, "He who stretches nets will catch himself in them, he who evilly digs a ditch will fall into it, he who sharpens a blade will have his own neck struck with it" (121). Finally, the description of old age in Koh 12₂ﬀ. is to be related to a passage in *Ptahhotep*: "Old age is come and age is descended. Weakness has come and we fall back into childishness. The weary man has lost his strength. The mouth is silent and no longer utters words. The sight is weak and the ears are deaf . . . The bones are ill with old age . . .". But another Egyptian work (*Insinger Papyrus* 17₁₁₋₁₄) contains, he thinks, a passage on old age which is even closer to the thought of Koheleth: "He who has lived sixty years has lived all that was before him. If he wants wine, he cannot drink as much as he would wish; if he wants food, he cannot eat as he used to. If his heart wants a woman he remains frigid(?) . . ." (122–123).

From these and other considerations Humbert concluded that Egyptian influence on Koheleth is clear and tangible, while the view that the work might be influenced by Greek thought is fraught with problems. Indeed Humbert sees such overwhelming Egyptian influence on the work that he assumes that Koheleth spent some time in Egypt and was acquainted with the Egyptian language. This, he thinks, explains our author's style and the literary mould in which the work is cast, as well as the breadth of his interests and the pronounced non-Jewish flavour of his thought (124). In a concluding paragraph he observes that Koheleth's use of אלהים – האלהים, with or without the article, corresponds exactly to the frequent use of *nṯr* (god) or *pꜣnṯr* (the god) which we frequently find in Egyptian moral literature (124).

Gemser, again, finds similarities between Koheleth and the collection of proverbs in the Egyptian *Instruction of ʿOnchsheshonqy*[9]. Some of these proverbs are but variations of those already noted by Humbert, but Gemser detects further points of contact. Thus he compares ʿOnchsheshonqy's saying "Do a good deed and throw it into the river; when this dries up you shall find it" with v. 1 of Koh chapter 11, "Cast your bread upon the waters . . .", and also with v. 4 which advises that a man about to sow his seed should not be concerned with the wind,

---

[9] The Instructions of ʿOnchsheshonqy and Biblical Wisdom Literature, in: VTS 7 (1960), 125–26.

and that a man about to reap should not regard the clouds. Koh 10₁₅, "The toil of a fool wearies him (?) so he does not know the way to the city", likewise resembles 'Onchsheshonqy 23. 1₁₂ "The way of God is open for everyone, the good-for-nothing does not know how to find it". So he thinks that *bêth 'ôlām* as the name of the grave in Koh 12₅ recalls the Egyptian "Let him attain his house of eternity (unconcerned)". These comparisons prompt Gemser to ask whether "in Koheleth an Egyptian background, or at least some connection with Egyptian Wisdom is not likely" (126).

It must be acknowledged that both Humbert and Gemser have brought to our attention interesting and relevant parallels between Egyptian Wisdom Literature and Koheleth. Yet Humbert's assumption of exclusive Egyptian influence on Koheleth is questionable in view of the parallels of thought also obtaining between our author and both Babylonian and Greek literature. Thus Humbert compares Koh 6₇₋₉ with material from the Egyptian *Song of the Harpist* recommending man to follow his heart, to dress in fine linen and anoint his person. But this passage in Koheleth may equally be compared with the extract from the Epic of Gilgamesh quoted above (152). Humbert again connected a passage in Koh (10₆₋₇), dealing with the reversal of the roles of the great and humble, with certain lines in the *Admonitions of an Egyptian Sage*, but in the Babylonian *Ludlul bel nemeqi* we also read, "I who strode along as a noble, have learned to slip by unnoticed. Though a dignitary, I have become a slave . . . my slave has publicly cursed me in the assembly" [10]. The pessimism in Koheleth with which Humbert compares the *Dialogue of the Weary Man* also occurs in Babylonian literature. Thus the sufferer in *The Babylonian Theodicy* complains:

> My body is a wreck, emaciation darkens (me).
> My success has vanished, my *stability* has gone.
> My strength is enfeebled, my prosperity has ended.
> Moaning and grief have blackened my features . . .
> Can a life of bliss be assured? I wish I knew how [11].

The chief character in *The Dialogue of Pessimism* displays the same attitude. Refusing to participate in the various occupations and pleasure of life, he finally says to his slave,

> To have my neck and your neck broken,
> and to be thrown into the river is good [12].

---

[10] Ls. 77–78. 89, as translated by Lambert, Babylonian Wisdom Literature, 1960, 35.
[11] Ls. 27f., as Lambert 73.   [12] Ls. 80f.

Concern over the uncertainty of the future and the unknown is, again, a theme in Koheleth and in the Wisdom Literature of both Babylonia and Egypt. Koheleth complains that it is impossible to find out what God's purpose for man is (3₁₁ 8₁₇), the author of *Ludlul bel nemeqi* asks, "Who knows the will of the gods in heaven? Where have the mortals learnt the way of a god?"[13], while in the Egyptian Petosiris inscription we read, "Nobody knows the day when death will come, it is the god who makes men's heart forgetful of this . . ."[14].

But some of these themes common to Koheleth and to Babylonian and Egyptian sages are also found in Greek works. That man should enjoy himself in life is emphatically stated by Amphis (4th cent. B.C.): "Drink and play, death ends our life, and short is our time on earth. But, once we are dead, there is no end of death"; and likewise, "One who is born to die and does not seek to add some pleasure to life . . . is a fool under heaven's curse"[15]. Again, commenting on the changes in the social order, Theognis could say: "Labourers rule; the base have the upper hand of the noble"[16]. So, of man's uncertainty of the future, Pindar complains: "No man upon earth has found a sure token from heaven of how it shall fare with him. Warnings of what will come are wrapt in blind darkness"[17].

---

[13] Ls. 36–38; cf. too The Babylonian Theodicy where we read "the plan of the gods is remote", 1.58.
[14] Text as Humbert 115.
[15] Gynaecocratia, as Cornford, Greek Religious Thought, 1923, 247.
[16] L. 679.
[17] Olympian xii i, as Cornford 115.

III. THE THEORY OF GREEK INFLUENCE

In view of such pronouncements on life it is not surprising that some scholars maintain that Greek influence is to be discerned in Koheleth. This claim was advanced as early as 1792 by Zirkel[18], and Greek elements in the work have subsequently been recognised by such commentators as Graetz, Plumptre, Siegfried, Wildeboer, Levy and Allgeier[19]. Again in a work entitled Ecclesiastes and the Early Greek Wisdom Literature (1925), Ranston argued in favour of this view, and thought that the influence of Theognis is particularly evident. Thus as Theognis claims "signal knowledge of wisdom"[20] (709), so Koheleth (1_{16} 2_9) claimed that he was more wise than any man before him in Jerusalem (15). Theognis again (133f., 165f.) attributes loss and gain, happiness and unhappiness to the deity, and Ranston thinks (16f.) that such passages in Koheleth as 2_{24} 3_{13} 9_7 and 11_5 are of similar purport. Koheleth 6_{10} which states that man is not able to contend with one stronger than himself is likewise reminiscent of Theognis line 687, "Tis not for mortals to fight with Immortals, nor to argue with them" (17). So, certain verses in Koheleth, referring to man's inability to tell the future (e.g. 3_{11} 6_{12} 7_{24}), are to be compared with Theognis 135ff., "No man toils, knowing within his heart whether the issue be good or ill ... Our thoughts are vain; we know nothing, the gods accomplish all things according to their own mind" (18). Theognis again protests at the indiscrimination which marks the fortunes of the righteous and the unrighteous: "How, then, Son of Kronos, dost thou think fit to deal out the same portion to wicked and just ...?" (377f.). "The unrighteous and wicked man, shunning the wrath neither of man nor the Immortals, waxes wanton, and is glutted with wealth, whereas the righteous are worn out distressed by sore poverty" (749ff.). Noting these lines of Theognis, Ranston points to such passages in Koheleth

---

[18] Untersuchungen über den Prediger.

[19] Graetz, Kohélet oder der Salomonische Prediger, 1871; Plumptre, Ecclesiastes 1885; Siegfried op.cit.; Wildeboer, Der Prediger, 1895; Levy, Das Buch Qoheleth: Ein Beitrag zur Geschichte des Sadduzäismus, 1912; Allgeier, Das Buch des Predigers oder Koheleth, 1925.

[20] The translation of Theognis here is that offered by Ranston.

as 2_{14-16} 6_8 3_{16} and 9_{11} and observes that they are in similar strain (19). Ranston again suggests (30) that Koheleth 4_2, where the dead are represented as being more fortunate than the living, is to be compared with Theognis' remark, "Of all things to men on earth it is best not to be born, nor to see the beams of the piercing sun, but, once born, as swiftly as may be to pass the gates of Hades and lie under a heavy heap of earth" (425 f.). But while Ranston thought that Koheleth was indebted to Theognis for the substance of these and other passages, he considers it unlikely that Koheleth actually consulted the writings of Theognis; rather his knowledge of the Greek writer depended on his acquaintance with the popular philosophy of the day (12. 61 f.).

Hesiod's *Works and Days* is another Greek work on which, in the opinion of Ranston, Koheleth was dependent. He would thus interpret (64–67) the material of Koheleth 4_{4-6} against the background of lines 11–41. In these lines Hesiod mentions that there are two kinds of rivalry; the one good and the other bad. The good has the effect of encouraging a man to emulate the worthy achievements of his neighbour: thus a potter strives to attain the high standards of a good potter, while a craftsman attempts to achieve the efficiency of a skilled craftsman. Such "rivalry is good for mortals" (l. 24). Evil rivalry, on the contrary, is productive of laziness and idleness, and creates envy and discontent amongst men. Ranston, then, regards (67) v. 4_{-6} of chapter 4 as a unit; that is to say, all toil and skilful arts have their origin in the rivalry of one man with another; the fool brings ruin on himself through laziness, and a few possessions enjoyed in quietness brings more happiness than much wealth amassed in care and sorrow. Koheleth's reference to the enthralling snares of a woman (7_{26}) is likewise, according to Ranston (68), to be compared with Hesiod's description of a woman as "deadly" and "a sheer snare from which there is no escape" (l. 83). Again, he thinks it possible (69) that Hesiod's dictum "the fitting time is best in all things" (694) is a primary source of Koheleth 3_{2-8} which expounds the theme of a season for everything. So when Koheleth exclaims, "Say not, why were the former days better than these"? (7_{10}), he is not referring to the sentiments which a man in old age may entertain of his youth. Rather, says Ranston (72 f.), there is a reference here to the Hesiodic view of the deterioration of the successive ages of the world. In 7_{13} Koheleth asks, "Who can make straight (לתקן) what he has made crooked": this again, argues Ranston (74), is not dependent on κοσμεῖν τἄκοσμα of the Stoic writer Cleanthes, but on the simple Hesiodic line "Easily he (Zeus) ἰθύνει σκολιόν—staightens the crooked" (7). But,

although Ranston discerns Hesiodic influences on these and other instances in Koheleth, he thinks that the Jewish writer does not offer a
translation of any of them. It is more likely that his knowledge of the
Greek author depends on remembering what he read, or possibly, on
the Hesiodic aphorisms current in his day.

Chapter 12₉, which states that Koheleth "taught the people knowledge, weighing and studying and arranging proverbs with great care",
led Ranston to confine Greek influence on the book to the gnomic
teaching of sages like Hesiod and Theognis. For he thinks that Koheleth would have been interested in practical aphorisms of this nature
rather than in the abstract philosophy of the Stoics and Epicurus (12).
It has, however, been contended not only that the influence of abstract
Greek philosophy is to be found in the book, but also that Greek literary
influence is to be discerned in it. Thus Plumptre regarded it as being
"throughout saturated with Greek thought and language" [21]. Allgeier
saw in the work the literary characteristics of the Stoic Diatribe [22], while
Levy recognised in it Cynic-Stoic and Cyrenaic ideas as well as influences
of the Greek language; for example, he would equate הבל in Koheleth
with τῦφος "illusion", and רעות רוח with κενὴ δόξα "empty wind" [23].
Again, as already noted under 3₁₂ and 5₁₇, commentators such as Wildeboer and Graetz regarded עשות טוב as the equivalent of the Greek εὖ
πράττειν, and טוב אשר יפה as καλὸν κἀγαθόν. More recently Braun has
argued that Koheleth was profoundly influenced by the language and
thought of the popular Greek philosophy of the third century B.C.
But, while scholars such as Ranston would limit Greek influence on
Koheleth to gnomic sayings of Hesiodic and Theognic origin, Braun
claims to recognise parallels in his work with the utterrances of almost
every known Greek writer, especially with Homer, Theognis, Euripedes
and Menander [24].

On the other hand, many scholars fail to see direct influence of
either Greek thought or language in Koheleth. McNeile indeed admitted
that some lines of Xenophanes (6th cent. B.C.) invite comparison with
a few passages in Koheleth. Thus Xenophanes' dictum that all things
come from the earth and ultimately return to it may be compared with
Koh 3₂₀, while again Xenophanes' view of man's uncertainty of the
future is reminiscent of Koh 7₂₃ and 8₁₇ [25]. But on the question of Stoic

---

[21] Op. cit. 32.   [22] Op. cit. 6 ff.   [23] Op. cit. 11 ff.
[24] Kohelet und die frühhellenistische Popularphilosophie *passim*, and especially
146 ff.
[25] An Introduction to Ecclesiastes 45 f.

influence on our author, McNeile observed that the Stoic founder Zeno
was of Phoenician descent whose followers came from such places as
Syria, Seleucia on the Tigris, and Carthage. In other words, Stoicism
had its origin in the Oriental and especially the Semitic mind. McNeile
accordingly declared that a study of Koheleth shows not that he wrote
under the influence of Greek philosophy, but that *as a thinking Jew he
had the makings of a Greek philosopher*[26]. Barton agreed with McNeile's
argument in respect of Stoicism, and added that if a similarity of thought
is to be discerned between Koheleth and Epicurus, it is due to their
teaching being based on an Old Babylonian concept which was, however, developed independently by each author[27]. He thus concluded that
the book of Ecclesiastes represents "an original development of Hebrew
thought, thoroughly Semitic in its point of view, and quite independent
of Greek influence"[28]. Gordis would disagree that Koheleth was entirely
independent of Greek influence, and rather thinks that he would have
been familiar with the popular doctrines of the Schools which formed
the intellectual climate of his age. Nevertheless, he contends that what
is remarkable about Koheleth is not his familiarity with such doctrines,
"but his *completely original and independent use of these ideas to express his own
unique world view*"[29]. Zimmerli expressed the opinion that Greek influence
on the book has not been satisfactorily proved, especially since his
critical attitude to life and its possibilities is discernible in ancient
Oriental literature[30]. Hertzberg was, again, doubtful if Koheleth reflects
a profound influence of Greek philosophy. He appears indeed to be
acquainted with the teachings of Theognis, Epicurus and the Stoics,
but his writings show no literary dependence on them[31]. That Koheleth
was aware of the intellectual movements of the day, but was not consciously influenced by them, is similarly the view of recent commentators
such as Kroeber, Strobel and Barucq[32].

---

[26] 44.   [27] Op. cit. 39–43.   [28] 43.
[29] Koheleth: The Man and His World 56.
[30] Das Buch des Predigers Salomo 128.
[31] Der Prediger 56–60.
[32] Kroeber op. cit. 47; Strobel, Das Buch Prediger (Kohelet), 15f.; Barucq,
Ecclésiaste, 31f. Cf. also Hengel, Judentum und Hellenismus, 1973², 210–237.

E. Reconstruction

I. ISRAELITE SOURCES

We certainly allow that there is Greek influence on Koheleth, but before offering our own interpretation of the nature of this influence, it will be an advantage to discern first the extent of his indebtedness to Israelite sources. Koheleth's familiarity with parts of the canonical Old Testament is commonly recognised[1]. For example, in saying that it is better to draw near to listen than to offer the sacrifice of fools, Koheleth (4₁₇ Heb.) seems to be aware of I Sam 15₂₂, "to obey is better than sacrifice and to hearken better than the fat of rams". Again, when he declares that a vow made to God should be fulfilled immediately, since its omission has unfortunate consequences (5₄. ₆ Heb.), he appears to be influenced by Deut 23₂₁, "When you make a vow to the Lord your God, you shall not be slack to pay it; for the Lord your God will surely require it of you, and it would be sin in you". Koheleth's remark that there is not a righteous man who does good and does not sin (7₂₀) is similarly reminiscent of I Reg 8₄₆ where we read "there is no man who does not sin". But Koheleth's familiarity with the Old Testament is, of course, in view of the sapiential nature of his work, more pronounced in respect of the book of Proverbs. Thus the good name which Koheleth regards as "better than ointment" (7₁) is clearly a reflection of Prov 22₁ where we find that "a good name is to be chosen rather than great riches". When we read in Koh 4₅ of the fool folding his hands and eating his own flesh we, likewise, recall Prov 6₁₀ "a little folding of the hands to rest, and poverty will come upon you like a vagabond". Koh 7₁₉, claiming that the strength of a wise man exceeds that of ten rulers, appears again to be based on Prov 21₂₂, "A wise man scales the city of the mighty and brings down the stronghold in which they trust". Similarly, Koheleth's saying "the lips of a fool consume him" (10₁₂) is to be compared with Prov 18₇, "A fool's mouth is his ruin and his lips are a snare to himself". Koheleth's observation that the patient in spirit is better than the proud of spirit (7₈) is likewise reminiscent of Prob 14₂₉ and 16₃₂.

---

[1] Cf. above 119f. where we noted the linguistic similarities between Koheleth and certain Old Testament passages.

Finally when Koheleth represents himself as king over Israel searching out by wisdom what is done on earth (1 12-13) we are reminded of Prov 25 2 which declares that "the glory of kings is to search things out".

The similarity of much of Koheleth's material with that of Ben Sira is also recognised. But, whereas it is commonly held that Ben Sira is dependent on Koheleth, we have previously contended that, on the contrary, Ben Sira is the earlier work. We have advanced this claim on grounds of language, but we have also drawn attention to the fact that while the material in question is invariably germane to the context in Ben Sira, it is usually in the form of proverbial adaptations in Koheleth, thus indicating its derivative nature. A corollary of the priority of Ben Sira is, then, the recognition of that book as a source for Koheleth.

Koheleth's obsession with the futility of toil and effort is a dominant theme of his work (e.g. 1 2. 12-13; *et passim*), but Ben Sira too could write, "A man who works and toils and presses on is so much the more in want" (11 11), and again, "Much labour was created for every man, and a heavy yoke is upon the sons of Adam from the day they came forth from their mother's womb till they return to the mother of all" (40 1). Koheleth was concerned for the man who amasses wealth only to leave it to another (2 18-21 4 8): so in Ben Sira we read, "There is a man who is rich through his diligence and self-denial and . . . says 'I have found rest, and now I shall enjoy my goods'" but "he does not know how much time will pass until he leaves them to others and dies" (11 18-19). Koheleth believes that there is nothing better for men than to be happy and to enjoy themselves as long as they live: "the feast is made for laughter and wine gladdens life" (10 19), and man should eat his bread with enjoyment and drink his "wine with a merry heart" (9 7). Ben Sira similarly urged that man should not deprive himself of a happy day nor let his share of desired things pass by, for in Hades one cannot enjoy luxuries (14 14. 16). So wine drunk in moderation is vital to men; indeed "What is life to a man who is without wine?" Has it not "been created to make men glad?" (31 27). Koheleth again says that a man should enjoy life with the woman he loves (9 9), while Ben Sira was eloquent about the charms and companionship of a loyal wife (26 2-3 13-16 40 23). Likewise both authors warn against the dangers of a treacherous woman. Koheleth refers to her heart as a snare and her hands as fetters (7 26), while Ben Sira spoke of the snares of an evil woman and the intrigues of a female singer (9 3-4).

Koheleth likewise seems to have been familiar with certain material of a proverbial nature in Ben Sira. Koheleth condemns dreams on the ground that they tend to increase foolish words (5₂ Heb), while in Ben Sira 34₅ we find that divinations, omens and dreams are but folly. Koheleth's advice that it is indiscreet to curse the king even in the most private circumstances (10₂₀) again recalls Ben Sira's teaching on the folly of repeating a conversation (19₇f.). In Koh 10₁₁ we read, "If a serpent bites before it is charmed, there is no advantage in a charmer", while Ben Sira remarked, "Who will pity a snake charmer bitten by a serpent"? (12₁₃). Ben Sira counselled "In all your work be industrious" (31₂₂) and "Excel in all that you do" (33₂₂), while Koheleth paraphrased, "Whatever your hand finds to do, do it with your might" (9₁₀).

There are also points of similarity between the views of Ben Sira and Koheleth on the fate of the living and the dead. Ben Sira thought that a man was "born to a curse" (41₉), that "death is better than a miserable life" (30₁₇) and that no man is "happy before his death" (11₂₈). Man is created from dust (17₁) and when at death he returns to it, he is consumed by "creeping things" and "worms" (10₁₁). Koheleth considered the dead more fortunate than the living (4₂): life is but a few short days which man passes as a shadow (6₁₂), and when at last his end comes, he returns to the dust from whence he came (12₇).

Finally we notice that wisdom occupies a basic place in the thinking of the two authors. Ben Sira believed that the attainment of wisdom is possible only to those in leisurely circumstances, and is beyond the reach of those engaged in agricultural and artisan pursuits (38₂₄₋₃₄). For it is only by intense searching that man may acquire the secrets of wisdom (6₂₇. ₃₂f.). The formulation of proverbs is a painful task (13₂₆) and he himself confesses that it was only after much thought that he was able to compose the work he leaves in writing (39₃₂). This work of Ben Sira seems to have been recognised as the standard treatment of the day on wisdom. For, in the Preface to the Greek translation of the book, Ben Sira's grandson commends it enthusiastically to his readers. Koheleth could hardly fail to take notice of a work of such established reputation. Like Ben Sira, he applies himself to wisdom (1₁₃. ₁₇ 2₁₂), and repeatedly assures us that all his conclusions on the problems of life are the result of the most searching deliberations (7₂₃. ₂₅. ₂₈. ₂₉ 8₁₆).

II. GREEK INFLUENCE

In investigating these problems, Koheleth's alert, inquiring mind
extends beyond the book of Ben Sira, and therefore it is not surprising
that much of his thought reflects a knowledge of Greek views on life
and existence. Greek influence has, as we have seen, often been maintained by scholars who place Koheleth as early as the third century B.C.;
and it is likely that Greek influence affected Hebrew thought and culture
at such a period. According to Diodorus, Hecateus of Abdera then
observed: "When the Jews became subject to foreign rule, as a result
of their mingling with men of other nations, both under Persian rule
and under that of the Macedonians who overthrew the Persians, many
of their traditional practices were disturbed"[2]. But the nature of Greek
influence in Koheleth presupposes a sustained contact with Epicurean
thought which could hardly be possible before the reign of Antiochus
Epiphanes (175–164 B.C.). Antioch, the capital of the Seleucid kings,
was an important centre of Epicurean studies, and, under the influence
of the philosopher Philonides, Antiochus Epiphanes became a convert
to Epicureanism[3]. As a system of philosophy Epicureanism was practical in outlook, and, however attracted to it personally, Antiochus conceived of it as a means of uniting the peoples of his realm. This was
doubtless his motive in attempting to impose Greek thought and culture
on the Jews[4]. Thus in I Maccabees we read that in the year 167 B.C.
he "wrote to his whole kingdom that all should be one people, and that
each should give up his customs. All the Gentiles accepted the command

---

[2] Diodorus XL 3 (as trans. by Walton, LCL, 1967, 286f.). See further Lifshitz, RB
72 (1965), 520f., who studies the influence of Greek language and culture on the
Jews in Palestine after the conquests of Alexander, and also Hengel op. cit. 108 ff.

[3] See Bevan, The House of Seleucus II, 1902, 276f., and the relevant source passage
(Rheinisches Museum NF 56, 1901, 395) reproduced in Appendix X, 304; also
De Witt, Epicurus and His Philosophy, 1954, 334f., and Farrington, Anales de
Filología Clásica, 7 (1959), 24–25.

[4] Tcherikover (Hellenistic Civilisation and the Jews 118ff.) disputes the view that
Antiochus' decrees were issued against the Jews to compel them to accept Greek
culture, but rather that they were a response to a previous revolt by the Jews.
But this would be no less reason for his attempting to impose a unifying culture
on them.

of the king. Many, even from Israel, gladly adopted his religion . . ."
(1 41-43). There was indeed much initial opposition to this new culture
(cf. e.g. I Mac 2–3; II Mac 11 24), but so captivated were some Jewish
priests and the most distinguished (κρατίστους) of the youth of the
country by Greek gymnastics (II Mac 4 11ff.) that in the course of a
decade or so Greek thought must likewise have made a considerable
impression on the more sophisticated sections of the community. In
such an environment, an inquisitive mind like Koheleth's could not be
indifferent to the claims of one of the major systems of philosophy of
the day [5]. Accordingly both on his view of God and on his reflections
on certain aspects of life we detect Epicurean influence.

Epicurus declared that his deity, dwelling in intermundial spaces,
"knows no trouble itself nor causes trouble to any other, so that it is
never constrained by anger or favour" [6]. So, according to the Epicurean
disciple Lucretius, "it must needs be that all the nature of the gods
enjoys life everlasting in perfect peace, sundered and separated far away
from our world. For free from all grief, free from danger, mighty in
its own resources, never lacking aught of us, it is not won by virtuous
service nor touched by wrath" [7]. The gods do not, therefore, participate
in the government of the world or intervene in the affairs of men, for
such activity would be injurious to their serenity [8]. The notion that God
is remote, self-sufficient and reluctant to communicate with man is
similarly to be detected in a few passages in Koheleth. Thus in 5 1 (Heb.)
we read that God is in heaven and that man on earth should behave with
deference before him. According to 3 11 God chose to leave man in
"ignorance" lest he should discover signs of the divine activity in the
world. Even the wise man has little hope of attaining to this knowledge
(8 17). The detached nature of the Epicurean gods naturally prompted
the notion that there could be no communication with them. It is thus
not surprising that Epicurus could say, "Prophecy does not exist, and

---

[5] The term אפיקורוס (אפיקרס) appears in the Mishna (e.g. Aboth 2 14; Sanhed
   10 1) with the general meaning of unbeliever or sceptic. It is thought, however,
   that it derives from a root פקר "to break through, to be free, to be licentious";
   see, e.g. Danby, The Mishna, 1933, 397 n. 4, and Jastrow I, 104.
[6] Principal Doctrines 139, as Bailey, Epicurus, 1926, 95.
[7] Lucretius II, 646, trans. by Bailey, Lucretius (De Rerum Natura) I, 1947, 271.
[8] Cf. Hicks, Stoic and Epicurean, 1962 edn., 290f. Cf. too Josephus who regarded
   the Epicureans to be mistaken in excluding "providence from human life, and refuse
   to believe that God governs its affairs or that the universe is directed by a blessed
   and immortal Being . . . but say that the world runs by its own movement without
   knowing a guide or another's care", Antiq Bk X 278 (LCL, 1937, 311f.).

even if it did exist, things that come to pass must be accounted as
nothing to us"[9]. Here he seems to imply that if a prediction made by
some diviner happened to materialise, no one could lend credence to
it, since it would not amount to a message from the gods who by their
nature do not commune with man. So Koheleth has moods in which
he is overwhelmed by his inability to discover the future. In 8₆₋₈ he
complains that "man's trouble lies heavy upon him, for he does not
know what is to be" and "who can tell him how it will be?"; and elsewhere (6₁₂) he exclaims "Who knows what is good for man while he
lives the few days of his vain life which he passes as a shadow?".

Yet life with all its uncertainties was for Koheleth preferable to
death. There is some hope for the living: "a living dog is better than
a dead lion; for the living know that they will die, but the dead know
nothing" (9₄₋₅). Man should try to interest himself in earthly affairs,
"for there is no work or thought or knowledge or wisdom in Sheol to
which" he is "going" (9₁₀). Even the memory of man and his achievements, so highly esteemed by Ben Sira (ch. 44), are of no account, since
at death the memory of man perishes (9₅). Moreover, in his nihilistic
estimate of the dead Koheleth doubts whether there is any difference
in the ultimate destiny of man and beast. It is obvious that both alike
die, but he thinks that "man has no advantage over the beasts". On
the contrary, "all go to one place; all are from the dust, and all turn
to the dust again", and then he exclaims, "Who knows whether the spirit
of man goes upward and the spirit of the beast goes down to the earth"
(3₁₉₋₂₁). Death has accordingly a finality for Koheleth which we do
not find elsewhere in the Old Testament. Such passages as Gen 37₃₅,
I Sam 28₃₋₁₉ and Job 3₁₇₋₁₉ envisage some mode of existence for those
departed to Sheol, but for Koheleth death seems to indicate complete
extinction in which the fate of man is indistinguishable from that of the
animal.

Here too Koheleth seems to be influenced by Epicurus. For Epicurus believed that with the death of the body life came to an end:
"Death is deprivation of sensation . . . when death comes, then we do
not exist. It does not then concern either the living or the dead, since
for the former it is not, and the latter are no more"[10]. But the soul
(ψυχή) too, which was regarded as corporeal, when released from the
body is dissolved and perishes at death; for if the bodily structure "is
dissolved, the soul is dispersed and no longer has the same powers . . .

---

[9] Bailey, Epicurus, 121 No. 3.   [10] Bailey, Epicurus, 85.

so that it does not possess sensation either. For it is impossible to imagine it with sensation ... when what encloses and surrounds it is no longer the same as the surroundings in which it now exists and performs these movements"[11]. This release of the soul appears to apply to the animal as well, for Lucretius later remarked that the soul (*anima*) of a serpent survives only as long as it is contained in the body[12].

Koheleth's description of the onset and occurrence of death may equally reflect Epicurean thought. For Epicurus, as we noted, conceived of the body enclosing the soul, but on the dissolution of the body the soul was released only to perish as well. This conception of the body as constituting a vessel for the soul finds more explicit expression in Lucretius who remarked, "since the body which was, as it were, the vessel of the soul, cannot hold it together, when by some chance it is shattered . . ."[13]. So having mentioned the approach of death, Koheleth continues, "the silver cord is snapped, the golden bowl broken, the pitcher is broken at the fountain and the wheel broken at the cistern, and the dust returns to the earth as it was, and the spirit to God who gave it" (12_6-7). The metaphor is here doubtless complex, but it is likely that the reference to the breaking of the bowl and the pitcher is an allusion to the Epicurean notion that at death the body is shattered and the soul released from it.

Unlike Epicurus, however, Koheleth has a certain apprehension of death. He resents the brevity of life (6_12), regrets the passing of youth (11_10) and regards the hereafter as a place of unrelieved gloom (11_8). So in the beginning of chapter 12 he draws a sombre picture of the approach of death. There will be a cessation of the functions of natural phenomena; the sun, moon and stars will be darkened and there will be no light. Terror will interrupt the normal activities of life. Strong men and keepers will retire in fear from their tasks. Terrified people will glance from their windows as the mills grind to a halt and the doors are shut in the streets. Mourners have already appeared, for man has reached the end of his life and goes to his eternal home (v. 1-5). Epicurus, on the other hand, believed that death has no terrors for man, since it was the extinction of all sensation. Thus in a letter to Menoeceus he wrote: "a right understanding that death is nothing to us makes the mortality of life enjoyable, not because it adds to an infinite span of time, but because it takes away the craving for immortality. For there

[11] Bailey op. cit. 41.   [12] Lucretius III, 657 ff.
[13] Lucretius III, 440 f., as Bailey, Lucretius (*De rerum Natura*), 325.

is nothing terrible in life for the man who has truly comprehended that there is nothing terrible in not living ... that which gives no trouble when it comes, is but an empty pain in anticipation. So death, the most terrible of ills, is nothing to us, since as long as we do exist, death is not with us; but when death comes, then we do not exist ..."[14].

Yet Epicurus is not indifferent to the claims and pleasures of life. He writes in his Ethics, "The beginning and the root of all good is this pleasure of the stomach (ἡ τῆς γαστρὸς ἡδονή)"[15], and again *On the End of Life* he observes, "I know not how I conceive of the good, if I withdraw the pleasures of taste (τὰς διὰ χυλῶν ἡδονάς) and withdraw the pleasures of love" (τὰς δὲ ἀφροδισίων)[16]. Elsewhere he remarks, "He is a little man in all respects who has many good reasons for quitting life"[17], and he considered it deplorable for a man to say "it is good not to be born" and "once born make haste to pass the gates of Death"[18]. Epicurus had a definite aim in life: it was to avoid anything which was injurious to the "health of the body and (the soul's) freedom from disturbance"[19]. "To this end", he says, "we always act, namely to avoid pain and fear". The good of the soul and body must not be affected by the absence of pleasure (ἡδονή), and pleasure is therefore "the first good innate in us"[20]. But when Epicurus maintains that pleasure is the end (ἡδονὴν τέλος ὑπάρχειν)[21], he does "not mean the pleasures of profligates and those that consist in sensuality, as is supposed by some ... but freedom from pain in the body and from trouble in the mind. For it is not continuous drinkings and revellings, nor the satisfaction of lusts ... but sober reasoning, searching out the motives for all choice and avoidance, and banishing mere opinions to which are due the greatest disturbances of the spirit"[22]. He later continues, "Of all this, the beginning and the greatest good is prudence (φρόνησις) ... for from prudence are sprung all the other virtues ... For the virtues are by nature bound up with the pleasant life (ζῆν ἡδέως) and ... is inseparable from them"[23].

This concept of hedonism seems to have made some impact on Koheleth. For in so far as Koheleth has a view of the good it appears

---

[14] Bailey, Epicurus, 85.   [15] Bailey op.cit. 134–135.
[16] Bailey op.cit. 122 and 123 (VI 10).
[17] Bailey op.cit. 111 No. xxxviii.
[18] Bailey op.cit. 87 No. 126.   [19] Bailey op.cit. 87 No. 128.
[20] Bailey op.cit. 87 No. 129.   [21] Bailey op.cit. 88 No. 131.
[22] Bailey op.cit. 89f. Nos. 131f. Cf. also Hicks op.cit. 167f.
[23] Bailey op.cit. 91 No. 132.

to consist of eating and drinking and enjoying oneself. Thus in 5₁₈ he says "Behold, what I have seen to be good and to be fitting is to eat and drink and find enjoyment in all the toil with which one toils under the sun during the few days God has given him, for this is his lot". Again in 8₁₅ he commends "enjoyment, for man has no good thing under the sun but to eat and drink and enjoy himself, for this will go well with him in his toil through the days of his life . . .". It is true that these sentiments also recall Amphis' advice to "drink and play" and "add some pleasure to life". That Koheleth was opposed to unseemly and immoderate feasting may be seen from 10₁₆₋₁₇ where he condemns feasting in the morning, and approves of it only at the proper time. It will further be noticed that Epicurus thought that it was through the attainment of "pleasure" that he could "fulfil the good of the soul and the good of the body". So Koheleth believes that "there is nothing better than that a man should enjoy his work, for that is his lot" (3₂₂). Elsewhere he confesses that while attaining pleasure he was able to pursue his work which he otherwise found unrewarding and distasteful: "I kept my heart from no pleasure, for my heart found pleasure in all my toil, and this was my reward for all my toil" (2₁₀). Finally, as Epicurus held that the basic and greatest good is prudence, so Koheleth declared that when he searched his mind how to cheer his body with wine, wisdom was his guiding principle (2₃).

Certain passages in Koheleth further suggest that he was aware of Stoic doctrine. There appears to be an allusion to the Stoic view of nature when he says, "That which is, already has been; that which is to be, already is" (3₁₅). The Stoics maintained that Zeus made all things and that they will perish in a universal conflagration which Zeus alone survives and initiates a new cycle of creation[24]. It is, of course, true that the notion of a recurring cycle is found in Pythagorean thought, and, as R. D. Hicks remarked, is probably a corollary of the Heraclitian theory of flux[25]. Like Koheleth (1₉), the Epicureans also believed that "nothing new happens in the universe" considering "the infinite time past"[26], while Lucretius later observed that the "same seeds" from which man is sprung "have often been placed in the same order as they are now"[27]. However, this doctrine of the periodic destruction and renewal

[24] Diogenes Laertius, VII 135–138, 141. For fuller extracts from earlier writers see Johannes ab Arnim, Stoicorum Veterum, Fragmenta, 1903–1905, § 9, 585 (181–183). See also Greene, Moira, Fate, Good, and Evil in Greek Thought, 1944, 339 f.

[25] Stoic and Epicurean, 36.

[26] Bailey op. cit. 135 (Fragment V).   [27] Lucretius III 864f.

of nature seems to have reached its fullest expression with the Stoics, and it is therefore likely that it is their view which Koheleth has in mind. It is likewise a Stoic tenet that "all things happen by Fate" which "is defined as an endless chain of causation, whereby things are, or as the reason or formula by which the world goes on"[28]. And since man is part of this cosmic process[29], he is subject to its movement and the unalterable decrees of Fate. According to Stoic teaching, "God is one and the same with Reason and Fate"[30], and it further regarded "the deity" as "a living being, immortal, rational ... admitting nothing of evil, taking providential care of the world and all that therein is"[31]. "Chance" (τύχη) was excluded from consideration, being regarded as "a mere cause inaccessible to man's reckoning"[32]. But the assumption of a world ordered in every detail by a divine power is clearly incompatible with the obvious fact of the existence of evil. Thus, while Koheleth was not the first Israelite to raise such issues (cf. e. g. Jer 12₁ Job 2₆ Hab 1₄), he seems to question this Stoic assumption of the moral government of the world when he declares that the wicked and the righteous, the good and the evil, are indiscriminately rewarded (8₁₄ 9₂). Again, commenting on the fact that "the race is not to the swift nor, the battle to the strong, nor bread to the wise", he says, "time and chance happen to all" (9₁₁). Epicurus, it may be noted, recognised the incidence of "Chance", but argued that it was only in "a few things it hindered a wise man, as reason (λογισμός) has ordered the most important matters in life"[33]. Koheleth, on the other hand, thought that one fate (מקרה) befalls the wise man and the fool alike (2₁₄).

Many of Koheleth's enigmatic references to man and the conditions of his existence receive, again, some illumination from Hesiod's *Works and Days*. We noted that in 1₁₃ he speaks of the unhappy lot which God has decreed for men, and that in 3₁₁ he attributes this to the "ignorance (עלם) which God has put into their heart so that man cannot discover what God has done from the beginning to the end". Now, we may wonder why Koheleth should think that God has so decreed the path

---

[28] Diogenes Laertius VII 149.
[29] Diogenes Laertius VII 143 where the world is referred to as "a living being ... endowed with soul, as is clear from our several souls being each a fragment of it", and also VII 156 where it is stated that the individual souls of animals are part of the universe.
[30] Diogenes Laertius VII 135.
[31] Diogenes Laertius VII 147.
[32] See Greene op. cit. 98 and 99; Arnim op. cit. II, 967 (281).
[33] Bailey op. cit. 98 and 99 No. xvi; so also 91 No. 134.

of man, and why, moreover, he should represent him as having implanted "ignorance" in man's heart. The notion seems to have had its
origin in Hesiod's *Works and Days* where we read, "For the gods keep
hidden (κρύψαντες) from men the means of life. Else you would easily
do work enough in a day to supply you for a full year even without
working ... But Zeus in the anger of his heart hid it, because Prome-
theus the crafty deceived him; therefore he planned sorrow and mischief
against men. He hid fire; but that the noble son of Iapetus stole again
for men from Zeus the counsellor in a hollow fennelstalk, so that Zeus
who delights in thunder did not see it. But afterwards Zeus ... said to
him in anger: 'Son of Iapetus, surpassing all in cunning, you are glad
that you have outwitted me and stolen fire—a great plague to you your-
self and to men that shall be. But I will give men as the price for fire
an evil thing in which they may all be glad of heart while they embrace
their own destruction'"[34]. That man finds it necessary to strive in order
to live on earth is, then, according to Hesiod, due to Zeus withholding
from him the means of life whereby he could easily subsist. Again,
referring to his own time, he says, "men never rest from labour and
sorrow by day, and from perishing by night; and the gods shall lay
sore trouble upon them" (176f.). He resumes this theme when later he
remarks, "Between us and goodness the gods have placed the sweat of
their brows; long and steep is the path that leads to her..." (289f.).
Thereafter Hesiod sees life as a struggle, and man only survives and
maintains himself by the most arduous efforts and diligent attention to
work (293–319).

It is thus probably this belief that Fate has decreed trouble and toil
for man which underlies Koheleth's concept of הבל. As we noticed
earlier הבל appears some 30 times in the body of the work, and the
fact that the editor inserted הבל הבלים at the beginning and end of the
book (1₂ 12₈) denotes that he was prepared to summarise Koheleth's
teaching by this phrase. We have considered the meaning of *hbl* under
1₂ and observed that as well as denoting what is evanescent and tran-
sitory it may also signify what is false, deceptive or disappointing. It
has been suggested that Koheleth's use of the term denotes what is incomprehensible[35]; but it is doubtful if it can be taken to suggest this
in more than one or two passages[36]. Again, when *hbl* is used in connec-

---

[34] Ls. 42–58 (as trans. by Evelyn-White, LCL, 1914).
[35] Staples, JNES 2 (1943), 95–104.
[36] E.g. in 8₁₄ where it is a *hbl* that the fortunes of the wicked and the righteous are
alike; but it might also denote "injustice".

tion with dreams in 5₆ (Heb.) it has obviously the primary meaning of
"evanescence" or "that which is without reality", while its application
to youth and the dawn of life in 11₁₀ similarly seems to denote "transi-
toriness". But, apart from such instances, *hbl* for Koheleth basically
denotes what is false and deceptive with particular reference to the
unrewarding efforts attending toil and work. And the fact that the term
is frequently used in conjunction with the phrase רעוּת רוּחַ—a" striving
after wind"—further suggests that which is intangible and unattainable.
Thus in 2₁₀ Koheleth says that his heart found pleasure in all his toil,
but in verse ₁₁ he confesses that when he reflected on all that his hands
had done and the toil involved he accounted it as *hbl* and a striving after
wind. Likewise in verse ₂₀ he gives his heart up to despair because of
the toil of his labours. And this is equally so in verse ₂₂: "What has a
man from all the toil and strain with which he toils beneath the sun?
For all his days are full of pain, and his work is a vexation; even in the
night his mind does not rest. This also is *hbl*." In 4₄ all toil and skill
are likewise *hbl* and a striving after wind; such efforts are not justified
even though they are motivated by envy of one's neighbour. Of similar
purport is 4₆: "Better is a handful of quietness than two hands full of
toil and a striving after wind"; that is to say, any advantage gained from
a second handful is offset by the toil involved. So in 5₁₄f. (Heb.), where
he refers to man leaving this world in the same natural state as he entered
it, he says, "He will take nothing from his toil", and in the next verse
he asks, "What gain has he that he toiled for the wind?". Again, the
man who lives many years and fails to enjoy life is compared with an
untimely birth which comes in *hbl* and goes in darkness (6₃f.); as the
untimely birth is an abortive effort, so this man's life is dismissed as a
failure.

Koheleth further expresses his dissatisfaction with life as he
contemplates the tyrannical oppression of the weak and helpless (4¹).
He accordingly comments, "I thought the dead who are already dead
more fortunate than the living who are still alive; but better than both
is he who has not yet been, who has not experienced the evil which is
done under the sun" (4₂₋₃). But this is, again, expressive of the view of
life entertained by more than one Greek writer before him. Ranston
has already drawn our attention to this notion as presented by Theognis,
but Homer had earlier said, "There is nothing more pitiable than man
of all things that breathe and move on earth"[37]. The poet Sophocles

---

[37] Iliad XVII 443f. (as trans. by Mackail, Select Epigrams from the Greek Anthology, 1890, 82).

(c. 496–405 B.C.), for all his energy and longevity, could write, "Never to be born is, past all reckoning best; next best, by far, when a man has come into the world, that, as soon as may be, he should return thither whence he came"[38]. Concerning the delight of man, Pindar (c. 522–442) commented, "in a little while it falls to the ground, shaken by adverse fate", while he regarded man as but "the creature of a day . . . the dream of a shadow"[39]. So later Menander (c. 343–290) considered "as most happy" the man "who, having gazed without grief on these august things, the common sun, the stars, water, clouds, fire, goes quickly back whence he came"[40]. Similarly Euripedes could say, "The life of man is all suffering, and there is no rest from pain and trouble. There may be something better than this life; but whatever it be, it is hidden in mists of darkness . . . What lies beyond is not revealed, and we drift on a sea of idle tales"[41]. This philosophy of pessimism was likewise so prominent in the time of Epicurus that, as we have seen, he was concerned to discourage it. Nor indeed was this view of life peculiar to Koheleth in Hebrew literature. In a moment of despair Job had earlier exclaimed, "Why was I not as a hidden untimely birth, as infants that never see the light? . . . Why is light given to him that is in misery, and life to the bitter in soul, who long for death, but it comes not . . . and are glad when they see the grave" (3₁₆ff.). So, as we noted previously, Ben Sira considered that "when you are born, you are born to a curse" (41₉), that "death is better than a miserable life" (30₁₇), and that we should "call no one happy before his death" (11₂₈).

But, while Koheleth was dismayed by the sorrow he observed in life, he could philosophically admit that there was a time for weeping as well as laughing and a time for mourning as well as dancing. Here again, as Ranston observed, we are probably to recognise the influence of Hesiod. For Hesiod concerned himself with Days as well as Works. He advises his brother Perses "to remember all works in their season" (640f.), and this is a theme he develops at length. There is thus a season of the year for ploughing, sowing and reaping (390f.; 448f.), and a time for winnowing and storing grain (597ff.). So there is a season for pruning the vines (564ff.) and a month to gather the grapes (609ff.). There is similarly a time and place for a man to drink and enjoy wine and to partake of choice food (588–595). Likewise there is a month of the year

---

[38] Oedipus et Colonnus, 1125 (as Cornford op.cit. 118f.).
[39] Pythian VIII 88 (as Cornford 113f.).
[40] Hypobolimaeus Fragment 2 (as Mackail 83).
[41] Hippolytus 189 (as Cornford 152).

to hew timber (420ff.) and a time to make ploughs (427f.), and a time
to build barns (502ff.). Again, there is a right day in the month for a
wise man to be born, and likewise for the birth of a boy and for the
birth of a girl (792ff.). So there is a right age to marry and a right month
of the year to bring home one's bride (800f.). Hesiod then proceeds to
mention other days when it is propitious to undertake certain domestic
and outdoor tasks, and finally comments: "These days are a great blessing to men on earth, but the rest are changeable, luckless, and bring
nothing ... Sometimes a day is a stepmother, sometimes a mother.
The man is happy and lucky in them who knows all these things and
does his work without offending the deathless gods" (822ff.)[42].

The thematic connection between these comments of Hesiod and
Koheleth's statement of the right time and season in 3 2-8 is obvious[43].
The significance of time and event, is, of course, a theme which we find
elsewhere. As noted earlier, we read in the Egyptian *Insinger Papyrus* that
"food is good in its time and ... sleep is good in time of feebleness"[44].
Again in Ben Sira we read that there is a time for rebuke (20 1), a time
to be silent (20 7), and a time to tell a story and quote a proverb (20 19f.).
It will be observed, however, that both Hesiod and Koheleth develop
the subject in some detail, and mention in common such topics as a
time to be born, a time to plant and a time to harvest. In view of such
correspondences it is, then, likely that it was Hesiod's treatment of the
theme which prompted Koheleth's composition[45].

---

[42] As trans. by Evelyn-White.
[43] Cf. J. A. Loader, ZAW 81 (1969), 240–242, who finds a complex Chiastic
structure in this passage.
[44] On the *Insinger* formulation of this theme, see the translation presented in
Schmid's Wesen und Geschichte der Weisheit, 1966, 221.
[45] Cf. Plöger ("Wahre die richtige Mitte: solch Maß ist in allem das Beste!", in:
Gottes Wort und Gottes Land, Hertzberg-Festschrift, 1965, 159–173) who
compares the biblical Wisdom literature to Hesiod's *Works and Days*.

III. COMMON PROVERBIAL MATERIAL

Koheleth's work further contains gnomic sayings which can be paralleled elsewhere in the literature of the ancient world. It will be recalled that we corrected אני פי מלך שמור in 8₂ to read אנפי מלך שמור (in the presence of the king be cautious) in accordance with *Aḥiqar* א[נ]פי מלך אלתקום (in the presence of the king do not delay)[46]. But in enjoining deference in the presence of a king, the passage in Koheleth as a whole (8₂₋₄) invites comparison with *Aḥiqar* ls. 101–103: "*In presence of a king* delay not . . . Do thou take heed to thyself. Let him not *show* it at thy *words*, that thou go away before thy time. *In presence* of a king if (a thing) is commanded thee . . . hasten, do it . . ."[47]. So Koheleth's saying that "a bird of the air carries the voice" (10₂₀) recalls *Aḥiqar* l. 98, "for a word is (like) a bird, and when he has sent it forth a man does not *recapture it*"[48]. When again Koheleth says, "All streams run to the sea, but the sea is not full" (1₇) he reminds us of the Greek poet Aristophanes (c. 450–385 B.C.) who observed that the sea is no fuller though all the rivers flow to it[49].

Koheleth's complaint that a man gathers possessions only to leave them to others (e. g. 2₂₁ 4₇) finds, as we have seen, a parallel in an Egyptian saying, but it appears too in the Psalms (39₆ 49₁₀) and Ben Sira (14₃₋₄). So Epicurus remarked "Some men throughout their lives gather together the means of life, for they do not see that the draught swallowed by all of us at birth is a draught of death"[50]. Koheleth's saying that "it is better to go to the house of mourning than to the house of feasting, for this is the end of all men" (7₂) similarly reminds us of Euripedes' view that "when a man is dead and has found rest from trouble, we should rejoice and carry him from the house with songs of gladness"[51]. Finally, Koheleth's estimate of dreams as vain and illusory (5₂. ₆ Heb.) already appears in Jer (23₂₆f.) and Ben Sira (34₁₋₇), while Epicurus regarded them as originating from the influence of images, having neither divine nor prophetic character[52].

---

[46] L. 101.

[47] As Cowley, Aramaic Papyri of the Fifth Century B.C., 223 (text 215).

[48] Cowley ibid.   [49] Clouds 1290–1294.

[50] Fragment V, Bailey, Epicurus, 111 No. XXX.

[51] Cresphontes, frag. 449, as Cornford op. cit. 153.

[52] Fragments V, Bailey op. cit. 109 No. XXIV.

IV. THE NATURE OF KOHELETH'S PROBLEMS

But while Koheleth draws on the concepts and proverbs of more than one literature to illustrate an opinion or to emphasise a mood, his spiritual problems were no nearer solution. For despite the novelty of his views, he still contemplates life from the standpoint of one who has his roots in Judaism. Thus, although man cannot find out what is done on earth, it is still God who does it (8$_{17}$), and what God does endures for ever (3$_{14}$). It is also God who is responsible for the beginnings of life, who gives and recalls the spirit (*ruaḥ*) of man, and who made all things (11$_5$ 12$_7$). It is again God who gives the good and evil day (7$_{14}$) and it is God who grants or withholds the aptitude to enjoy one's possessions (6$_2$). The pleasures of eating and drinking are similarly regarded as gifts of God (2$_{24-25}$ 5$_{18}$ 8$_{15}$), and it is likewise God's will that man should take pleasure in his toil (3$_{13}$). So a man who can enjoy his work has reason to thank God, and as long as God can keep him occupied with joy in his heart he will not have to dwell on the unpleasantness associated with labour (5$_{17-18}$ Heb.). Even evil, which was so problematical to Koheleth, was to some extent due to man's indifference to his fellows (8$_9$). Again, God helps those who please him (2$_{26}$ 7$_{26}$), and it will be well for those who fear him (7$_{18}$ 8$_{12}$)[53].

Accordingly such passages indicate that although Koheleth questioned the purpose of life (1$_{2-3}$. $_{14}$ etc.) he did not question the existence of God[54]. Indeed his problems arise from this issue. For, on the one hand, he seems reluctant to abandon traditional Israelite belief, and, on the other, he exhibits a scepticism towards it. This would seem to account in some measure for the apparent contradictory nature of many passages which a number of scholars regard as secondary. Thus McNeile thought that 2$_{26}$ 7$_{29}$ 8$_{12-13}$ and 11$_{16}$ are the work of the *Ḥᵃsidim*[55]. So Rankin regarded such instances as 3$_{17}$ 4$_5$ 6$_7$ 9$_{17}$–10$_3$ 10$_{8-14a}$. $_{15}$. $_{18}$. $_{19}$

---

[53] Cf. Pfeiffer, Die Gottesfurcht im Buche Kohelet, in: Gottes Wort und Gottes Land, 133–158.

[54] Cf. Zimmerli, Die Weisheit des Predigers Salomo, 1936, 13 ff., and Lauha, VTS 3 (1955), 183–191.

[55] Op. cit. 24–26.

as the work of the pious glossator[56]. Other scholars[57] again would explain seeming inconsistencies in the book in terms of the literary influence of the Greek Diatribe which is characterised by interruptions, interjections and unusual co-ordination of clauses[58]. But while there may be some substance in this, it is also possible that some passages may represent the effusions of Koheleth's thought, uttered in moments of uncertainty regardless of logical consistency. There are doubtless secondary elements in the book, but, because of its complex literary structure, claims to their detection and extent can only be arbitrary and subjective[59]. Certainly we cannot suspect every passage of a religious nature in the work, since even an editor would not have accorded it initial recognition unless it contained some genuinely orthodox material. It is, then, the conflict between the traditional notion of God's goodness and activity with his own observation of life which constitutes Koheleth's problem, and which he analyses in the light of wisdom.

It is thus through wisdom that he discovers that what befalls the fool also befalls the wise man, and that the wise man is remembered no more than the fool (2_{13-16}). It was again when he applied his "mind to know wisdom" that he was able "to consider the work of God" and to learn that man cannot find out the work that is done on earth (8_{16-17}). It was likewise through wisdom that he discerned that "the righteous

---

[56] Op. cit. IB 5,12. See also Baumgartner, The Wisdom Literature, in: The Old Testament and Modern Study, 1951, 223, who observes that such passages as 3_{17} 7_{18b} 8_5 12_{12-14} are normally accepted as glosses inserted in the interests of orthodoxy.

[57] In addition to Allgeier above (p. 158) we may mention Miller, MB 2 (1934), 106–117, and S. de Ausejo, EstBib 7 (1948), 390 ff. So, it may be noted, Bertram, ZAW 64 (1952), 26, recognises the style of the Diatribe in the Septuagint.

[58] For the characteristics of the Diatribe, see Hertzberg op. cit. 56 f. who refers to Bultmann's, Der Stil der paulinischen Predigt und die kynisch-stoisch Diatribe, 1910, 10 ff.

[59] It is, e.g. generally accepted that 12_{8-12} is editorial, but, while some commentators recognise at least two hands here, Loretz (op. cit. 290) contends that the evidence does not enable us to decide whether it is from one or more hands. No less arbitrary is the determination of secondary material on the basis of theories of the literary structure of the book. Thus Ellermeier (Qohelet 22–129) has recently offered a complicated analysis of the work into *Gattungen* consisting of such subdivisions as "mashal", "proverb", "maxim", "counsel", "reflection" and "sentences", but regards as glosses elements which cannot conveniently be assigned to any of these units (especially 93, 100–103. 125 ff.). Cf., on the other hand, Zimmerli, VT 24 (1974), 221–230, who, although he would not claim that the work has the definite theme of a tractate, nevertheless, contends that it is more than a lose collection of Sentences.

and the wise and their deeds are in the hand of God" but that their
destiny is "vanity", since one fate comes to all (9₁-₂). But even wisdom
to which Koheleth ardently aspired (e.g. 7₂₅) was not without its dis-
illusionment and embarassment[60]. For "in much wisdom is much vexation" (1₁₈), and a man with wisdom is not much better than a man
without it (6₈). Koheleth himself sought to be wise, but wisdom only
taught him that the world is incomprehensible (7₂₃-₂₄), while no less
disconcerting is his discovery that even a wise man cannot understand
the ways of God (8₁₇).

In considering his problems Koheleth could find little refuge in the
attitude to pessimism and suffering portrayed in the ancient literatures
with which he seems to have been acquainted. As we know from such
compositions as *Ludlul bel nemeqi* and *The Theodicy*, the Babylonians had
experienced the question of evil and suffering. In *Ludlul bel nemeqi* we
read of one Subsi-mesre-Sakkan who complains that he cannot discover
the will of his god, that he is ignored by his friends and suffers from
various bodily diseases. Yet despite such afflictions, due sacrifice and
priestly incantations suffice to appease the deity[61]. *The Theodicy* presents
us with a dialogue between a sufferer and a friend. The complainant
cites his miseries as an example of a man neglected by his gods, but the
friend, rather in the manner of Job's friends, remonstrates with him
and finally persuades him that his god will listen to his plea[62].

Likewise in Egyptian sources we read of the frustrations and dis-
illusionments of the individual, and of anarchy in the social order. As
Humbert has noted, both in *The Lamentations of Khekheperre-Sonbu* and in
The Dialogue of the Weary Man the individual bemoans his grief and speaks
in sorrow to his heart[63]. So *The Prophecy of Neferrohu* mentions the
dangers overshadowing the land, treachery and murder even in family
circles, and the ruthless confiscation of property[64]. Yet the Egyptians
do not appear to have complained of the mysterious ways of deity,
while belief in a future existence offered the hope of retribution and
blessing in another world[65].

---

[60] Cf. Würthwein, Die Weisheit Ägyptens und das Alte Testament, 1960, 14; H.
Gese, Die Krise der Weisheit bei Kohelet, in: Les Sagesses du Proche-Orient
ancien, 1963, 139–151.

[61] See Lambert, Babylonian Wisdom Literature, 39f.

[62] Lambert 63–91.

[63] Humbert op. cit. 108.

[64] ANET 445.

[65] See Erman, Die Literatur der Ägypter, 1923, 316f.

Hesiod too complained of injustice and evil, but could only admit that man was helpless in their grasp. Of the age in which he himself had the misfortune to live he speaks, as we have already noted, of the endless suffering which man endures and of the callous indifference of the gods. It was, moreover, an age when the just and the good win no favour, when men rather praise the evil-doer, and the wicked overthrow the worthy. It is thus with passive resignation that he concludes "and bitter sorrows will be left for mortal men and there will be no help against evil"[66].

Again, acknowledging the existence of pain and evil, Epicurus thought that they must be borne passively and could not be assigned to any particular cause. He thus remarked, "All bodily suffering is negligible; for that which causes pain has short duration, and that which endures long in the flesh causes but small pain"[67]: and again, "Let us not blame the flesh as the cause of great evils, nor blame circumstances for our distresses"[68]. In any case, evil could hardly be considered in the context of man's notion of God; for the deity not only dwells in a sphere remote from man[69], but men must conceive of him as "a being immortal and blessed ... and not assign anything alien to his immortality or ill-fated to his purpose"[70]. So for the Stoics evil did not theoretically constitute a problem, since God was conceived as an immortal being, admitting nothing of evil and as taking providential care of the world and its inhabitants[71].

While Koheleth seems to have been aware of such attempts to accept or ignore the problem of pain and evil, he was not reassured by them. His bold, agile mind penetrated their religious assumptions and philosophical compromises, and he constantly asserted his inability to discern justice or purpose in the events of life. Job had indeed earlier experienced similar problems but his rediscovery of faith enabled him to acquiesce in the traditional belief that God's dealings with man are beneficent though mysterious (42_{1-6}). But Koheleth could entertain no comparable sentiment. For while he occasionally assents to conventional doctrine, he repeatedly returns to such issues as the moral government of the world, the incidence of chance and injustice, and the "vanity"

---

[66] Works and Days 174–201 (as Evelyn-White).
[67] Fragments A iv (as Bailey, Epicurus, 107).
[68] Fragments D 63 (as Bailey 135).
[69] See above p. 166.
[70] Epicurus to Menoeceus 123 (Bailey 83).
[71] See above p. 171.

which characterises all human activities. Even Wisdom to which he appeals as a last resort proved inadequate and disappointing. To the authors of such compositions as Proverbs chapter 1–9 and the book of Ben Sira *Wisdom* was God's gift to the pious (e.g. Prov 2₆) and through which he reveals his secrets to men (e.g. Ben Sira 4₁₈) [72]. But to Koheleth's more secular and realistic outlook wisdom was not only a means of investigating and exposing the conditions of human existence, but also of examining the nature of God's relationship with man. And because these constituted problems to which he could find no satisfactory answer he maintained to the end a questing, negative attitude to life [73].

---

[72] Cf. Whitley, The Genius of Ancient Israel, 1969, 143 ff.

[73] We can thus scarcely agree with Blieffert, Weltanschauung und Gottesglaube im Buch Kohelet, 1958, 13 f., that the problem of Kohelet can be solved theologically. So while Castellino, CBQ 30 (1968), 15 ff., recognises the difficulties confronting Koheleth, his suggestion that he becomes reconciled to them through Wisdom (26–28) hardly accords with Koheleth's own utterances.

V. CONCLUSIONS

Our analysis of the thought of Koheleth, then, shows that it is complex, discordant and challenging. Not only does he show a familiarity with earlier Hebrew books such as Job, Proverbs and Ben Sira, but the major themes of his work have obvious affinities with material in the gnomic and prudential literatures of Egypt, Babylonia and Greece. Thus the pessimism which characterises so much of his thought is to be found in Egyptian and Babylonian literature, while the notion that it were better not to be born is particularly prominent in Greek authors from Homer onwards. The compensating attitude of *carpe diem* is likewise no less obvious in these literatures. The remoteness and indifference of the deity is a basic assumption of Epicurus, while the unalterable cycle of nature is a cardinal doctrine of Stoicism. The motif of the right time is adumbrated in the Egyptian Insinger Papyrus, developed in some detail by Hesiod, and is the subject of a sonnet by Koheleth. The burden of old age and the gloom of death are again themes appearing in more than one literature of the ancient Near East. But, apart from certain Hebrew books, there is no evidence of literary dependence on the literature with which Koheleth's thoughts have affinities; it may be that he consulted certain sources and presented their substance in his own words, or again such material may have been current in oral form in the intellectual world of his day.

Although Koheleth displays a wide knowledge of proverbial and gnomic literature, it was hardly his intention to compose a work of a conventional nature which offered positive instruction on the problems of life. Podechard indeed thought that the work was composed for the wisdom schools where its teaching was discussed by the pupils of the day[1]. But its approach seems to be too critical and negative for that. Koheleth had certainly an extensive knowledge of Wisdom Literature,

---

[1] L'Ecclésiaste 187. So Gordis thinks that Koheleth was "undoubtedly trained in the Wisdom academies and perhaps taught there" himself (Koheleth: The Man and His World, 28) while Hengel similarly regards him as a teacher of Wisdom (op. cit. 214).

and his editor is justified in referring to him as a wise man and a collector of proverbs (12₉); but in adding that he "also taught the people knowledge" he doubtless wished to represent him as being in the tradition of orthodox Israelite wisdom literature (cf. e.g. Prov 1₄ 15₇ 22₁₇ Ben Sira 44₃₋₄). The term *Koheleth* is commonly thought to denote one who convokes an assembly, but, assuming that this were the case and that the duty of such a person included the reading of material to a collected assembly, it is doubtful if a composition so unorthodox in content and disjointed in structure would be so read. Moreover, as we noted earlier, there is some reason for thinking that it signified "a sceptic", and therefore it was probably applied to the author of our work because of his sceptical and challenging attitude to conventional thought.

Koheleth has been regarded as an original thinker by some scholars[2], but in view of the number of parallels which can be adduced for so many of his sayings this is questionable; and indeed Koheleth himself was probably aware of the common place nature of his materials when, like Epicurus before him, he remarked that there is nothing new under the sun. His achievement rather consists in the candour and realism he brought to his work. And this was an approach prompted by the intellectual and religious climate of his day. For, due to the influence of Greek thought in the recent reign of Antiochus Epiphanes (175–164 B.C.), there was a more discriminating attitude to traditional Judaism. Moreover, despite the nationalistic aspirations which attended the Maccabean revolt, the people as a whole experienced the sufferings and deprivations inseparable from such a struggle (cf. IMac 2₄₃ 5₂ IIMac 15₁₈₋₁₉). In the circumstances, many of the more liberal minded Jews must have regarded the optimism of the book of Daniel exaggerated, while Koheleth, informed and courageous, was tempted to question accepted belief and to offer his own thoughts on human experience.

But in committing these thoughts to writing he achieved little literary success. Not infrequently is his style inelegant and his meaning obscure. The disturbed conditions of the day would hardly be favourable to the composition of such a work, but he was also labouring under two further difficulties: one is that when he was writing, the Hebrew language was in a state of transition from classical to Mishnaic Hebrew and therefore he was using a linguistic medium which was largely experimental; the other is that the material he adapted from non-Israelite sources did not always find facile expression in Hebrew. Again, much

---

[2] E.g. Barton op.cit. 43; Rankin loc.cit. (IB 5) 15a; Gordis op.cit. 156ff.

of his teaching is in the form of proverbial sayings and loosely connected observations on life. Rarely does he develop a theme beyond a few verses and there is consequently little logical coherence in the book. Yet it seemed to meet with the approval of some at least of his contemporaries. For in accepting the work they recognised it as an assessment of life which was relevant to the uncertainty of events in Judah during the middle of the second century B.C.

Bibliography

TEXT AND VERSIONS

The Hebrew Text

G. S. Baer and Franz Delitzsch, Quinqua Volumina, Leipzig 1886.
R. Kittel, Biblia Hebraica[3], Stuttgart 1937 and later.
Biblia Hebraica Stuttgartensia, 1968 and later

The Septuagint

H. B. Swete, The Old Testament in Greek, Cambridge 1937[3].
A. Ralphs, The Old Testament in Greek, Stuttgart 1936.

Aquila, Symmachus, Theodotion

F. Field, Origenis Hexaplorum quae supersunt, Oxford 1875.

The Vulgate

Marietta Edition, Roma 1959.

The Peshitta

Edition of A. M. Ceriani (ex Codice Ambrosiana, Facsimile), Milano 1876.

Syro-Hexaplar

Codex Syriaco-Hexaplaris, ed. Henricus Middeldorpf, Berlin 1835.

Targum

Biblia Sacra Polyglotta, ed. Brian Walton, London 1657.
The Bible in Aramaic, by Alexander Sperber. Leiden 1959–1973.

JEWISH SOURCES

The Mishna

Ed. Philip Blackmann, New York 1964[2].

The Talmud

Babylonian, ed. Lazarus Goldschmidt, Leipzig 1906.
Jerusalem, Krotoschin edn. 1866.

Midrash Rabbah

(Ruth and) Ecclesiastes, Vol. 8 ed. H. Freedman and M. Simon, Eng. edn.
London 1939.

Josephus

Jewish Antiquities, Books vi and xii, Loeb Classical Library, London, 1928
and 1957.

ANCIENT CLASSICAL WRITERS

Aristotle, Cicero, Diodorus Sicullus, Diogenes Laertius, Herodotus, Hesiod, Plato, Pliny, Plutarch, Terence and Thucydides, cited as in Loeb Classical Library.

WORKS CONSULTED

Ackroyd, P. R., Two Hebrew Notes, ASTI 5 (1966–67), 82–86.

Albright, W. F., Some Canaanite-Phoenician Sources of Hebrew Wisdom, in: Wisdom in Israel and in the Ancient Near East (Rowley Festschrift, eds. M. Noth-D. W. Thomas) VTS 3 (1955), 1–15.

Allgeier, Arthur, Das Buch des Predigers oder Koheleth, Bonn 1925.

Arnim, Johannes ab, Stoicorum Veterum Fragmenta, Teubner-Leipzig, 1903–1905.

Ausejo, S. de, El género literario del Ecclesiastés, EstBib 7 (1948), 390 ff.

Autran, C., Phéniciens (Essai de contribution à l'histoire antique De La Mediterranée) Paris 1920.

Avigad, N., Aramaic Inscriptions in the Tomb of Jason, IEJ 17 (1967), 101–111.

—, The Seal of Abigad, IEJ 18 (1968), 52–53.

Bailey, Cyril, Epicurus: The Extant Remains, Oxford 1926.

—, Lucretius (De Rerum Natura), Oxford 1947,

Baillet, M., Les petites Grottes de Qumran, RB 63 (1956), 54 ff.

Barth, J., Die Nominalbildung in den semitischen Sprachen, Leipzig 1913.

Barr, James, Comparative Philology and the Text of the Old Testament, Oxford 1968.

Barton, G. A., The Book of Ecclesiastes, ICC, Edinburgh 1908.

Barucq, André, Ecclésiaste (Qohéleth), Paris 1968.

Batten, L. W., David's Destruction of the Syrian Chariots, ZAW 28 (1908), 188–192.

Bauer, H., Die hebräischen Eigennamen als sprachliche Erkenntnisquelle, ZAW 48 (1930), 73–80.

Baumgarten, J.-Mansoor, M., Studies in the New Hodayot (Thanksgiving Hymns), JBL 74 (1955), 115–124.

Baumgartner, W. The Wisdom Literature, in: The Old Testament and Modern Study (ed. H. H. Rowley), Oxford 1951, 210–227.

Bergsträsser, G., Hebräische Grammatik (Parts 1–2), Leipzig 1918–1926.

Bertram, Georg, Hebräischer und griechischer Qohelet, ZAW 64 (1952), 26–49.

Bevan, E. R., The House of Seleucus II, London 1902.

Bezold, Carl, Babylonisch-assyrisches Glossar, Heidelberg 1926.

Bickerman, Elias, The Maccabees (Eng. trans.), New York 1947.

Birkeland, Harris, The Language of Jesus, in: II Hist.-Filos. Kl., No. 1, 6–40, Oslo 1954.

Blieffert, Hans-Jürgen, Weltanschauung und Gottesglaube im Buch Kohelet, Rostock 1958.

Bode, D. F. A.-Nanavutty, P., Songs of Zarathustra, London 1952.

Braun, Rainer, Kohelet und die frühhellenistische Popularphilosophie, BZAW 130, Berlin 1973.

Brekelmans, C., The Preposition b = from in the Psalms according to Dahood, UF 1 (1969), 5–14.

Brockelmann, Carl, Lexicon Syriacum, Halle 1928.

Budde, Karl, Der Prediger, HSAT, Tübingen 1922⁴ (ed. A. Bertholet)

Burkitt, F. C., Is Ecclesiastes a Translation? JTS 23 (1922), 22–26.
Burrows, Millar-Trevor, J.C.-Brownlee, W. H., The Dead Sea Scrolls of St. Mark's Monastery, II. Fascicle 2: Plates and Transcription of the Manual of Discipline, BASOR, New Haven 1951.
Castellino, G. R., Qohelet and His Wisdom, CBQ 30 (1968), 15 ff.
Chomsky, William, How the Study of Hebrew Grammar Began and Developed, JQR 35 (1943–44), 281–301.
—, What was the Jewish Vernacular during the Second Commonwealth?, JQR 42 (1951), 193–212.
Cook, S. A., A Glossary of Aramaic Inscriptions, Cambridge 1898.
Cooke, G. A., A Textbook of North Semitic Inscriptions, Oxford 1903.
Cornford, F. M., Greek Religious Thought, London 1923.
Corré, A. D., A Reference to Epispasm in Koheleth, VT 4 (1954), 416 ff.
Cowley, A. E., Aramaic Papyri of the Fifth Century B. C., Oxford 1923.
Cross, F. M., Jr.-Freedman, D. N., Early Hebrew Orthography: A study of the Epigraphic Evidence, New York, 1952.
Cross, F. M., Jr., The Ancient Library of Qumran, London 1958.
Dahood, Mitchell J., Canaanite-Phoenician Influence in Qoheleth, Bibl 33 (1952), 30–52, 191–221.
—, Qoheleth and Recent Discoveries, Bibl 39 (1958), 308–318.
—, Qoheleth and Northwest Semitic Philology, Bibl 43 (1962), 349–365.
—, The Phoenician Background of Qoheleth, Bibl 47 (1966), 264–282.
—, Ugaritic-Hebrew Philology, Roma 1965.
—, The Psalms I, AB 16, New York 1965.
—, Three parallel pairs in Ecclesiastes 10:18, JQR 62 (1971), 84–87.
Danby, H. D., The Mishna, Oxford 1933.
Delitzsch, Franz, Commentary on the Song of Songs and Ecclesiastes (Eng. trans), Edinburgh 1885.
Delitzsch, Friedrich, Prolegomena eines neuen hebräisch-aramäischen Wörterbuchs zum Alten Testament, Leipzig 1886.
De Rossi, J. B., Variae Lectiones Veteris Testamenti III, Parma 1786.
De Witt, N. W., Epicurus and His Philosophy, Minneapolis, 1954.
Di Lella, A. A., The Hebrew Text of Sirach, The Hague, 1966.
Donner, H., Ugaritismen in der Psalmenforschung, ZAW 79 (1967), 322–350.
Dornseiff, Franz, Das Buch Prediger, ZDMG NF 14 (1935), 243–249.
Driver, G. R.-Miles, J.A.C., The Babylonian Laws II, Oxford 1955.
Driver, G. R., The Judean Scrolls, Oxford 1965.
—, Studies in the Vocabulary of the Old Testament, JTS 32 (1931), 250–257.
—, Problems and Solutions, VT 4 (1954). 225–245.
—, Reflections on Recent Articles, JBL 73 (1954), 125–136.
—, Forgotten Hebrew idioms, ZAW 78 (1966), 1–7.
—, Review of The Assyrian Dictionary, xvi, 1962, JSS 9 (1964), 346–350.
—, Once Again Abbreviations, Textus 4 (1964), 76–94..
Driver, S. R.-Gray, G. B., The Book of Job Pt. II, ICC, Edinburgh 1921.
Drower, E. S.-Macuch, R., A Mandaic Dictionary, Oxford 1963.
Du Plessis, S. J., Aspects of Morphological Peculiarities of the Language of Qoheleth, in: De Fructu Oris Sui: Essays in Honour of Adrianus Van Selms (ed. I. H. Eybers), Pretoria Oriental Series, 9 Leiden 1971, 164–180.

Eissfeldt, O., Kleine Schriften II, Tübingen 1963, ed. Rudolf Sellheim and Fritz Maass.

Eitan, I., La particle emphatique "la" dans la Bible, REJ 74 (1922) 1–16.

Elbogen, Ismar, Der jüdische Gottesdienst in seiner geschichtlichen Entwicklung, Hildesheim 1962⁴.

Ellermeier, Friedrich, Das Verbum חוש in Qoh. 2₂₅, ZAW 75 (1963), 197–217.

—, Die Entmachtung der Weisheit im Denken Qohelets. Zu Text und Auslegung von Qoh. 6₇₋₉, ZThK 60 (1963), 1–20.

—, Qohelet (Teil I, Abschnitt I). Herzberg, 1967.

Ehrlich, A. B., Randglossen zur hebräischen Bibel 7, Leipzig 1914.

Erman, Adolf, Die Literatur der Ägypter, Leipzig 1923.

Farrington, Benjamin, Lucretius and Memmius, Anales de Filología Clásica 7 (Buenos Aires 1959), 13–31.

Fensham, F. C., Ugaritic and the Translation of the Old Testament, in: The Bible Translator, 18 (1967), 71–74.

—, The First Ugaritic Text in Ugaritica V and the Old Testament, VT 22 (1972), 296–303.

Fernández, Andrés, Es Ecclesiastés una Versión, Bibl 4 (1922), 45–50.

Fitzmyer, J. A., The Aramaic Inscriptions of Sefîre (Biblica et Orientalia 19), Roma 1967.

Fohrer, Georg, Introduction to the Old Testament (Eng. edn. New York 1968).

Forman, C. C., The Pessimism of Ecclesiastes, JSS 3 (1958), 336–343.

Freedman, D. N., Notes on Genesis, ZAW 64 (1952), 190–194.

—, Archaic Forms in Early Hebrew Poetry, ZAW 72 (1960), 101–107.

Friedrich, Joh., Altpersisches und Elamisches, Orientalia 18 (1949), 1–29.

Friedrich, Joh.-Röllig, W., Phönizisch-Punische Grammatik (Analecta Orientalia 46), Roma 1970.

Galling, Kurt, Der Prediger, in: Die Fünf Megilloth. HAT 18, Tübingen 1969.

—, Das Rätsel der Zeit im Urteil Kohelets (Koh. 3₁₋₁₅), ZThK 58 (1961), 1–15.

Gemser, B., The Instructions of ʻOnchsheshonqy and Biblical Wisdom Literature, VTS 7 (1960), 102–128.

Gese, H., Die Krise der Weisheit bei Kohelet, in: Les Sagesses du Proche-Orient ancien, Paris 1963, 139–151.

Gevirtz, Stanley, The Ugaritic Parallel to Jeremiah 8₂₃, JNES 20 (1961), 41–46.

—, On the Etymology of the Phoenician Particle אש, JNES 16 (1957), 124–127.

Ginsberg, H. L., Studies in Kohelet, New York 1950.

—, The Structure and Contents of the Book of Koheleth, VTS 3 (1955), 138–149.

—, Koheleth 12₄ in the Light of Ugaritic, Syria 33 (1956), 99–101.

—, The Quintessence of Koheleth, in: Biblical and Other Essays (ed. Alexander Altmann), Harvard 1963, 47–59.

Ginsburg, C. D., Coheleth or The Book of Ecclesiastes, London 1861.

Gordis, Robert, Koheleth—The Man and His World, New York 1951.

—, Koheleth—Hebrew or Aramaic? JBL 71 (1952), 93–109.

—, Was Koheleth a Phoenician?, JBL 74 (1955) 103–114.

—, Qoheleth and Qumran—A Study of Style, Bibl 41 (1960), 395–410.

Gordon, C. H., Ugaritic Textbook, Roma 1965.

—, Azitawadd's Phoenician Inscription, JNES 8 (1949), 112–115.

—, North Israelite Influence on Post-exilic Hebrew, IEJ 5 (1955), 85–88.

Goshen-Gottstein, M. H., Linguistic Structure and Tradition in the Qumran Documents, in: Scripta Hierosolymitana IV, Aspects of the Dead Sea Scrolls (eds. C. Rabin-Y. Yadin), Jerusalem 1965², 101–137.

Graetz, H., Kohélet oder der Salomonische Prediger, Leipzig 1871.

Greene, W. C., Moira, Fate, Good, and Evil in Greek Thought, Harvard 1944.

Greenfield, J. C., Lexicographical Notes II: IX The Root שׁמח, HUCA 30 (1959), 141 ff.

—, Review of: The Literary and Oral Tradition of Hebrew and Aramaic amongst the Samaritans, Vol. III Pt. 2 by Z. Ben-Hayyim, Bibl 50 (1969) 101.

Grintz, J. M., Hebrew and the Spoken and Written Language in the Last Days of the Second Temple, JBL 79 (1960), 32–47.

Habermann, A. M., Megilloth Midbar Yehuda, Jerusalem 1959.

Hammershaimb, E., On the so-called *infinitivus absolutus* in Hebrew, in: Hebrew and Semitic Studies Presented to G. R. Driver (eds. D. W. Thomas-W. D. McHardy), Oxford 1963, 85–94.

Harris, Z. S., A Grammar of the Phoenician Language, New Haven 1936.

—, Development of the Canaanite Dialects, New Haven 1939.

Hauer, C. E., Who was Zadok?, JBL 82 (1963), 89–94.

Haupt, Paul, The Book of Ecclesiastes, Baltimore 1905.

Held, Moshe, A Faithful Lover in an Old Babylonian Dialogue, JCS 15 (1961), 1–11.

—, The Action-Result (Factitive-Passive) Sequence of Identical Verbs in Biblical Hebrew and Ugaritic, JBL 84 (1965), 272–282.

Hengel, Martin, Judentum und Hellenismus, Tübingen, 1973².

Hertz, J. H., The Authorised Daily Prayer Book (Jewish, rev. edn.), London 1964.

Hertzberg, H. W., Der Prediger, Gütersloh 1963.

—, Palästinische Bezüge im Buche Kohelet, in: Baumgärtel-Festschrift (ed. J. Herrmann), Erlangen 1959, 63–73.

Hicks, R. D., Stoic and Epicurean, New York 1962.

Hitzig, Ferdinand, Der Prediger Salomos (KEH² by W. Nowack) Leipzig 1883.

Hoftijzer, J., Review Article in BiOR 24 (1967) 28–29.

—, Remarks concerning the Use of the Particle ʾT in Classical Hebrew, Oud Stud 14 (1966), 1–99.

Horton, Ernest, Jr., Koheleth's Concept of Opposites, Numen 19 (1972) 1–21.

Huesman, John, Finite Uses of the Infinitive Absolute, Bibl 37 (1956), 271–295.

Humbert, Paul, Recherches sur les sources égyptiennes de la litterature sapientiale d'Israël, Neuchâtel 1929, 107–124.

Hummel, H. D., Enclitic MEM in Early Northwest Semitic, especially Hebrew, JBL 76 (1957), 85–107.

Hurvitz, A., The Chronological Significance of "Aramaisms" in Biblical Hebrew, IEJ 18 (1968), 234–240.

Irwin, W. A., Ecclesiastes 8₂₋₉, JNES 4 (1945), 130f.

—, Eccles. iv₁₃₋₁₆, JNES 3 (1944), 255–257.

Jastrow, M., Jr., A Gentle Cynic, Philadelphia 1919.

Jenni, Ernst, Das Wort 'ōlām im Alten Testament, ZAW 64 (1952), 197–248.

Jirku, Anton, Zum Infinitivus Absolutus im Ugaritischen, in his: Von Jerusalem nach Ugarit, Gesammelte Schriften, Bonn-Graz, 1966, 36 ff.

Joüon, Paul, Sur le nom de Qohéleth, Bibl 3 (1921), 53 ff.

—, Notes philologiques sur le texte hébreu de l'Ecclésiaste, Bibl 11 (1930), 419–425.

—, Glanes Palmyriennes, Syria 19 (1938), 99–100.

Kadman, L., The Hebrew Coin Script, IEJ 4 (1954), 150 ff.

Kahle, Paul E., The Cairo Geniza, Oxford 1959.

Kamenetzky, A. S., Konjecturen zum hebr. Texte des Koheleth, ZAW 24 (1904), 237 ff.

Kautzsch, E., Die Aramaismen im Alten Testament I, Lexikalischer Teil, Halle 1902.

Kennicott, Benjamin, Vetus Testamentum Hebraicum; Cum Variis Lectionibus II, Oxford 1780.

Knudtzon, J. A., (ed. with Weber, O., and Ebeling, E.). Die El-Amarna-Tafeln, II, Leipzig 1915.

Kroeber, Rudi, Der Prediger, Berlin 1963.

Kropat, Arno, Die Syntax des Autors der Chronik verglichen mit der Seiner Quellen, BZAW 16, Gießen 1909.

Kuhn, K. G., Konkordanz zu den Qumrantexten, Göttingen 1960.

Kutscher, E. Y., The Language and Linguistic Background of the Isaiah Scroll (1 Q Isaª), Leiden 1974.

Lambert, G. W., Babylonian Wisdom Literature, Oxford 1960.

Lauha, Aarre, Die Krise des religiösen Glaubens bei Kohelet, in: Wisdom in Israel and in the Ancient Near East (Rowley-Festschrift), VTS 3 (1955), 183–191.

Leahy, T. W., Studies in the Syntax of IQS, Bibl 41 (1960), 135–157.

Lévi, Israel, The Hebrew Text of the Book of Ecclesiasticus (Semitic Studies Series No. iii), Leiden 1951 reprint.

Levy, Ludwig, Das Buch Qoheleth: Ein Beitrag zur Geschichte des Sadduzaismus, Leipzig 1912.

Lidzbarski, Mark, Ephemeris für Semitische Epigraphik III, Gießen 1915.

Liebermann, Saul, Hellenism in Jewish Palestine (Studies in the Literary Transmission, Beliefs and Manners of Palestine in the I Century B. C. E.–IV Century C. E.), New York 1950.

Lifshitz, Baruch, L'Hellénisation des Juifs de Paléstine, RB 72 (1965), 520–538.

Loader, J. A., Qohelet 3₂₋₈—"A Sonnett" in the Old Testament, ZAW 81 (1969), 240–242.

Loewenstamm, S. E., The Seven Day-Unit in Ugaritic Epic Literature, IEJ 15 (1965), 121–133.

Loretz, Oswald, Qoheleth und der Alte Orient, Freiburg 1964.

Mackail, J. W., Select Epigrams From the Greek Anthology, London 1890.

MacDonald, D. B., Old Testament Notes, JBL 18 (1899), 212 ff.

MacDonald, John, The Particle את in Classical Hebrew: Some New Data on its use with the Nominative, VT 14 (1964), 264–275.

McNeile, A. H., An Introduction to Ecclesiastes, Cambridge 1904.

Malamat, Abraham, Origins of Statecraft in the Israelite Monarchy, BA 28 (1965), 34–65.

Mansoor, M., The Tanksgiving Hymns (Studies on the Text of the Desert of Judah, 3), Leiden 1961.

—, The Book and the Spade, Wisconsin 1975.

Margoliouth, D. S., Book of Ecclesiastes, JE 5 (1903), 32–34.

Margulis, B., A Ugaritic Psalm (RŠ 24. 252), JBL 89 (1970), 292–304.

Megia, Jorge, El Lamed enfático en nuevos textos del Antiguo Testamento, EstBib 22 (1963), 179–190.

Mercer, S. A. B., The Tell El-Amarna Tablets, Toronto 1939.

Merrill, E. H., The Aphel Causative: Does it exist in Ugaritic?, JNSL 3 (1974), 40–49.

Middendorp, Th., Die Stellung Jesu ben Siras zwischen Judentum und Hellenismus, Leiden 1973.

Milik, J. T., Un Contrat juif de l'An 134 après J. C., RB 61 (1954), 182 ff.

—, Fragments d'un midrash de Michée dans les manuscrits de Qumran, RB 59 (1952).

Miller, A., Aufbau und Grundproblem des Predigers, MB 2 (1934), 104–122.

Mittwoch, Eugen, Some Observations on the Language of the Prayers, the Benediction, and the Midrash, in: Essays Presented to J. H. Hertz (eds. L. Epstein, L. Levine, C. Roth), London 1942, 325–330.

Montgomery, J. A., Notes on Ecclesiastes, JBL 43 (1924), 241–244.

Moor, J. C. de, Studies in the New Alphabetic Texts from Ras Shamra II, UF 2 (1970), 303–327.

Moore, G. F., The Caper-plant and its Edible Products: With reference to Eccles. XII 5, JBL 10 (1891), 55–64.

Moran, W. L., The Use of the Canaanite Infinitive Absolute as a Finite Verb in the Amarna Letters from Byblos, JCS 4 (1950), 169–172.

Morgenstern, Julian, The Hasidim—Who were They?, HUCA 38 (1967), 59–73.

Müller, Hans-Peter, Wie sprach Qohälät von Gott?, VT 18 (1968), 507–521.

Murtonen, A., The semitic Sibilants, JSS 11 (1966), 135–150.

—, The Living Soul, StOR 23 (1958), 63 ff.

Muilenburg, James, A Qoheleth Scroll from Qumran, BASOR 135 (1954), 20–28.

—, The Linguistic and Rhetorical Usage of the Particle כִּי in the Old Testament, HUCA 32 (1961), 135–160.

Naveh, J., Dated Coins of Alexander Janneus, IEJ 18 (1968), 20–25.

Nötscher, F., Zum emphatischen Lamed, VT 3 (1953), 372–380.

Nougayrol, J., Le Palais Royal d'Ugarit III, Paris 1955.

Odeberg, Hugo, Qohaelaeth, Uppsala 1929.

Pedersen, Johannes, Sceptisisme israélite, RHPR 10 (1930), 317–370.

Perles, Felix, A Miscellany of Lexical and Textual Notes on the Bible, JQR NS 2 (1911/1912), 130 ff.

Pfeiffer, Egon, Die Gottesfurcht im Buche Kohelet, in: Gottes Wort und Gottes Land, Hertzberg-Festschrift (ed. H. G. Reventlow), Göttingen 1965, 133–158.

Pfeiffer, R. H., Introduction to the Old Testament, New York, 1941.

—, History of New Testament Times, New York, 1949.

Plöger, Otto, Wahre die richtige Mitte; solch Maß ist in allem Beste!, in: Gottes Wort und Gottes Land, 159–173. (ed. H. G. Reventlow)

Pope, M. H., Ugaritic Enclitic-m, JCS 5 (1951), 123–128.

—, "Pleonastic" WAW before Nouns in Ugaritic and Hebrew, JAOS 73 (1953), 123–128.

—, Marginalia to M. Dahood's Ugaritic-Hebrew Philology, JBL 85 (1966), 455–466.

—, Job, AB 15, New York 1965.

Plumptre, E. H., Ecclesiastes, Cambridge Bible, 1885.

Podechard, Edouard, L'Ecclésiaste, Paris 1912.

Power, A. D., Ecclesiastes or the Preacher, London 1952.

Prijs, Leo, Ein „WAW der Bekräftigung"?, BZ 8 (1964), 105–109.

Rabin, Chaim, The Zadokite Documents, Oxford 1954.

—, The Historical Background of Qumran Hebrew, in: Scripta Hierosolymitana: IV, Jerusalem 1965², 144–161.

—, The Ancient Versions and the Indefinite Subject, Textus 2 (1962), 60–76.

Rabinowitz, Isaac, Sequence and Dates of the Extra-Biblical Dead Sea Scroll Texts and "Damascus Fragments", VT 3 (1953), 175–185.

Rabinowitz, J. J., Graecisms and Greek Terms in the Aramaic Papyri, Bibl 39 (1958), 77–82.

Rainey, A. F., A Study of Ecclesiastes, CTM 35 (1964), 148–157.

Rankin, O. S., Ecclesiastes, IB 5, Tennessee 1956.

Ranston, Harry, Ecclesiastes and the Early Greek Wisdom Literature, London 1925.

Renan, Ernest, L'Antichrist, Paris 1873.

—, L'Ecclésiaste, Paris 1882.

Reider, J., Etymological Studies in Biblical Hebrew, VT 2 (1952), 113–130.

Rosenthal, Franz, A Grammar of Biblical Aramaic, Wiesbaden 1961.

Roth, Cecil, The Historical Background of the Dead Sea Scrolls, Oxford 1958.

Roth, W. M. W., The Numerical Sequence $X/X + 1$ in the Old Testament, VT 12 (1962), 300–311.

—, A Study of the Classical Hebrew verb ṢKL, VT 18 (1968), 69–78.

—, The Zadokite Fragments and the Dead Sea Scrolls, Oxford 1952.

—, Menelaus and the Abomination of Desolation, in: Studia Orientalia Ioanni Pedersen, Copenhagen 1953, 303–315.

Rowley, H. H., The Zadokite Fragments and the Dead Sea Scrolls, Oxford 1952.

Rubinstein, A., A Finite Verb continued by an Infinitive Absolute in Biblical Hebrew, VT 2 (1952), 362–367.

Rüger, H. P., Text and Textform im hebräischen Sirach, BZAW 112, 1970.

Sarna, N. M., The Interchange of the Prepositions BETH and MIN in Biblical Hebrew, JBL 78 (1959), 310–316.

—, The Mythological Background of Job 18, JBL 82 (1963), 315–318.

Saydon, P. P., Meanings and Uses of the particle את, VT 14 (1964), 192–210.

Schechter, S., Fragments of a Zadokite Work (vol 1, Documents of Jewish Sectaries), Cambridge 1910.

— (with Taylor, J.) The Wisdom of Ben Sira, Cambridge 1899.

Schmid, H. H., Wesen und Geschichte der Weisheit, BZAW 101, Berlin 1966.

Schunck, K. D., Drei Seleukiden im Buche Kohelet?, VT 9 (1959), 192–201.

Scott, R. B. Y., Proverbs, Ecclesiastes, AB 18, New York 1965.

Segal, M. H., A Grammar of Mishnaic Hebrew, Oxford 1927.

Siegfried, Carl, Prediger Salomonis und Hoheslied (2nd edn. W. Nowack), Göttingen 1898.

Smith, J. M. Powis, Micah, Zephaniah and Nahum, ICC, Edinburgh 1911.

Smith, R. Payne, Thesaurus-Syriacus (I–II), Oxford 1879–1901.

Sperber, Alexander, A Historical Grammar of Biblical Hebrew, Leiden 1966.

Speiser, E. A., The "Elative" in West-Semitic and Akkadian, JCS 6 (1952), 81–92.

—, The Semantic Range of dalāpu, JCS 5 (1951), 64–66.

Staples, W. E., The "Vanity" of Ecclesiastes, JNES 2 (1943) 95–104.

Stevenson, W. B., Grammar of Palestinian Jewish Aramaic, Oxford 1924.

Strobel, Albert, Das Buch Prediger (Kohelet), Düsseldorf 1967.

Talmon, S., The "Manual of Benediction" of the Sect of the Judean Desert, RdQ 8 (1960), 475–500.

—, The Calendar Reckoning of the Sect from the Judean Desert, in: Scripta Hierosolymitana: IV, Jerusalem 1965², 162–199.

Tcherikover, Victor, Hellenistic Civilisation and the Jews (Eng. trans.), Philadelphia 1961.

Thomas, D. W., A Note on במדע in Eccles. X. 20, JTS 50 (1949), 177.

Torczyner (Tur Sinai), H., „Dunkle Bibelstellen", in: Vom Alten Testament Karl Marti zum siebzigsten Geburtstage gewidmet (ed. K. Budde), BZAW 41 (1925), 279 ff.

Torrey, C. C., The Question of the Original Language of Qoheleth, JQR 39 (1948), 151–160.

—, The Problem of Ecclesiastes IV 13-16, VT 2 (1952), 175–177.

Ullendorff, Edward, The Meaning of קהלת, VT 12 (1962), 215.

Van der Ploeg, J., Notes Lexicographiques, Oud Stud V (1948), 142–150.

Van Dijk, H. J., Does Third Masculine Singular *Taqtul exist in Hebrew?, VT 19 (1969), 440–447.

Vaux, Roland de, L'Archéologie et les manuscrits de la Mer Morte (Schweich Lectures 1959), London 1961.

Virolleaud, C., Palais Royal d'Ugarit II, V, Paris 1957, 1965.

Vischer, W., Der Prediger Salomo, München 1926

Von Soden, W., Grundriß der akkadischen Grammatik, Roma 1952.

Vriezen, Th. C., Einige Notizen zur Übersetzung des Bindewortes ki, in: Von Ugarit nach Qumran, Eissfeldt Festschrift, (ed. J. Hempel-L.Rost) BZAW 77, Berlin 1958, 266–273.

Wagner, Max, Die lexikalischen und grammatikalischen Aramaismen im alttestamentlichen Hebräisch. BZAW 96 Berlin 1966.

Watson, W. G. E., Archaic Elements in the Language of Chronicles, Bibl 53 (1972), 191–207.

Wehr, Hans, Arabisches Wörterbuch für die Schriftsprache der Gegenwart, Leipzig 1956.

Wevers, J. W., A Study in the Hebrew Variants in the Books of Kings, ZAW 61 (1945), 45–76.

Whitley, C. F., The Genius of Ancient Israel, Amsterdam 1969.

—, Some Functions of the Hebrew Particles BETH and LAMEDH, JQR NS 62 (1972), 199–206.

—, The Positive Force of the Hebrew Particle בל, ZAW 84 (1972), 213–219.

—, Has the Particle שׁם an Asseverative Force?, Bibl 55 (1974), 394–398.

—, The Hebrew Emphatic Particle *l* with Pronominal Suffixes, JQR NS 65 (1975), 225–228.

Wildeboer, G., Der Prediger, in: Die fünf Megillot, 18, Tübingen 1898.

Winckler, Hugo, Zum Kohelet, in: Altorientalische Forschungen I, Leipzig 1896, 351 ff.

Wright, A. G., The Riddle of the Sphinx, CBQ 30 (1968), 313—334.

Wright, C. H. H., The Book of Koheleth, London 1883.

Würthwein, E., Die Weisheit Ägyptens und das Alte Testament, Marburg 1960.

Yadin, Yigael, The Ben Sira Scroll from Masada, Jerusalem 1965.

—, A Note on DSD IV 20, JBL 74 (1955), 40–43.

Zapletal, Vincent, Das Buch Koheleth, Freiburg 1911².
Zimmerli, Walther, Die Weisheit des Predigers Salomo, Berlin 1936.
—, Das Buch des Predigers Salomo, ATD, Göttingen 1962.
—, Das Buch Kohelet-Traktat oder Sentenzensammlung?, VT 24 (1974), 221–230.
Zimmermann, Frank, The Aramaic Provenance of Qohelet, JQR N S 36 (1945–46), 17–45.
—, The Question of Hebrew in Qohelet, JQR 40 (1949), 79–102.
Zirkel, G., Untersuchungen über den Prediger mit philosophischen und kritischen Bemerkungen, Würzburg 1792.

Abbreviations

AB	The Anchor Bible (Garden City, New York)
ANET²	Ancient Near Eastern Texts relating to the Old Testament, ed. J. B. Pritchard, Princeton 1955²
Antiq	Josephus, Antiquities
AASOR	Annual of the American Schools of Oriental Research (New Haven)
ASTI	Annual of the Swedish Theological Institute (Jerusalem, Leiden)
ATD	Das Alte Testament Deutsch (Göttingen)
Aq	Aquila
BA	The Biblical Archaeologist (New Haven)
BASOR	Bulletin of the American Schools of Oriental Research (New Haven)
BDB	Hebrew and English Lexicon of the Old Testament, F. Brown-S. R. Driver-C. A. Briggs (Oxford 1952 impression)
BH³	Biblia Hebraica, ed. R. Kittel, 1937 and later (Stuttgart)
BHS	Biblia Hebraica Stuttgartensia, 1968 and later (Stuttgart)
Bibl	Biblica (Roma)
BiOR	Bibliotheca Orientalis (Leiden)
Bodl 2333	A Babylonian Yemenite MS in the Bodlean Library Oxford. See Y. Ratzabi, Textus 5 (1966), 93–113.
BZ	Biblische Zeitschrift (Paderborn)
BZAW	Beihefte zur Zeitschrift für die alttestamentliche Wissenschaft (Berlin)
CAD	The Assyrian Dictionary of the University of Chicago (Chicago 1963 and later)
CBQ	Catholic Biblical Quarterly (Washington)
CIS	Corpus Inscriptionum Semiticarum (Paris 1899–1911)
CML	Canaanite Myths and Legends (Old Testament Studies No. iii), G. R. Driver (Edinburgh 1956).
CTM	Concordia Theological Monthly (St. Louis)
DISO	Dictionnaire des inscriptions sémitiques de l'Ouest, C.F. Jean-Jacob Hoftijzer, (Leiden 1965)
EstBib	Estudios Bíblicos (Madrid)
Freytag	Lexicon Arabico-Latinum, by G. W. Freytag (Halle 1830–1837)
G	Greek
GK	Gesenius' Hebrew Grammar, ed. E. Kautzsch, 2nd Eng. edn. by A. E. Cowley (Oxford 1910)
HAT	Handbuch zum Alten Testament (Tübingen)

Hier	Hieronymus
Hist.-Filos Kl.	Historisk-Filosofiske, Klasse II, No. 1, 1954 (Avhandlinger Utgitt av Det Norske Videnskaps-Akademi I, Oslo)
HSAT	Die Heilige Schrift des Alten Testaments (Tübingen 1922⁴)
HUCA	Hebrew Union College Annual (Cincinnati)
IB	The Interpreters' Bible (New York)
ICC	International Critical Commentary (Edinburgh)
IEJ	Israel Exploration Journal (Jerusalem)
JAOS	Journal of the American Oriental Society (New Haven)
Jastrow	A Dictionary of the Targumim, the Talmud Babli and Yerushalmi, and the Midrashic Literature, by Marcus Jastrow, I–II (London-New York 1903)
JBL	Journal of Biblical Literature (Philadelphia)
JCS	Journal of Cuneiform Studies (New Haven)
JE	Jewish Encyclopaedia (London 1903)
JNES	Journal of Near Eastern Studies (Chicago)
JNSL	Journal of Northwest Semitic Languages (Leiden)
JSS	Journal of Semitic Studies (Manchester)
JTS	Journal of Theological Studies (Oxford)
JQR	Jewish Quarterly Review (Philadelphia)
K	Coptic
KAI	Kanaanäische und aramäische Inschriften, I/III, H. Donner-W. Röllig (Wiesbaden 1962–64)
KAT	Kommentar zum Alten Testament (Göttingen)
KBL³	Lexicon in Veteris Testamenti Libros L. Koehler-W. Baumgartner (Leiden 1967 and later)
K-de R	Benjamin Kennicott, Vetus Testamentum Hebraicum; Cum Variis Lectionibus ii (Oxford 1780), and J. B. de Rossi, Variae Lectiones Veteris Testamenti iii (Parma 1786)
KEH	Kurzgefaßtes exegetisches Handbuch zum Alten Testament (Freiburg)
KHC	Kurzer Hand-Commentar zum Alten Testament (Freiburg)
Lane	An Arabic-English Lexicon, E. W. Lane (London 1863–1893)
LCL	Loeb Classcial Library (London)
LHAVT	Lexicon Hebraicum et Aramaicum Veteris Testamenti, ed. F. Zorell (Roma 1965 and later)
LXX	The Septuagint
MB	Miscellanea Biblica (Roma)
MT	The Massoretic Text
NEB	New English Bible
Oud Stud	Oudtestamentische Studiën (Leiden)
Q	Qere

RB	Revue Biblique (Paris)
RdQ	Revue de Qumran (Paris)
REJ	Revue des Études Juives (Paris)
RHPR	Revue d'Histoire et de Philosophie Religieuses (Paris)
RSV	Revised Standard Version
S^h	Syro-Hexaplar
StOR	Studia Orientalia (Helsingfors)
Sym, Σ	Symmachus
T	Targum
Theod	Theodotion
UT	Ugaritic Textbook, C. H. Gordon (Analecta Orientalia 38) (Roma 1965)
UF	Ugarit-Forschungen (Neukirchen-Vluyn)
V	Vulgate
VT	Vetus Testamentum (Leiden)
VTS	Supplements to Vetus Testamentum (Leiden)
WUS	Wörterbuch der ugaritischen Sprache, Joseph Aistleitner (ed. O. Eissfeldt, Berlin 1967)
Y	Jerusalem Talmud
ZAW	Zeitschrift für die alttestamentliche Wissenschaft (Berlin)
ZDMG	Zeitschrift der Deutschen Morgenländischen Gesellschaft (Wiesbaden)
ZThK	Zeitschrift für Theologie und Kirche (Tübingen)

Subject Index

W
DE
G

Walter de Gruyter
Berlin · New York

Beihefte zur Zeitschrift für die
alttestamentliche Wissenschaft